THE COUNSELLOR

A powerful true story about
addiction, grief and love.

ALISON KERWIN

Published by Alison Kerwin

facebook.com/thecounsellorbook
instagram.com/thecounsellorbook/
twitter.com/alisonkerwin

Cover design by Ounce Studio.

Editing by Fred Johnson.

ISBN: 978-1-8382954-0-0

Born in 1977, Alison Kerwin grew up in a small town called Leyland in the North West of England. She spent her formative years living in a three-bed semi with her mum, dad, brother Danny, and sisters Rachael and Claire.

Alison infamously won a calculator in a school competition when she was eight years old and once had five numbers come up in the lottery the week after she'd left the syndicate.

Considered 'the posh one' by her siblings—as her kids eat houmous and fajitas—she currently lives in Birkdale, Southport with her husband Eddie, children Peter and Lily, and their pet rats, Remy and Rizzo.

The Counsellor is Alison's first book.

Dedicated to Mum—for allowing me to share our story and for loving us so much it made it a story worth sharing.

I believe that we're all born with an incredible power, but it's locked away in a treasure chest. It's usually only a crisis or trauma that gives you the key to open that chest. Empowerment, for me, is finally opening that box of treasure and using what's within. Everyone's box is unique and what triggers one person may not trigger another.

- Rachael Newsham

Prologue

2019

22 NOVEMBER

Dear Danny,

I'm sitting here, trying to write your eulogy. Your eulogy! But the words aren't flowing.

I think it's because all I can think about right now is my grief. And to do you and our family justice, I need to speak for all of us—to get your story right. Get *our* story right.

So, like a ghost that needs to be exorcised, I need to get my own thoughts down on paper. I need you to know what you meant to me. How my life will be irrevocably changed without my devilishly handsome, incredibly witty and often impossible big brother.

You and me. Me and you. Oh Danny, I miss you so, so much.

I just can't believe we'll never pick up the phone to call each other at exactly the same time ever again.

I can't believe the person I had the most banter with in the entire world won't be around to tell me how crap my trainers are or to take the piss out of every promotion I ever had. Who else will tell everyone that I simply make tea for my colleagues in the office?

I can't believe we won't get to hug again. Those silly hugs you gave people that lasted too long—on purpose, of course, to make them uncomfortable. But they never made me uncomfortable, Danny. I loved being in your embrace. What I would give for one of those bear hugs right now.

I can't believe you won't wind Peter up saying, 'What? What?', and won't get to tell Lily how she has the most beautiful eyes. I'll tell her that every day, Danny.

Mostly, though—and this is what I really want to say—I can't believe I couldn't save you.

It was my job, wasn't it? To fix you. Always: to pick you up and put you back together. To remind you to be strong. To tell you that you already were.

Being your little sister was the best label I ever had—the best one I ever will.

I'll always adore you, Dan. I'll follow you to the moon and back. Just as I always have; just as I always will.

Sleep tight, big brother.

Alison
xxx

A true story

2019

18 NOVEMBER

06:20

The alarm takes a long time to pull me from sleep. When finally my eyes ease open, I exhale slowly before reaching for my phone on the nightstand. I mash the snooze button and push Peter, my skinny little eight-year-old, to the far corner of the bed. He murmurs sleepily.

I blink at the bright screen. I've missed a call, I see—strange. Who would have called me in the middle of the night?

I stifle a yawn and refocus. Forty-six missed calls.

I jump out of bed and frantically begin scrolling.

Rachael (3)

Claire (4)

Rachael (7)

Rachael (2)

Claire (2)

Rachael (9)

Claire (5)

Rachael (14)

Shit. Shit. *Shit.*

3

I stride from the room, the phone to my ear. I'm calling—I don't even know who. All I know is that something is terribly, irreversibly wrong. My heart is already thudding in my chest—my forehead feels hot, clammy. I can't stand still.

My sister Rachael answers. *'Ali—'*

I can still hear it: my tiny little name drawn out over what felt like minutes. So familiar yet so foreign.

'No, no, no, no!' I shriek. I know I am moaning; I don't even recognise the sounds coming out of my mouth.

'Ali,' she continues, her voice steady as always, 'it's not what you think'—correctly assuming I'd jumped to the conclusion that we'd lost a parent.

I stop for a second. Take a long, haggard breath. And she continues.

'It's our Danny, Ali. It's Danny.' Her voice cracks. 'He's dead.'

Something sharp and tremulous tears its way from my throat. My legs waver and I clutch at the bannister, pressing myself against it.

'I'm so sorry,' Rachael is saying. She sounds like she's laughing, but I know she's not. Her voice sounds so distant. It's her but not her.

She goes on, trying to comfort me, but her words seem foreign, empty—floating up and away like so many lost balloons. My brother is dead. Our brother. Danny.

Danny. Danny. *Danny.*

I fly downstairs, the phone forgotten, and burst into the kitchen. Eddie's pouring cereal for Lily. She's waiting patiently at the kitchen table, her eyes fixed on the iPad in front of her.

He looks up, startled by the speed at which I've arrived.

Before he can speak, I begin to yell.

He is quickly by my side. Holding me—so tight. He gently strokes the back of my head, holding me still, letting me sob into his shoulder.

Slowly, I start to take in the enormity of what I've been told. As my breathing starts to steady, the same two words play over and over in my head:

He's dead. He's dead. He's dead.

My chest tightens and I break away, running back upstairs. All I remember from talking to Rachael is that my sisters are coming to get me. We have to tell Mum and Dad.

Fuck! I stop suddenly. Mum and Dad.

We can't tell them their son is dead. We just can't.

I call back. Not sure who I'm calling.

'Are you sure?' I plead. I'm sobbing. My voice is fast and fragile, unrecognisable. Dimly, I realise I must sound like a madwoman.

'How do we know?' I shout again, 'how do we know it's really him? Is it really him? Are you really sure?'

It's my other sister, Claire. She is crying too.

'It's him, Ali. I'm so, so sorry, but it's him. We're sure.'

I throw random items—whatever's on the bed, in the top drawer, the first things I grasp in the wardrobe—into an overnight bag and head back downstairs.

When I reach the kitchen, I notice my children as if for the first time. They're looking up at me, wide-eyed. Their bewildered faces, so perfect, follow mine, and the tears come again. Eddie puts his arms around me.

I look at my little Peter. My son, who'd been lying next to me in bed just ten minutes before. His breathing has quickened, and he has fear written all over his face. What has happened to my mummy, it said. No one should be so frightened at eight years old.

And there, my darling Lily. She is standing with her arm around her brother. She looks at me expectantly.

'I'm sorry, darlings,' I splutter, 'but Mummy has just had some really bad news.'

I pause and take a deep breath so I can get the words out in one go.

'Uncle Danny has died.'

Saying it nearly chokes me. Their beloved Uncle Danny has died. It can't be; it shouldn't be.

They both rush towards me and wrap their arms around my legs. The four of us stand, holding one another, the slow world going by outside. Peter strokes my thigh. Lily looks up at me awkwardly, wondering what on earth she is supposed to do.

Eddie does the talking. He explains everything, his voice quiet, gentle, and they watch him as if transfixed. I have no idea what he's saying, but I am grateful. I straighten my hair (why, why, why?!) and throw my make-up in the overnight bag. It's most definitely a no make-up day.

I text my best friend, Kelly.

Ring me as soon as you get up.

Then, with nothing left to do, I stand in the living room and wait: for the car to turn up, for Kelly to ring back—for something, anything, to change.

Finally, the phone rings. It's Kelly. I don't give her a chance to speak.

'Danny's dead, Kelly. He's dead. I've lost my brother, just like you did. I knew I would. I always knew I'd lose him. I told you. I knew…'

Tears. Pain. The unbearable knowledge that I'll never see my brother again. I replay the conversations I had with Kelly following her own brother's death all those years ago. I'd known then, deep down, that I'd one day go through the same thing—but now that the time has finally come, I find that I don't know what to do.

She cries with me. For me. For him. For her brother.

It can't be true. It can't be.

I'd thought hearing of my brother's death would be the worst I'd ever feel, but I'm soon proved wrong. Less than two hours after getting the news, I'm left facing the unenviable task of telling my mum and dad that they'll never see their son again.

In the car on the way to our parents' home, my siblings and I debate how best to tell them. We want to do it together, but we know that the sight of the three of us (plus Linda, Danny's partner) will communicate more than words ever could. On top of that, we want to catch Mum and Dad together, but that seems unlikely—my dad has a chronic lung condition, so it'll be Mum who answers the door. She'll know as soon as she sees us, meaning Dad will be alone when he hears her break down, unable even to rise to see what the matter is. We can't face that.

Reluctantly, we decide it should be one of us. Me. The others will wait a few minutes around the corner.

'How will we know when you've told them?' Claire asks, her voice flat.

'Claire, they'll know the moment they see my face,' I reply. It's eight o'clock on a Monday morning, the sky is a pale English grey, and I live half an hour away. It's the news we've all dreaded but, on some level, expected. They'll know—I just want to make sure they find out together.

As luck would have it, the front door is open, and I can hear Mum upstairs with Dad. It is a small mercy on the most horrific of days.

I shout something—I don't remember what—as soon as I enter, and hurry upstairs. They turn as I ease my way into the room, eyes fixed on the wooden floor. When I finally look up, they're gazing at me expectantly.

I watch my mum's eyes as she scans my face. Slowly, horribly, her face darkens. No one says anything.

They know. Of course they know. Right then, I want to freeze time, to preserve this precious moment in which nothing is confirmed. If I don't speak, I can stop everything from falling into place.

'Please don't tell me,' Mum pleads softly, the colour already gone from her small face.

'I'm so sorry,' is all I manage. I had more than this, I'm sure—the words I'd been rehearsing in my head on the way here—but they just won't come.

And with that, she falls to the floor, her whole body voluntarily crumpling beneath her. She's still only for a moment—then she's knelt over the bed, slamming her fists into the duvet.

'Why Dan-i-el?' she screams. 'Why, why, why?'

Before I know it, my sisters have joined me in the room, Linda alongside. We divide ourselves up and cradle our parents. I haven't yet found the strength to look at my dad, but now I turn and steal a glance at his face. He's wide-eyed—frightened, confused. His cup of tea steams gently, forgotten, on the bedside table.

We hold them as they go through the same emotions we'd experienced only a few hours earlier. Disbelief: are we sure? Horror. Anger. And then nothing left but pain—visceral, burrowing pain.

As we sit there, holding each other through the tears, realisation begins to sink in: My big brother is gone and my parents are broken. My whole family has been torn apart.

2014

17 DECEMBER

Message to: Alison

From: Danny

09:32

Hi al hope your ok,am gonna jump in swift here,jones has left me in a shit situation,can explain later,basically I would be great full of a six hundred pound loan,please don't just say no think about it basically I was letting him have 60 saga figures at ten pound each as agreed,anyway car dealer say no more I am still putting them on ebay as we speak,I fainted again Monday so work is 50'50 and I am ringing drug helpline next job and mum is going with me I took more drugs with Alison,please think about Alison I can't have another Xmas like last year,I won't let you down like Rachael though I don't take sides as it's my job to love you all unconditionally,.xx

Message to: Danny

From: Alison

11:46

Hi Dan.

I am really glad you are getting the support you need. I was really worried about you. I still am.

9

With regard to money though, I am afraid I am in no position to help. I just can't afford to lend it out.

I really am sorry you are having a hard time and I will help in any way I can, but I just can't with money. I have been let down before and I can't risk that ever happening again. It's too stressful, Danny.

Get your Star Wars stuff on buy and sell or eBay. You'd definitely sell it.

x

Message to: Alison

From: Danny

14:24

I am booked in for 14 of jan,alison I won't let u down with money I just need more time to sell this Star Wars stuff am on it now,trust me,I can't physically get it,this stuff will go,if I wasn't desperate I would not ask if I could get all my shopping in and bills paid least I could have a face on that makes other people happy,I know I will sell it,£600 is a lot of money but I promise you I can get it back to you,can you not at least speak to eddy about it. if you can't physically do it I understand but if you could put trust in me would mean a lot it really would,and the thing is it's all about Shay and making up for last year if you don't trust me I still love you,it just means I can get in the spirit now.thats all I can say xx

Message to: Danny

From: Alison

16:48

But Danny, I don't have it. We have just done our Christmas shopping and we have enough left to get home for Christmas, Claire's birthday, and a bit of shopping—and that's it.

I am sorry but I am just not in a position to loan anyone anything.

I feel absolutely terrible that you've asked me as I can't help and I feel like I will now be responsible for you having a shit time but I just don't have money to loan out. X

Message to: Alison

From: Danny

16:51

If u can't u can't don't tell mum please

X

28 DECEMBER

Message to: Alison

From: Danny

01:43

Hi al sorry to wright so late,I've got a big weight on my shoulder I need to bare,since my 40 th and losing my job I've been really down, anyway to cut a long story short since the end of November I started to dabble in heroin, I told the drs and drug clinic what I was up too they finally got me an appointment at the drug clinic on the 14th of jan I am going to try and get it brought forward,it's all a long story and something I am not proud off I decided to quit it just before Xmas but it isn't that easy you body needs it to function.with insomnia and depression well any excuse I've fucked up,until I get to the drug clinic I need to spend 25 a day on it that's just at night it does not get me high and I won't take anymore than that,I am dependant on it I don't think anyone has even noticed I take it,I have no option but to keep takeing it until I get a substitute or rehab which ever they advise,I am going to tell Claire tom and rach but I don't want mum to know,I will try my best to get this appointment moved forward,I needed to get this off my chest,I am so sorry,I love u please don't worry two weeks earlier and I could of just stopped at lease to won't it to stop now,sorry for always being a burden xxxx

07:36

Heroin. *Oh my god.*

He's going to die. I'm going to lose him.

11

I call Rachael.

I have no idea what we speak about. How do two clean-living working mothers in their mid-thirties deal with a heroin abuser? We knew he was using drugs—neither of us can remember a time he wasn't taking Valium, diazepam, or whatever else—but heroin? This is another level. We've worried about him for the last five years, but this is a line we never thought he'd cross.

Fuck, Danny.

2019

AUGUST

Dad's lung condition means he can't walk very far without getting breathless. He's also a home bird; getting him to venture out is becoming harder and harder.

Mum, though, likes to be out and about. She's always been busy, and her advancing years haven't slowed her down (despite the protests of her children!). She's been spending a lot of time at our house, but increasingly worries about leaving Dad, so one weekend I manage to get them both to stay. I told Dad he could bring Amber, his beloved dog, to sweeten the pill.

Once in the house, he relaxes. The kids make him laugh—they run around the garden pretending to be him on his scooter, and act out an argument with Mum, their nana, about eating all the pies. He's enjoying himself watching them even if he won't admit it.

And Mum relaxes too. Never one to completely switch off, she busies herself in the kitchen with me, drinking endless cups of tea and meticulously wiping down my surfaces every five minutes.

On Sunday, we venture to Ainsdale Beach, which is only a ten minute drive from my house. We stop at the local supermarket en route to buy a fisherman's chair so my dad has somewhere to sit. We park directly on the sand and, before we have chance to set up Dad's seat, the kids have already taken Mum by the hand and dragged her off toward the sea. I get Dad comfortable and then watch him as he leans back, sipping his steaming brew and smoking a cigarette. It's the first time he's been in years, and it's wonderful to see him looking so content in the great outdoors. I look out towards the sea and spot Mum in the distance. She is far away but I can easily make out her slim frame, her trademark sunglasses covering half her face. Her face breaks into a huge smile as she notices me and she stretches

13

her arms into the air before glancing over to Dad. He gives her a sneaky wave, his fag hidden behind his back.

She has no idea—she's at the edge of the sea with the kids. Paddling, splashing, laughing. Trying to beat me to 10,000 steps by walking farther and farther away.

It's one of those days I know I'll treasure forever. It feels like my parents are young again, alive again—they're out in the sunshine, relaxed, enjoying family time. Mum is happy that Dad is with us, and Dad is content in the fresh air, knowing that we're overlooking him smoking because we don't want to ruin the moment.

When we get back to my house, salt-swept and revitalised, I make us each a fresh brew.

Mum and Dad sit under the balcony Eddie built in the garden, looking on as the children play with Amber.

'What're your happiest memories?' I ask, settling down next to them. It's a warm afternoon, gentle and balmy, and my parents are quiet, content. I hand them their drinks.

'Holidays,' they say in unison.

They go on, the dam suddenly split, recounting cruises they've enjoyed; Turkey, Greece, Barbados. Oh, they *loved* Barbados. All holidays without us kids, I think with a wry smile, but I don't point that out.

'And your worst?' I ask after a moment's pause.

I already know the answer—or, at least, I think I do. They lost a baby girl, Tracy, before my siblings and I were born. Mum still spoke about her sometimes; it was the fact they'd never got to say goodbye that really tore at her. As their faces darkened, I winced, wanting to kick myself for ruining the moment.

'Danny,' they say at once.

I feel tears prick my eyes. I wasn't expecting that.

'We just worry about him so much,' Mum says sadly. 'I can't relax here for worrying about what he's doing at home.'

And with that, our perfect weekend is tainted.

31 OCTOBER

Message to: Danny

From: Alison

16:42

Dearest Brother.

Your firstborn replied in the affirmative. He shall join you at the gymnasium. Kindest regards,

Your Amazing Sister

Message to: Alison

From: Danny

16:49

Oldest of the three younger ones. message received and appreciated.one will see you shortly xx

Message to: Danny

From: Alison

16:50

One shall look forward to that. Message received and understood.

'Awwww,' I coo, 'did you have a lickle bit of tuna and pasta for your dindins?'

Danny laughs, taking his lunch box from his bag and popping it in the sink.

'Yes, it was yummy scrummy in my tummy,' he replies, matching my sing-song voice and shooting me a sarcastic look.

'Did you just fancy something different for a change?' I continue, safe in the knowledge that he's eaten that same lunch every day since he was a teenager.

'Shut it, Al,' he shoots back, pretending to scold me and softly punching my arm.

It's just a normal exchange between two siblings. Only, I'm forty-two and he's forty-five.

'Where're What-What and Lily-pod—' he begins, just as they barge into the kitchen. Lily is dressed as a 'pretty' witch, while Peter is a hot dog.

Danny scoops Peter up, laughing at the sight of his nephew dressed as junk food on Halloween. It's typical Peter to utterly disregard social norms. Danny asks if he can eat him for his tea. Peter giggles for a second, writhing in his uncle's arms, but then seems to seriously reconsider.

'No,' he says sternly.

Danny grins and lowers Peter to the floor. He turns back to me.

'Can you give me and Shay a lift to the gym later?' he asks as Peter runs out to join his sister and cousins.

'Sure,' I reply.

Shay walks in, hands in his pockets, and Danny bolts upright. 'There's only one Shay!' he chants, clapping his hands.

'There's only one S-h-a-y!' we both continue.

Shay, Danny's shy fifteen-year-old, blushes. You can see how embarrassed he is to be the centre of his childish auntie and dad's attention.

I've not seen Shay for a while—he's spent most of the summer at his mum's.

'You're looking handsome,' I tell him sincerely. Because he was.

'Isn't he gorgeous?' his dad jumps in. I can see the pride written all over his face.

'Daaaadddddd,' Shay protests, visibly wincing and trying to hide his face from our view. 'Are we going in a bit?'

'In a bit, mate. Just let me grab a quick shower.'

When I drop them off later that day, I sit for a while in the car, watching them stride away. Dad and son. Two peas in a pod. I'm struck by the sight of them; Shay has grown so big. With his broad shoulders and beaming white smile, he's looking more and more like his dad. I'm no longer looking at my brother and his little boy; instead, I see two people turning into one another. Buddies. Pals. Best mates. I smile to myself, stealing one last look before turning the car around and heading back toward my mum's house.

That was the last time I saw my brother alive.

2014

28 DECEMBER

Rach arrives at mine with a forlorn Danny. We'd agreed that he needed to get away from Leyland, so she's brought him to my house in York. Eddie is worried about having him in the house with the kids—they're only three and, you know, heroin. But it's Danny. *My* Danny. Where else can he go?

It's late when she arrives so she's eager to get going before it gets too dark. We briefly hug, neither of us saying anything, before she announces she has to get going on the long drive back home. She wipes a tear from her cheek, blows her nose, and is gone.

'I'm sorry, Al,' Danny says when we find ourselves alone in my living room. He has a small overnight bag with him. I fight the urge to rifle through it.

'It's okay, Dan,' I reply. And it is—agreeing to let him stay was instinctive, just like everything concerning Danny. He's my brother. I don't get to choose when to help.

In the short time we had to process the fact that Danny is using heroin, my sisters and I decided that he should stay with me and go cold turkey. We've all educated ourselves on heroin abuse, courtesy of Google. Looking back, all the signs were there: the itchy skin. The eyes. Oh, the eyes. The desperate pleas for money.

We feel that if he stays in Leyland, he'll be too close to his 'friends'. So here he is—getting away from it all. From everyone.

One of my sisters, I can't remember which now, had the unhappy job of telling Mum and Dad. Their worst fears have at last been realised: he's gone down a path of no return, one far too dark—even for him.

It's my job to lead him back. To feed him. Talk to him. Be with him.

I'd imagined that he'd writhe in his bed, caked in cold sweat, that I'd have to restrain him as he desperately called out for a fix. I've seen *Trainspotting*—I know how this works.

But, of course, it isn't like that. It's nothing like that.

Now, when I look back at that time, I do so with fondness. I remember a brother and sister and an unbreakable bond.

He spent the first twenty-four hours in bed, refusing the food we offered and barely speaking a word; but, by day two, he was able to get up in the evening. He was well enough to communicate, so we all watched a film together. His appetite had returned, so we raided one of the kids' selection boxes and ate chocolate until we felt sick. I giggled every time he asked if there was any more. It became a part of our routine, something we did every day until he left.

30 DECEMBER

We're sitting in the living room after putting the kids to bed. Eddie is scrolling through Netflix, looking for a film for us to watch.

Danny looks across at him.

'Ed, I really appreciate you having me here. I know it's Christmas and it's hard with the kids. I really am so grateful, mate.'

'Don't worry about it,' Eddie replies before turning back to the TV. He's really relaxed since Danny first arrived, but is content to leave the deep discussions to us.

Danny gives a small smile and settles back in his chair. He playfully pushes my feet away from his legs before picking up his cup of tea and taking a big gulp. He reaches for his mobile.

Message to: Alison

From: Danny

20:07

I love you too and can't thank you enough for guiding me back to life,you and Eddie both make me welcome didn't want you to feel left out,xx

Message to: Danny

From: Alison

16:50

Do you fancy watching a movie after you've spoken to Shay? I will make a brew and give you some chocolate? x

That's if you've not eaten it all.

31 DECEMBER

In late 2006, inspired by an article I had read in a magazine, I wrote a cosmic order which delivered me my husband (so I like to think). So, as we sit in my living room on New Year's Eve, I persuade Danny to do the same thing. It's a cold dark night and Eddie, Danny and I are tucking into a curry I've ordered. I'm desperately trying to make the night feel special as I'm acutely aware Danny is pining for his son. Glasses of barely touched prosecco gently fizz next to us as we each take turns to refill our plates, despite already feeling uncomfortably full.

We'd spent days talking about his relationship with drugs—his past, how he'd got here. He was desperate to put some positivity back into his life.

He missed Shay terribly, but knew he had to get himself well again. He'd be a much better dad if he just took some time out.

I'd persuaded him to read my copy of Rhonda Byrne's *The Secret*, and was amazed when he announced he was actually enjoying it. My friend Cath, who was also Danny's ex, had recommended it years ago, and I'd spent quite a long time trying to do as the book said and attract positive things into my life. I thought Danny could do with some positivity of his own.

Once we've finished eating, Danny takes on my cosmic order challenge with both hands. We both do. We create two lists: the first contains all the things we want to leave behind in 2014. Danny's list makes me sad; people, relationships, drugs. It paints a rich picture of how he got where he is. We burn these just before midnight, two Witches of Eastwick cackling in my back garden. Eddie can't contain his laughter at the sight of us, but we don't care. Danny tells me it feels cathartic and I hug him tight.

We write down our wishes, seal them in envelopes, and I put them in the frame behind my wedding photograph in my living room. Safely tucked away—ready for the universe to get its hands on. I chink my now flat glass of prosecco with his.

When we said cold turkey, that didn't include alcohol, right?

I feel like we're entering the new year with a spring in our step. We've done it—we've pulled him back from the brink. He reaches out and I grab him. It's only been a matter of days, but I see a huge change in him already. It's like all he needed to do was tell someone—a problem shared and all that.

The drink goes straight to my head. I feel dizzy with excitement.

Have I got you back Danny? I feel like I have.

2019

17 NOVEMBER

The day before Danny died, I was dusting and polishing in my living room when the picture frame fell apart. As I bent down to clear up the mess, I found our envelopes protruding from the board. Smiling, I unfolded our notes one by one.

Danny's contained more of himself than he'd perhaps intended: of course he wanted to be clean, to be a good dad to Shay (he already was), and to be healthy, but he'd also asked for a girlfriend, ideally dark-skinned because, at the time, he had a thing for Nicole Scherzinger. I had to laugh.

It's good to dream, Dan.

That was my brother: always taking it one step too far.

2001

JULY

Mum is in the hospital—she's just had her bunions removed. Personally, I can't remember a time she didn't have them, but apparently after all these years the pain finally got the better of her. I'm driving to Chorley to pick her up with Danny, Rachael, and Claire all packed into my little Renault Clio. We're behaving like she's just undergone a triple heart bypass: we have balloons, snacks, and enough magazines to keep her occupied for weeks—only, she's an outpatient. Hmm.

It's a gorgeous summer day and it feels wonderful to be in the car with all my siblings. I can't remember the last time we were all sandwiched together like this. The windows are down and I can feel the warm breeze brush against my face as the road unravels beyond the windscreen. Danny, sitting in front, cranks up the stereo; it's a song by Five, Claire's current favourite band.

'Turn it up,' she screams excitedly from the back. I wince—it's loud enough already and I hate drawing attention to myself, but I don't say a word. Danny cranks it up and we all begin to sing.

Everybody get up singing

One, two, three, four, Five will make you get down now

Claire's beautiful voice rises above the rest of our discordant shrieks, and Rach and I attempt to drown her out. Danny points out at passers-by as he shouts the numbers *one, two, three, four* out the window. I laugh—my brother singing along to one of the least 'cool' songs of the year. At that moment, I realise I don't want to reach our destination; I want to stay here, singing with my siblings forever and ever.

23

Mum is in a bed surrounded by elderly people, so we easily spot her. She has a cotton nightdress on covered with tiny flowers. She's fixing her hair using a small mirror when she notices us. We're weighed down with gifts, and she laughs.

'You know you are taking me home, don't you?' Mum says, giggling as we approach her bed.

Although it was a routine operation—and a minor one at that—Mum being in hospital is scary. She takes care of us; it's not the other way around. We haven't spoken about it, but I can tell that we're all more than a little freaked out. When I asked my siblings whether they wanted to come with me to pick her up, they all jumped at the chance.

Mum asks Danny to leave the cubicle so we can help her get dressed. She's determined to be ready before the consultant comes around; she doesn't want to be in her nightwear during daylight hours any longer than she has to be.

We're pulling a jumper over her when she jerks suddenly. Before we can do anything, she lurches forward and throws up all down her top.

'I'm okay,' she insists, wiping her mouth. She's not. Catching our worried looks, she adds, 'It's just the anaesthetic. I shouldn't have moved that quickly.'

The consultant arrives just as we finish getting her dressed. I have her overnight bag in my arms, ready to get going.

He's a tall, harried-looking man with thinning brown hair. He greets us with a tight smile before running an eye over Mum's foot, prodding gently. Apparently satisfied, he scribbles something on a notepad, nods once, and turns to us. 'She's good to go,' he says matter-of-factly before turning to Mum. 'Just take it easy.'

'I will,' she lies.

Pulling back the curtain, I find Danny standing in front of us with a wheelchair. He beams at Mum.

'I am not going in that, Dan-i-el!' she declares, crossing her arms.

'You bloody well are,' he insists, 'I just heard you being sick. You're not walking anywhere.'

'I'm bloody well not,' Mum replies.

We exchange looks—Mum never swears. It must be the anaesthetic.

Rach, Claire, and I walk behind as Danny wheels Mum down the long corridor. We're still laden with bags and gifts, and can hear her giggling as Danny picks up speed, the wheelchair gaining momentum in front of him. I hear something else too, something above her laughter: he's singing.

Everybody get up singing

Five will make you get down now.

2015

2 JANUARY

Beyond our immediate family, only a couple of people knew about Danny. I'd been with our cousin Kat on the day I'd found out, so I'd told her. I'd also told Cath and my best friend, Kelly, because I told her everything.

Cath was Danny's ex and my friend. Despite living on the other side of the world, she had a mystical way of always knowing what was going on. I'd often get a *Is Danny okay?* message out of the blue, only to discover that he wasn't. Despite their romantic relationship lasting only a short time, they'd retained a strong bond, and she was as much his friend as mine.

I messaged her shortly after he arrived at my house in York. She'd kind of known, she said—she always did, and she vowed to send healing and all sorts of spiritual goodness our way.

I was never truly sure what I believed, but I believed in Cath; and besides, at this point and I'd would take anything I could get.

While I tried to focus on getting Danny physically well, Cath tried to help him recover mentally. She recommended books and videos. Anything that focused on positivity and healing and he couldn't get enough of it.

Each day he'd wake up with a bit more energy and a new positive affirmation to try. He was desperate to reinvent himself, make a fresh start and Eddie and I got caught up in his enthusiasm. As Danny talked about his desire to have a fresh new look, I felt such a rush of love for my husband who listened to him attentively without pointing out that the smart jeans, retro Adidas tops and trainers combo had been staples of Danny's wardrobe ever since he'd known him.

4 JANUARY

I found a support group in York for people with alcohol and drug dependencies, and was thrilled when Danny agreed to attend.

The meeting was held in a historic building, just inside the city walls. It looked far too grand to be a sanctuary for addicts and I wondered whether the people passing by had any idea what it was. I waited in the trendy cafe directly opposite, half expecting him to come walking out as quickly as he'd walked in. But he didn't.

One hour and two strong cups of coffee later, he returned. He seemed lighter. He was walking taller.

'Good meeting?' I said as he sat down across from me.

'Yeah, Al,' he said, frowning slightly, 'it was good. I met a bloke, a bit like you, a professional fella who went to work and did a really big job and then went home and sank a bottle of vodka every night. He was a normal guy.'

'As are you,' I reminded him with a smile.

'Mmmm,' he said, and turned to peer out the misted window at the busy street outside.

'Come on,' I said, standing up. We left the café, coats wrapped tight around us against the morning chill. As we passed a barbershop, Danny nudged me and said he fancied a professional shave.

'Will you treat me?' he asked cheekily.

'I think I've treated you enough,' I said with a stern look.

'Yeah I know, Al,' he said, his voice softer now. 'I am grateful, you know.'

'I know, Danny.' I gave a small smile. 'I know you are.'

Once I'd got him to that first support group, the rest came quickly. First, I decided we were going to walk around the block every night. That quickly turned into a light jog and, before we knew it, we'd agreed to start using my couch-to-5k app—or perhaps I forced it upon him. I can't remember.

In true Alison Kerwin style, I decided that we were ready to enter our first race once we'd been out a couple of times.

'We need a goal,' I told him, 'to keep us motivated.'

And so we entered the Great North Run. Or, rather, I entered us.

He was slowly coming back to us. As each day passed, I got a bit more of my brother back. His humour was returning. His love for my kids and for me. I'd watch when Peter and Lily climbed up onto his knees, taking it in turns to run their hands across his shaved head. He'd pretend to be cross before pulling them close for a cuddle. During those moments, he'd often catch my eye and give me the biggest smile.

During those dark days, we often talked about the heroin. What it felt like. How it had drawn him in. 'It's euphoria, Al,' he told me. 'It's fuckin' bliss. That's what makes it so hard.'

It sounds ridiculous now, but we spoke about how similar my addiction to food was to his addiction to drugs. We both recognised the same compulsion, the same draw, the same propensity to indulge without thinking about it.

Looking back, he was kind to indulge me; to let me feel that we were the same, when of course we weren't. A tendency to eat too much junk food isn't the same as indulging in an activity that could kill at any given point. But I loved him for letting me believe that it was.

8 JANUARY

'What am I going to do without you?' I joked when Rachael arrived to take Danny home.

'Eat less chocolate,' he laughed.

I grinned—yes, there was that.

It hadn't been two weeks, but Danny was already a different man. Positive. Determined. Strong.

He was our Danny again.

'God, he looks well,' Rachael commented once he was out of earshot.

I nodded. 'He does, Rach, but the real journey starts now. Being back in Leyland will be hard. You all need to keep a close eye on him.'

She nodded, and we hugged.

And then, just like that, they were gone. My big brother and little sister setting off back home. He was bandaged but still broken; he'd need a lot of love and care to get himself fixed up, but we were all determined to get him there. If any family could love him back to good health, it was us.

28 FEBRUARY

'Thirty days clean, Al.' He sounded so happy.

'I know, Dan. We're so proud of you.'

2020

SEPTEMBER

He was obsessed with days. Thirty-one days, fifty-four days, 114 days. At first I made a fuss—we all did. I'd make a mental note of milestones; a fortnight, a month, three months, and I'd send him messages to tell him how proud I was and how he needed to keep going. But after a while, my life began to get in the way; I'd be so wrapped up in what was happening that I'd forget to check in on him.

'I thought you might have called, Al.' His tone was both accusing and self-pitying, and it would immediate get my back up. I'd take a deep breath before replying, reminding myself of all that he'd been through and how far he'd come. He didn't need to know that I'd been tearing my hair out with the kids, arguing with Eddie, or having a hard time at work. He needed me to notice him and recognise how hard he was trying—that was the deal I'd signed up for. I was his support. So I'd apologise for my lack of contact and ask him how many days it had been now and he'd instantly relax, letting his frustration go, and tell me it was fifty-six or ninety-one or something else. The truth is, I never paid attention. The number didn't matter to me; the only thing that mattered was him staying clean.

But the numbers mattered to him. It was like the higher they got, the further away he was from the foot of the hill and the closer he was to the summit. Only, there was never a summit. There was no magic number he had to reach. He had to stay clean *forever*. He had to not use again *forever*. And the thought of that overwhelmed him and, if I'm honest with myself, it overwhelmed me too.

I'm spending an evening, as I often do, going through everything in my head. I'm trying to sort it all into compartments so that hopefully, one day soon, I can stand back and see it all neat and tidy and realise that it all makes sense. And I'm thinking about the way he used to talk about addiction. How quick he was to label himself an addict and how unashamed he was to say he always would be. I'm running through all those conversations about days and months and milestones in my head and wishing I'd tried harder to make a fuss while, at the same time, knowing that it wasn't my praise he needed; it was his own. He knew he'd never reach the summit, but he wanted to get as far away from the foot of the hill as he could. Maybe if he couldn't see it any more, things would get easier.

And that's the tough thing about overcoming addiction: it's a commitment you have to make to yourself every single day. You aren't ever getting off that hill. You just have to try your hardest to keep walking until, one day, and here's the hope, walking becomes so natural to you that you almost forget you're even walking at all.

2017

SEPTEMBER

'Of course he is!' Claire huffed, shaking her head, 'but, as usual, Mum's in complete denial and won't hear any of it.'

We were in Claire's kitchen. All six of our kids were running around the house, screaming at one another. We were trying to have a normal conversation in the way you do while refereeing several different arguments.

Claire spent a lot more time at Mum's than I did as I lived so far away. As such, she saw more of Danny, which, evidently, was both a good and a bad thing. Frustration and anger were written all over her face.

'And Dad knows, of course. He's not stupid.'

Cups smashed against each other as Claire filled the sink with hot soapy water, adding more noise to the already chaotic household.

I knew where she was coming from. As much as we loved our brother, we all had an in-built need to protect our mum and dad—and with Danny clearly using again, we weren't able to do that. To make matters worse, he was lying about it.

For Claire, it was the shiftiness; the 'popping out'; the endless cans of Cherry Coke; the weekends in bed. And, of course, the eyes that looked like someone had stolen his pupils, leaving tiny pinpricks in their place.

For me, though, it was about communication. He'd bounce between periods of total radio silence and unprompted waves of manic phone calls. Recently, it had been the latter. He's always been wronged in some way: someone at work. A doctor. Someone from some company or other.

As for me, I was always frustrated. Firstly, I'd try to reason. I'd listen intently for as long as I could, but then I'd get snippy as we went over the same things again and again and again.

Was he ok? I'd ask. Was he using? Was he being honest with me?

That one always got him. I don't know why I even bothered asking—I knew well enough that his response would only be defensive. I'd piss him off and him lying would piss me off. I knew that while he was in this place, he'd never furnish me with the truth.

So instead we went around the roundabout. Him calling each evening. Me answering. A strained conversation. A slightly tense goodbye.

Night after night after night after night.

I understood Claire's frustration. Our experiences were different, but we saw the same thing: he was using, he was in denial, and he was hurting Mum and Dad.

'The thing is,' I began slowly, 'maybe denial is a good place for Mum. I mean, what can be gained by convincing her that he's using?'

When Claire didn't answer, I went on, choosing my words carefully. 'None of us can stop him. We can't fix him, so maybe believing it's not happening is easier?'

Finally, she nodded—a sad, tired nod. She turned back to the sink.

As I processed the words that had just left my mouth, I started to feel envious of Mum. How different my life would be if I could only see the best in my brother. How lovely it would be to think he called me each evening because he just wanted to chat with his sister. How wonderful it would be to go about my daily life believing he was fixed and happy instead of tormented and sad.

I shook my head, my reverie falling apart. I wasn't Mum.

I saw Danny deeper than he saw himself. And, just like Claire, I knew he was using again. I knew the lying and hiding were thicker than they'd ever been before. I knew he'd gone even farther down the rabbit hole.

But what I didn't know—what none of us knew—was how on earth we could get him out.

2019

2 DECEMBER

Drank coffee.

Listened to 'Step On' by the Happy Mondays.

Decided the Happy Mondays are underrated.

Realised Danny never underrated them.

Cried.

Drank coffee.

Cried.

Thought about getting dressed.

Listened to 'Music is the Answer' by Danny Tenaglia.

Cried.

Decided music is, in fact, not the answer.

Music hurts.

Everything hurts.

2016

6 JUNE

'Hiya Mum.'

I embraced her after dumping our bags on the kitchen table.

She kissed me on the cheek, dusting the flour from her hands as she did so. Peter and Lily flung their arms around her in unison and gave her a tight squeeze. She held her arms out, careful not to get them dirty but bent down to give them both a kiss. Her short golden brown hair tickled Lily's face and she pulled away giggling.

'Your dad's in the living room,' she said, smiling down at them, 'having a nap.'

I flick the kettle on, desperate for a brew after a long drive from York and head off to say hello to my dad.

The kids trailed behind me. 'Grandad!' they shouted as they entered the living room, waking my semi-conscious father.

'Hello my little teapots,' Dad mumbled, shuffling up on the leather sofa and opening his arms for a cuddle.

The kids settled themselves beside him and I bent down to give him a kiss. His face was full of stubble so I rubbed my hand against it disapprovingly and he shook his head and laughed.

Leaving the kids with Dad, I walked back into the kitchen. He once made the mistake of taking them to the shop and letting them get bubble gum, and now they expected it every time.

'Where's Dan?' I asked as I began to take cups out of the cupboard.

35

'In bed,' Mum answered. 'He's ill.'

Claire looked up from her seat at the kitchen table and rolled her eyes. *Not again*, I thought.

I only went to my mum's every couple of months, if that. It was a two-hour drive from York, and the journey was hard to fit around the kids' activities and my work. This was my third visit that year—and the third time Danny had been in bed. It was beginning to piss me off. Lily and Peter adored Uncle Danny and yet he'd barely said more than two words to them in about six months. It just wasn't on.

Claire stood, slipped a cigarette from the pack in her handbag, and left the room. I followed her outside.

'What's going on?' I asked as she lit up, eyes on the horizon.

'The usual,' she said, her voice flat. 'Mum's in denial, but he's not been in work for weeks. He's talking shit. I can't be arsed anymore—I have enough problems of my own.'

I was quiet for a moment, weighing it all up in my head. 'I know, Claire,' I said at last—and I did. 'He needs to sort himself out. He's a joke.'

8 JUNE

I am hanging the kids' school bags on the pegs under the stairs when my phone begins to ring. I still have my coat on after collecting the kids from after-school club, and I reach into my pocket to answer. It's Danny.

'Hi Al,' he says, 'sorry I missed you at the weekend. I had flu.'

Yeah, yeah.

'When are you down again?'

Bugger off, will you?

'I'm not sure,' I reply tersely. A tense silence drags on. Finally, I say, 'The kids miss seeing you.'

I'm being snippy and I know it, but I can't help but bite. I'm angry—hurt, even. Not only for my kids, but for me. For him.

'I was ill, Al,' he spits, a familiar edge entering his voice.

I already can't be arsed.

'Okay.' I don't want to get into the usual conversation: the one where he lies and I call him out and he lies some more.

'Well,' he says, 'I'm sorry I didn't see you. I couldn't help being ill.'

And with that, he hangs up.

Just fuck off, Danny.

2019

21 NOVEMBER

The guilt. How much time had I spent being angry with him? Disappointed in him? Frustrated by him?

It took his death for me to realise how much I loved him. I mean, of course I knew I loved him. But to really know what that meant.

I'd always felt empathy for people who'd lost a loved one; I thought I could feel some of their pain. But I was so wrong. I didn't have a clue.

Losing Danny was like losing a piece of myself. Who am I if I am not his little sister? What do I do if I'm not looking out for him? I felt lost. I fear I always will.

A few days after his death, I was back home with my husband and kids, crying in the kitchen. Being held in a way that has become so familiar now. Cradled.

'I've slagged him off so much, Eddie,' I managed. 'I've spent so much time being angry with him.'

I wondered dimly whether my husband found my reaction to Danny's death strange. I'd spent so much time badmouthing him and being angry with him that my sorrow must seem contradictory, even hypocritical.

'It's because you loved him so much, Ali,' Eddie said, stroking my hair. 'You were angry because you knew he was better than that. You believed in him. You idolised him. You couldn't save him, Ali, and that's why it hurts—but it's not your fault.'

I sobbed. Big, fat, ugly sobs. I cried into my husband's shoulder so hard that my head started to throb.

Eddie knew me better than I knew myself.

7 DECEMBER

A good day. Well, as good as could be expected.

I was starting to understand what people meant when they described grief as a kind of numbness.

When my sister called me that morning, in pieces and unable to talk, I was calm. When my mum spoke about being angry at everyone about everything, I reasoned with her. Then, as if everything were normal, I took the kids to do the shopping. Made lunch. Folded clothes.

On the way back from my parents' house, my kids and I sang silly songs in the car. We laughed at the top of our voices and competed with each other to sing in the silliest voice.

And then I pulled up at the railway crossing near my house. The barriers were down. Waiting there together for the train to pass.

In a bar on the corner, eager Saturday night revellers were already sitting with drinks in hand. A screen on the wall showed that night's football game. The camera flicked away from the pitch and to a blue, sterile studio, where a man was being interviewed. Big. Bald.

It was Danny.

Of course, I knew it wasn't. But I allowed it to be. His arms folded underneath his armpits; the serious expression on his face as he spoke about his passion. His eyebrows. I'd never noticed them before, but now I saw them clearly: blond and bright. His teeth perfect and white but flat somehow, without the gleam he'd had when he smiled.

The barrier lifted. As if waking from a dream, I lifted the clutch and let the car drift on. 'I don't have onion rings, not even chocolate!' I sang, my voice mingling with Lily's. It was a song she'd made up just five minutes before. By the road, the ocean stretched on.

I dropped Lily at her friend's house for a sleepover and drove Peter back home. Eddie and I had promised to do whatever Peter wanted; it wasn't often he got his parents to himself. Peter decreed we were to visit Hickory's Smokehouse. So be it.

It was 5:15 p.m. The restaurant was full, so we took a seat at the bar. Football was on the big screen: Man United, his favourite team, were playing Man City.

Danny. Danny. *Danny.*

'Mummy?' Peter asked. He was peering up at me, his little brow furrowed.

I found I couldn't answer.

2015

JULY

Danny was the only person I could really talk to about myself. I worried that comparing my problems with food to his with drugs might make him feel I was trivialising his problems, but Danny said it made him feel like we understood each other.

When I told him my physiotherapist had advised me not to continue running, he was devastated, as much for me as he was for himself.

The Great North Run had been our thing, our pact to help get us both back into a healthy place. It was the thing that had kept us united throughout the year and focused on a goal.

Me crashing out was bitterly disappointing for both of us, but an old knee injury had come back to haunt me—it was simply too painful to carry on.

'I'm gutted, Al,' he told me sadly, 'you were doing so well.'

I knew he was worried about doing it alone, but I could sense he was worried I'd go back to my old ways too. I was lighter, fresher, and happier than I had been for years, and I knew he didn't want to see me undo all the good that I'd done.

'I'll still do something, Dan,' I told him, 'I just can't run. I'm not going to give up.' I was referring to my eating habits. Running had really helped me sort out my life and take back a bit of control, and I didn't intend to let those benefits slip away. 'But you need to carry on. You're doing it for both of us now.'

I didn't want to give him an opportunity to back out. I'd already done the Great North Run back in 2006; I already knew what it felt like to run through those crowds. I so desperately wanted him to experience it too.

'And I'll be beside you all the way, Danny!'

13 SEPTEMBER

We woke ridiculously early on the day of the run. Danny, Mum, Shay and I rushed to get ready as Eddie and my kids slept soundly upstairs. I set about making porridge for Danny.

I doubled the quantities to give him a good start, but somehow managed to go wrong—even after ten minutes, the porridge oats were floating on top of a pool of milky liquid.

We had to go.

'I'll just have it like that, Al,' he said, taking the bowl from my hands and gulping it down in one go.

'Come on,' he motioned, 'we'll be late.'

I'd managed to get us on a coach with a group of runners from York, and had four spaces reserved.

It was a Lycra-fest, as you'd expect. One couple were in fancy dress. Each and every runner clutched a bottle of water—except Danny, that is, who'd snuck in two cans of Monster Energy under his hoodie.

Once we were on the road, Mum and I got chatting to a guy who'd battled cancer. He was only my age. She was in awe—I could tell because she put on her posh voice when asking about his struggle. It turned out that running had, quite literally, saved his life. He didn't look like a typical runner, but he was clearly a cherished member of the local runners' community.

If only they knew what Danny had battled, I thought. There's a modern-day hero right here. But heroin wasn't the kind of thing you brought up with strangers. At least, it wasn't then. These days, I can't stop talking about it.

Mum and I were sat behind Danny and Shay, and as the bus rolled on I listened to them chatting away. Shay was clearly shattered, but I could hear the excitement in his voice. His dad went on and on, spouting random facts, tales of jobs he'd been on, nights out, football trips—

Some of it was clearly fabricated—that was the way it went in our family. We all love a good story. We get that from Dad. But Shay was enraptured.

When the bus finally pulled up in Newcastle, we gaped out the windows: people were everywhere. Chaos. Excitement. Anticipation.

Danny began to weave his way toward the starting line, and we followed. He'd sank both cans of Monster and was ready to go.

Mum and Shay hugged him, a little too enthusiastically. Mum kept telling him how proud she was.

'You can do this Dan-i-el!' she shouted as he disappeared out of sight.

I felt a pang of sadness—I'd wanted to join him, but my knee injury was still causing me pain. It had been our pact, after all, our thing—but I quickly shook it off. This was his day. I was simply proud; so bleedin' proud. Look at him, I thought. Look how far he's come.

We climbed back on the bus, which dropped us near the finish line, and got some breakfast at a greasy spoon in South Shields. The atmosphere was already electric: families and friends had gathered in anticipation, and the September sun was bright in the sky.

Shay was as excited as a kid at the fair. At eleven years old, he was old enough to enjoy a little independence, but was still happy to spend time with his family. It was wonderful to have him just to ourselves.

Sitting with my mum and Shay on the grassy bank overlooking the track is a memory I'll treasure forever. A steel band played nearby, and my mum sang along to every song, waving her arms in the air as though she were at a carnival. Hours passed like minutes, and the first runners appeared on the horizon—at their head, Mo Farah. We jumped up.

This was it!

We began cheering and clapping wildly, calling out his name, shouting our congratulations. We didn't stop for over three hours!

Although I'd run the Great North Run before, I'd never truly appreciated the sheer scale of the event. There were thousands upon thousands of runners. Many had the names of loved ones emblazoned upon their chests, while others ran in fancy dress costumes. Young, old; black, white—just a sea of people. Bloody amazing people.

We scanned every single face, searching for Danny. Rather ambitiously, we started looking for him as soon as we'd seen Mo. Such was the faith we had in that man!

Quite how we managed to pick him out of that crowd I'll never know, but there he was: limping, sure, but running.

'There he is!' I shouted, arm outstretched.

My mum stood taller, waving her arms as though her life depended on it. 'Go Dan-i-el!' she cried, 'go Dan-i-el! Go, go, go!'

And then Shay saw him.

'Dad!' he screamed, and before we knew it, he was off, running toward the barrier. Running alongside his dad. Running to bring him home.

We quickly grabbed our things and dashed after him. But, within seconds, both father and son had disappeared. A sudden cold spread through my chest as exhilaration turned to fear.

'We can't tell Danny we've lost his son,' I said to mum as we hurried towards the finish line.

'He's going to bloody kill us!'

There were crowds of people everywhere: families hugging, bands playing. However would we find him?

But, after what felt like hours, there they were.

Danny was on the floor, practically horizontal, wrapped in what looked like a big sheet of tin foil. Shay lay on the grass beside him. They were both eating and drinking their way through Danny's goodie bag.

We ran over, relief rushing through me. I glanced at Mum, and I could tell she felt the same as me: so bloody happy.

'You did it!' I exclaimed, locking eyes with my brother.

'I'm going to fucking kill you, Al,' he shot back before opening his arms to give me a great big hug.

2019

18 NOVEMBER

On the day he died, we all stayed at Mum and Dad's. We took turns crying, the rest of us dutifully hugging the current weeper. Nothing made sense. And no matter how many words of comfort we offered one another, no matter how many cups of tea we went through, nothing made anything better.

By lunchtime, talk had turned to practicalities. Rachael reluctantly mentioned the funeral. His body, she remembered the police telling her, would be taken to a funeral home in Preston once it was released.

It was Rachael who'd received Danny's clothes and belongings. Unable to touch them, she'd thrown them into her room and closed the door. It couldn't have been more than a few hours since he'd passed, but already our beloved brother was being treated like just another corpse. A process and procedure had kicked in the second he was declared dead.

'We're using Harvey's,' my dad said as soon as the question of a funeral home was raised. They were the first words we'd heard him say all day. It was good to hear him finally communicate, but sad to hear he had such a strong view on something so painful.

'Okay, Dad,' Rach said dutifully reaching out to squeeze his arm. After a pause, she added, 'also, the police said someone needs to identify him.'

Mum let out another one of the painful moans that had already become familiar. It had only been a few hours; we weren't ready.

'I'll do it,' I said instinctively.

There was no question; this was, of course, what I needed to do.

I watched as relief spread across my sisters' faces and brushed aside the 'are you sure?'s that followed. I was sure; I wasn't simply trying to be a martyr. This was what I did: I sorted shit out for him.

Linda quickly jumped in: 'I'm coming with you.'

'Me too,' Gemma, my niece, said, cautiously.

I looked around the room—first to Linda, then to Gemma, and back to Linda again. Without speaking, I knew what we were all thinking. Maybe, just maybe, it wasn't actually him.

By 2 p.m. we were all mentally exhausted, so we packed Mum off to bed and my dad went for a lie down in the living room. None of us had eaten and the prospect of food felt insane. We all felt that same hole in our gut that food wouldn't fill.

My sisters left for a while, and Gemma and I found ourselves alone in a quiet house. Her youthful face, normally bright and pretty, looked tired and lost as we both tried to busy ourselves in the kitchen, but with little success. Every time we started, we'd forget what we were doing and instead end up aimlessly picking things up and putting them back down again.

Suddenly, my dad appeared behind us.

'Okay Google,' he instructed, hunched over the Google Home. 'Play "Mother" by Pink Floyd.'

'"Mother" by Pink Floyd,' Google repeated in its mechanical voice, and the words began to flow out of the little white box.

Mother, do you think they'll drop the bomb?

Mother, do you think they'll like this song?'

My dad sang along.

'He was singing this in the shower last week,' he said, smiling softly.

And then he broke.

'Fuckin' hell, Danny,' he sobbed.

And sobbed and sobbed and sobbed. He was like a child—his face contorted, giant, uncontrollable sobs leaking down his wrinkled face.

Gemma and I instinctively put our arms around him while he continued to say Danny's name. I reached out and stroked the back of Gemma's soft hand, trying to be the grown-up, trying to protect the family I so desperately loved. Tears were streaming down our faces, our heads pressed against his strong shoulders. We stayed like that for a long time.

8 DECEMBER

Pringle socks.

Hugo Boss.

Man United.

Happy Mondays.

'You're twistin' my melon, man!'

Hoodies.

Adidas trainers.

Tattoos.

Orange.

Bear hugs.

Music.

Vinyl.

Decks.

'Call the cops!'

Tuna and pasta.

    Garlic bread.

    No onions!

    Corona.

    Brandy.

    Thirty-three.

    Love.

Warmth.

Loyalty.

Banter.

'Get in the shower, Shay!' (For the millionth time.)

Danny.

1995

SUMMER

It was a blazing hot summer's day, but the thick floral curtains were drawn in the living room. Danny and his mates were sprawled across the sofas. The TV was blaring.

Mum was in the kitchen, busying herself with washing, silently cursing him for having the curtains drawn in the middle of the day. I could read her thoughts on her tightly drawn face: *What will the neighbours think?*

'Riders on the storm . . .'

I walked into the lounge. It smelt like sweaty boys. One of his friends—I can't remember who now—lifted his legs so I could sit down.

'You watching this, Al?' Danny said as I plonked myself down on the pink patterned sofa.

'Yeah,' I replied, adding an *'obviously'* in my head as I did so. Where else would I be if not with Danny and his mates?

It was a movie about The Doors. I remember rain on windows and something about Jim Morrison being in a bath, but not much else. It was never about watching the movie—it was about hanging out with my brother. Or *hanging on*, which is probably closer to the truth.

We were all shattered but unable to sleep. Conversation was difficult and laboured, so a movie made sense. It occupied our scrambled brains.

Danny was fascinated by The Doors—or, more specifically, Jim Morrison. He loved the darkness and poetry of the music, and was strangely drawn to the story of Morrison's life. Even in his early twenties, Danny was fascinated by drugs and the journeys they took people on; the wild highs and crushing lows. He was the happiest, most fun guy you could meet but, looking back, it's clear that he was perversely addicted to tragedy and sadness.

The night before, my friends and I had joined Danny and his mates at the Park Hall nightclub in Charnock Richard. We were kids of the '90s; Friday night raves were our thing!

I'd been going since before I turned eighteen (sorry Mum!) and although we went separately, Danny and his friends always made sure I went home with them.

The Park Hall was, to our teenage brains, one of the best nights out in Lancashire. Our home town, Leyland, had pubs aplenty but if you wanted to go to a nightclub you had to travel. When we were young there were two choices. You could venture to Tokyo Jo's in nearby Preston for cheesy music or The Park in Charnock Richard for dance. It was almost always, dance. Everyone who was anyone was there, many of us underage with faces thick with make-up and jangly car keys clutched in-hand so as to convince the bouncers we were old enough. I vividly remember the queues—it felt like they went on for miles.

Drugs were as much a part of the rave scene as alcohol, and, while it's strange to say, it was never a big deal. At least, not to me.

We started with speed. Girls would smuggle Rizla-wrapped bombs to the toilets in their bras, while the lads hid them in their socks.

Speed left you wasted. You'd be dancing in the taxi on the way home even when there wasn't any music playing. Manic chatter; tired and weary, but with enough energy left to run a marathon.

That's where the pot came in. Just as speed would take you up, marijuana would bring you down. Danny and his mates would start rolling spliffs in our parents' living room as soon as they got home from a club.

I never got involved with pot. I was passionately anti-smoking (still am!) and it was never for me. Still, I'd sit with Danny and his mates as they smoked, laughed, ate, and laughed some more. I felt like the coolest little sister in the world.

Before long, speed turned to ecstasy and the Park was replaced by 'proper' clubs. We travelled all over the North West—Liverpool, Manchester, Leeds—frequenting new venues: Cream, the Hacienda, Back to Basics, Bowlers. Always a coach-load of merry revellers, utterly mad for it. Always a group of zombies crashed out on the way back.

Unlike speed, ecstasy could take you either way. Sometimes, you felt the tingle of the blood pumping through your veins in time with the music, all the hairs standing up on the backs of your arms and neck, a deep love for everyone around you, even people you'd never met—everyone was one big, amazing family.

Or . . .

It took you down. You felt like a zombie. It was impossible to get a smile on your face. You felt the music but it moved through you rather than inside you. You weren't sad, exactly—you were just a bit numb.

Once, Danny and our friends were at Feel in Preston for a club night hosted by the University of Central Lancashire's students' union. He saw that I was on a downer—dancing in a trance-like state amid a sea of thrashing lunatics.

'Come on!' he shouted and grabbed my arm.

He led me up the stairs to the chillout room. It was smaller, darker, the music duller but still going—a gentler beat.

'Just feel it,' he said, pushing me onto the dancefloor and standing in front of me, closing his eyes.

I can still picture him now: his arms outstretched, his eyes closed. He really felt music. He became it.

For some reason, he still had his huge, thick tan coat on. He must have thought it was cool at the time; Danny was the coolest dresser I've ever known.

He took it off and placed it across my shoulders. It weighed heavy on me, like a thick blanket trying to drag me to the floor, but I kept it on.

He closed his eyes again, gently rocking to the music. Arms stretched wide; a huge smile across his beautiful face.

I followed suit, trying to capture his mood—closing my eyes, forcing myself to take it all in, soak it all up.

And we danced. And we danced. And we danced.

1996

SPRING

Mum was raging. I'd never seen her so angry. It was at that moment that I began to understand where the saying 'steam coming out of your ears' comes from.

'I will not have that stuff in my house!' she shouted upstairs.

A door slammed in response.

'I am *so* disappointed in you, Dan-i-el!'

I skulked around the kitchen, not wanting to get in her way.

After many months of that distinctive smell wafting through our house, my poor mum had finally found out what it was: marijuana. Drugs.

Dad tried to calm her down, but she quickly bit his head off. He retreated hastily to the living room, shooting me a 'keep away from her' look as he went. I followed him.

'Shit! She's angry,' I said to Dad.

'Yeah, I know,' Dad replied, settling himself into his chair flicking on the telly.

I sighed. It was no big deal to my dad; he was ex-army, a man of the world. Smoking a bit of pot was just another rite of passage.

But it was different for Mum. She cared what people thought more than was wise, but mostly she cared for him. All she knew about drugs was that they led to bad places.

I'd better not tell her about me, I thought.

I waited until the evening before pouring out a couple of glasses of wine. Danny had gone to the pub with his mates, so now was the best opportunity I'd get to have a chat with Mum.

'Mum,' I began cautiously.

She looked up, taking the offered glass silently.

'I know pot is a massive thing to you, but honestly, everyone does it. It just isn't a big deal.'

'You don't, do you?' my mum shot, eyes narrowing to slits.

'No, of course not!' I replied. Best not to completely tip her over the edge by telling her I'd taken far worse.

She told me she was scared that it would lead to other things, that it would take him down a path he couldn't get off of. He was a fitness fanatic, a footballer—she didn't want him to ruin it all.

Slowly, I talked her round. She began to relax.

'It doesn't lead to anything, Mum. It's a smoke at the end of the night—it's no big deal. Trust me.'

And, to my shame, she did. *Little did I know.*

A couple of hours later, the boys were back from the pub. They were clearly drunk, and more than a little lively. But apprehension hung above them like a dark cloud.

Danny and his friend Sant poked their heads around the living room door.

'She's okay,' I said, beckoning them in.

They sat down.

'Not in my house,' Mum said with a stern look, and then took a sip of her wine.

The boys nodded. Message received and understood.

2000

JULY

My cousin Helen asked me to house sit while she and her husband went travelling around Southeast Asia. Rachael had left home when she was sixteen, while I was still there at twenty-three! Naturally, I jumped at the chance to move out. I convinced my friend Anna to move in with me too, and, a few months later, Danny joined us.

It was a deceptively spacious terrace in Chorley. Only a 10-minute drive from Mum and Dad – close enough to pop in but far enough away to feel that I could spread my wings. The high ceilings and modern décor were a world away from the room, adorned with cherished teddy ornaments, that I had previously shared with my youngest sister. Anna and I had spacious rooms upstairs, while Danny took over the second reception room on the ground floor. His decks came with him and his constant music broke the calm Anna and I had briefly enjoyed.

Before long, she left to join her boyfriend and Danny's friend Jonesey replaced her. There was always music, always weed—always strangers bobbing in and out. When Helen and Joe returned from their travels, we all bumbled about the huge shared house, an eclectic mix of young people trying to live side by side.

It was during this time that Danny and I first met Cath, who was a friend of Helen's. It was love at first sight for both of us (for Danny in a romantic sense!). She was beautiful, captivating, and incredibly warm. With huge brown eyes and silky dark hair he was instantly drawn to her and was desperate to take her out.

Personally, I felt an immediate connection. I just knew we'd be friends. She was wise and spiritual, and had an air of confidence I couldn't help but envy. Cath and I were the same age, but I felt like she'd been here before.

It wasn't long before Danny and Cath began to date, and she soon became a fixture in our house. She challenged him to think differently about relationships by continuing to see and stay with her male friends, much to Danny's frustration, and, slowly, taught him to love and to trust again. Something he had struggled to do since the end of his last serious relationship. Prior to meeting, she had already made the decision to go travelling and, while he was hopeful she'd change her mind, she was adamant that she had to go. Her single-mindedness and determination were part of the reason he loved her, but they hurt him too.

Cath and I kept in regular contact via email, but Danny found it tough. He wasn't good with technology, and found having intimate chats over MSN Messenger impersonal and unnerving.

And so, before too long, I had to break the news to her that he'd met someone else: Kelly.

Only, Kelly wasn't just someone else. She became the mother of his son, his wife—and then, at last, his ex-wife.

She was the love of his life.

2019

19 NOVEMBER

A woman named Laura ran the funeral home. She was disconcertingly young and pretty, which felt rather odd considering her profession, but it became quickly clear that she knew what she was doing.

Of course, everything felt too soon. But, in twenty-four hours, we'd made at least some of the decisions about the kind of send-off we wanted to give Danny.

I was conscious of time as I had arranged to be at the hospital to identify his body at midday and it was already 10:30, so I asked if we could get started even though we were still waiting for Shay and his mum to arrive.

We filed into the living room, filling it to the brim. Rachael took a seat on the floor with her daughters—Gemma, Hannah, and Becky—around her, while Claire perched on the chair behind them, her hands covering her face. My mum and dad sat together on the two-seater sofa, their hands clutching each others tightly. I motioned to Laura to sit alongside Claire and I took a seat underneath the window, the curtains tightly closed behind me.

When Kelly and Shay arrived ten minutes later, they took a seat by the door. We were already in full flow and immediately started firing questions at Shay. Even now, I shudder at the things we asked of a fifteen-year-old boy:

'Are you happy with him being cremated? Grandad wants that . . .'

'You should choose his clothes, Shay. Your dad would like that.'

'Any particular songs you'd like?'

'Are you happy if the boys carry him, or did you want to?'

He was fifteen years old, and had just lost his dad—his guide, his best friend in the whole world. But somehow trying to keep him included felt better than leaving him alone. We were desperate to do the right thing.

A few days later, a friend sent me a text me a Gary Barlow quote: 'Planning a funeral is like planning a party when you're really sad.'

It was exactly that.

'He liked Johnny Cash,' Claire suggested tentatively, lifting her head from her hands. Danny had loved music, so it was important we got it right.

'No, god no,' I said, rather too abruptly shaking a painful memory of Danny listening to Johnny Cash from my mind. She looked crestfallen, so I quickly tried to move us on. 'Coldplay?'

'Yes, of course. "Yellow"' Claire said, determined.

For me it was 'Magic', but I didn't have the heart to say this now. So I nodded.

We all fell silent. It was as though we had momentarily run out of steam, so Laura shuffled her paperwork on her knee and nodded gently. 'Right. So I'm going to need to know who to send the forms to.'

'I'll be the contact,' I said quickly. 'Send everything through me.'

Rachael and I got back into gear and took control. We selected a coffin without really looking and agreed to every one of Laura's suggestions. Yep, yep, yep, it was all fine. Money was no object; We'd sort it.

And then came the question of the eventual ashes. Mum decided that she wanted to lay her son to rest in the cemetery where he was christened, St. Mary's. It was close enough for Mum and Dad to visit and, ultimately, it felt right.

Laura asked whether we wanted an urn or a box.

'Eddie will make that,' I said without thinking. Eddie was an incredible craftsman; he'd be happy to do it.

But as soon as the words had left my lips, I realised what I'd said. I was going to ask my husband to make a box for my brother's ashes.

Was this even real? What was happening?

Without warning, tears began to stream down my face. My parents turned to me, staring, and Claire's tear-stained eyes went wide. *Shit*, I could see them thinking. *If Alison's broken then we're all screwed.*

Once we were finished I stood on the doorstep with Laura. My family were inside, each of them coming to terms with the coming funeral. Bright light played on the concrete step, and I stared past Laura in silence. Finally, I said, 'What should I expect?'

When she didn't immediately answer, I added, 'You know, when I identify him.'

She drew a deep breath and then began. She told me that it would be hard, that mortuaries weren't the same as a chapel of rest. They wouldn't have prepared him for viewing, so it was likely to be shocking.

'Yes, I can imagine,' I said automatically, with no clue what on earth I was talking about. 'I guess they won't have stitched his eyes together yet.'

She gave a small smile and put her head to the side. 'We don't do things like that, but his eyes may be open. You need to consider whether you can handle that.'

She asked if anyone else could do it, but I assured her I'd be okay; I just wanted to know what to expect.

Before I had a chance to catch my breath, Becky had driven Linda, Gemma, and I to Preston and we were waiting in the mortuary. When a young man with kind grey eyes entered the room, we all began speaking at once:

'What does he look like?'

'Is he ok?'

'Are his eyes open? Is it scary?'

He dutifully went back and forth between my brother and us, doing his best to answer all our questions. It was surreal knowing that Danny was in the room next door—so close and yet so far away.

'He's peaceful,' the man assured us. You could tell he meant it.

Finally, the police officer arrived and got to work. She was lovely but inexperienced, and tried to make small talk as she took details. I found it irritating rather than comforting, and gave her very little back. *If you don't mind, I'm just about to identify my dead brother so I haven't really been giving much thought to the traffic on the A59.* Of course, I didn't say any of that out loud, but I hope I conveyed it with my eyes.

Once the formalities of the statement had been drafted, we finally entered. Me first, followed by Linda and Gemma. Becky waited behind, determined not to see him.

And, all at once, there he was.

Danny. My Danny. *Our* Danny.

It hit us all at once with the force of a double-decker bus. Each of wept, Gemma so deeply that it actually hurt. We told him we loved him. We were proud, we said. We were sorry.

'It's him,' I confirmed as soon as I could find the words. 'It's definitely him.'

And it was; there was no doubt. The tiny hope I'd held in my heart that it was all a bad dream had at last been eradicated. It was him. His face, his stubble, his eyes, his lips, his freshly cut blond hair—it was Danny.

Except, at the same time, it wasn't. It was a perfect mannequin of my brother. While it looked like him, it didn't feel like him. I knew instinctively that everything that had made Danny *Danny* had long since left that body.

I realised then that Danny wasn't gone; he was everywhere.

2015

MARCH

Shortly after leaving my house that January, Danny had started sessions with a drug counsellor. In between seeing her and the community meetings, he was finally beginning to sort his head out.

His counsellor was teaching him to be kinder to himself; to focus on what he had achieved rather than what he'd done wrong. He was starting to sound positive again. Hopeful, even. Each day, he'd find and document something positive: a silly saying that Shay had come up with, perhaps, or something beautiful he'd seen. A lyric. Anything to connect him to the good in life.

During one of our regular calls, he first mentioned the word 'relapse'. It sent a shiver down my spine.

He told me his counsellor had said relapse was a good thing. The way he was talking, it sounded inevitable.

I felt crushed. I knew it had been too easy.

He assured me that relapse was the furthest thing from his mind, but I felt that a seed had been planted. In one fell swoop, he'd gone from 'never again' to 'I hope not'. Looking back, it's clear things were already beginning to unravel.

2019

9 DECEMBER

I keep thinking about turning forty-six. It's a milestone I don't ever want to reach.

At forty-six, I'll be older than him for the first time in my life. No longer his little sister.

I can't bear the thought of it.

I don't want to get old and wrinkly only for him to stay the same. Not because it's not fair, but because it's not right.

He should turn into our dad. He should get cranky and short-tempered. He should become a grandfather, the kind that continues to enjoy a kickabout long after his knees have started creaking. He should have a wife who tells him to be more careful, wagging her finger at him through the kitchen window.

He should be sharing his stories, making us all laugh, keeping us all light.

He should be here. He should just be here.

2013

28 DECEMBER

Winter had truly set in—the air was crisp and cold, the days growing shorter and shorter. Our car was filled to the brim with Christmas presents from the two sides of our family, and the kids were excited to get home and unwrap them all. Only one thing had been conspicuously missing over the Christmas weekend: Danny.

'Can we just pop into Alison's on the way back?' I gingerly asked Eddie, knowing how he hated to be delayed.

He huffed, sighed, and then looked at his watch dramatically before proceeding to switch on the satnav.

'Where am I going?' he asked curtly.

'I'll direct you,' I said confidently, ignoring his tone.

Danny had been staying at then-girlfriend Alison's for Christmas. He'd had a haemorrhoid operation just before the holidays, and had been in quite a lot of pain since. I was upset with him for not making it to Mum's to see us, but thought he must have been quite unwell to have not been in touch at all.

When we arrived, Alison's daughters showed us into the living room and informed us that Danny was in bed. Alison had gone out running errands but we were informed she was due back soon, so we sat awkwardly on the sofa, waiting with the girls. Peter and Lily couldn't keep still and Eddie and I were on eggshells.

After what felt like hours but was in fact only minutes, Alison bustled in, greeting us with warm hugs and immediately berating her daughters for not offering us tea.

As she switched on the kettle, she turned to me.

'Have you seen him?' she asked.

'No, he's in bed. I didn't want to—'

'Oh, bugger that,' she responded, grabbing my arm and leading me upstairs.

She pushed her bedroom door open. It was pitch black, even though it was a sunny winter's day outside. The room had that stuffy smell you get when it's too warm and someone has been in bed for too long. Alison strode to the window and swept open the curtains, flooding the room with sudden light.

'Your Alison's here to see you,' she said brightly.

'Hi Dan!' I told him cheerfully.

He didn't move; I couldn't even see his face.

'Sorry Al,' came his hoarse whisper, 'I'm just too ill. I'll ring you.'

I felt anger rise in my stomach. It would be months before I could see him again, and he couldn't even look me in the eye. I glanced at Alison, and her cheerful, slightly sad smile stopped me saying anything further.

I kissed my hand and placed it on top of the duvet covering my brother.

'I'll see you soon,' I said. 'I love you.'

He didn't even murmur in reply.

Alison and Danny had been together for a few years. They'd known each other as teenagers but had reconnected when he'd started cleaning her windows (one of his many business ventures!). He'd seduced her with his banter, making her feel like a teenager again. It was such a cliché, but a story we all enjoyed.

Alison was the definition of lovely. My family and I all thought the world of her, and were so pleased when Danny appeared to fall in love again after the breakdown of his marriage. She was kind and driven, and so unbelievably strong. She had lost part of her leg and the use of her arm in a motorcycle accident years before, but you would never have known it from the way she carried on. Alison was the pinnacle of positivity and she made Danny happy. What was not to love?

Danny had practically moved in with Alison and her three teenage daughters but he found being around them, when he didn't have Shay, unbelievably hard. It was a vicious circle: he wanted to move on and be happy, but he couldn't shake the feeling of guilt when he wasn't with his son. Whenever things began to look up for him, the guilt would arrive to knock him back down.

Alison set about refilling our cups and I noticed Eddie looking at the clock.

'We'll have to get going, Alison,' I told her, 'it's a two-hour drive.'

'Sorry,' she told me, abandoning the drinks and reaching out to give me a hug.

She held me tight, giving me a loving squeeze. She was only a few years older than me, but had a hard-earned wisdom about her that made me feel I was being embraced by someone much older. As she let me go, she looked me straight in the eye.

'I promise I will tell him you came. I'll make sure he calls you.'

I nodded, feeling my eyes fill with tears. It was like she could see straight into my soul.

As we said our goodbyes and got the kids settled in the car, I looked up at the window. The curtains were once again drawn.

I wrapped my coat tighter around me. 'Why's he so ill?' I asked.

Alison's face twitched, and a deep sadness rose in her eyes. She sighed. 'It's the painkillers, Alison. They've been giving him morphine.'

Uppers and downers. Upper and downers. Down, down, down, down.

2004

2 MAY

I was on my way to meet some friends in Liverpool when I got the call. I'd just walked past the bombed-out church and was turning down Bold Street—and there it was, finally, his name on my buzzing phone's screen.

Danny.

My life had changed dramatically since our house-sharing days in Chorley. I'd travelled the world, bought my own place, started to talk about my job as 'my career'. I was a world away from the pill-popping young woman who'd hung onto her big brother's every word.

But we'd remained fiercely close. The kind of bond we had couldn't be broken just because our lives had taken us down different paths.

It was the call I'd be waiting for.

'Well!' I answered expectantly.

'He's here, Al,' he began excitedly, 'he's here and he's bloody gorgeous.'

You could hear everything in his voice: the pride, the love, the sheer sense of relief. It was beautiful.

He explained it had been a difficult birth. He mentioned a Hoover, which I later discovered referred to vacuum extraction. Kelly had done so well. Apparently Shay's head looked a bit weird, but Danny hoped it would be okay. You could hear his nervousness. (Just for the record, Shay's head is perfect now!)

He was overjoyed. A big, silly grin spread across my face.

Danny and Kelly's journey to have a child of their own had been rocky. Kelly already had a son, Ben, who Danny adored, but he was desperate for a child of his own.

After a heartbreaking miscarriage and a tentative toe dipped into the world of IVF, Kelly fell pregnant with their 'miracle' baby. They were so excited, but understandably nervous. As I'd later find out myself, pregnancy after a miscarriage is a frightening thing—you want to be excited, but are so worried about falling in love again that you hold back, which causes tremendous guilt.

He had more calls to make, more excitement to share, so we said our goodbyes and I promised to visit the next day after work.

'I'm so bloody proud of you,' I said.

'I'm bloody proud of myself!' he laughed.

When I arrived at the pub where I'd arranged to meet my friends, I strode straight to the bar and bought us an ice-cold bottle of champagne. If we were to celebrate Shay's arrival into the world, we'd do it Danny-style.

2007

SPRING

Often, when a difficult marriage ends, both parties harbour a lot of anger and resentment. Danny and Kelly were no different.

They loved each other so much, but no matter how hard they tried, they couldn't make things work as a couple; slowly, their love became corrosive and their relationship toxic.

Sadly, Shay was caught in the middle.

Danny hoped that by taking himself out of the family home he could make life easier for everyone, but that hope soon faded. He went from spending all his free time looking after and playing with his boy to long periods without seeing him, and I could see it eating away at him.

He'd always been a hands-on person, ever since he was a little boy. When there was something he was interested in, he wanted to get involved—he wanted to wade in shoulders-deep. With Shay, this impulse was turned up to eleven!

After his marriage fell apart, he confided in me that not having Shay around felt like a part of him was missing. He said that he couldn't bring himself to enjoy his new-found freedom; he simply pined for his boy.

This was when drugs became less about having a good time and more about keeping going, about feeling nothing at all.

He started to talk about Valium and uppers and downers. By now, this language was completely foreign to me—I just knew that, when he wasn't with Shay, he spent a lot of time in bed.

A 'normal' person might have gone to the doctor then and there, but illegal drugs were such a familiar part of Danny's world that it seemed sensible, to him at least, to medicate himself.

For us, his family, that was when things started to go so horribly wrong.

2019

10 DECEMBER

I'm back in the office. Everyone's been very understanding, but I can't help but wonder whether it's socially acceptable to respond with, 'I will never be okay again,' when the next person asks me how I'm doing.

Okay, perhaps not.

Life feels kind of surreal now. Everything keeps moving: people keep talking, projects keep progressing. I'm hoping my zest will come back. Aside from wanting work to distract me from endless thoughts of Danny, I have a mortgage to pay and kids to feed.

My colleagues have spread Christmas cheer across the office. There is tinsel everywhere, boxes of half-eaten chocolates spilling out over desks. Try as I might, I can't seem to catch onto the widespread good will.

I just want to be back with my mum and dad, pouring them cups of tea, trying to stitch our broken family back together.

My lunch break sets me off again. I glance at one of the big fridges as I stand in the queue at Tesco, armed with my sandwich and a bottle of sparkling water. Bottles of Corona in long, gleaming rows.

Danny. Corona. Danny. Corona.

His favourite beer.

11 DECEMBER

I marched to our designer's desk on my way back from a meeting, plonking his designs on his desk.

Olly looked up at me, an eyebrow raised.

'Can I steal a coloured pen?' I asked softly, plucking one from his stash without waiting for an answer.

I began to colour in one of his designs and write several words underneath.

'This has been approved,' I said, gingerly looking at him, 'but I thought we could add some colour here and align it to these words . . .'

Olly dutifully agreed(!) and offered to send me the new version ASAP.

I walked back into my office with a spring in my step. I was back.

But no sooner had the thought entered my brain, I remembered.

My brother is dead.

2007

LATE SUMMER/EARLY AUTUMN

I was living in a flat I'd bought in Liverpool and travelling to work, at Edge Hill University in Ormskirk, every day. Parking on the large campus was a nightmare and each morning and evening, I would traipse what felt like miles (it wasn't) from the car to the office and back again.

So many of these treks involved calls from Danny.

'Can you send me some money so I can come home from Tenerife?'

'I want to find a new job. Can you update my CV?'

'I'm setting up a business. Can you build me a website when you have a minute?'

'Can you chuck my money in for Dad's birthday and I'll sort you out later?'

In recent months the calls had only been about one thing: Kelly. Things had been as dramatic as ever—Danny and Kelly had the kind of relationship that bounced between incredible and horrific. To an outsider, it looked like there wasn't a lot in between. It was a bit like the children's rhyme: when they were good, they were very, very good, but when they were bad, they were horrid.

I'd recently met Eddie, my future husband, and was in a brilliant place in my life. Unfortunately, Danny was not.

He and Kelly had only married in January, but they'd quickly found that marriage had only papered over the cracks in their relationship. Now, that paper was sloughing away in drifts.

He called me, distressed. Things were really bad and he was worrying about the impact on Shay. There was no question they both adored him, that they wanted the best for him; they just couldn't put aside their enmity for one another.

Danny was looking after the boy he loved more than anything in the world, and was frightened about the impact his and Kelly's sparring was having on Shay. After all, Shay was only three years old, and Danny felt his innocent eyes had already seen too much. He loved Kelly desperately, but knew things couldn't carry on. He wanted to protect Shay.

Finally, after going round in circles for months, Danny left.

2016

JANUARY

To say Danny lived for Shay would be an understatement. From the moment Shay was born, he was the centre of his father's universe.

I think most parents would admit to feeling the same but, after Danny's divorce, this bond—a reliance, really—became even stronger. All of Danny's decisions were based on what they'd mean for Shay.

I spent one evening watching a public lecture on the adolescent brain by a brilliant professor from UCL. She spoke of her research into brain development during adolescence and its impact on the way teenagers behaved. She gave examples: teenagers take more risks, for example, and become more concerned with peers than parents. Essentially, they go a bit astray.

What we'd known for centuries was now science: it was no longer up for debate. It was a matter of fact.

I called Danny the second I got home, eager to explain how it had helped me understand my own teenage years—but also eager to warn him about Shay.

The bond Danny and Shay shared was beautiful. Shay genuinely loved his dad's company, and Danny certainly loved Shay's. Every time you saw them, they'd have a new funny story to tell. Even when Danny was telling Shay off, there was a lightness about it. He could never stay cross for long.

Oh, how I loved to hear him shout, 'Get in that shower, Shay!'

At some point, though, if the professor was to be believed, Danny would feel like he was losing his boy. Dad would no longer be Shay's best pal, his playmate of choice; like every other teenager before him, Shay would care more about his friends than his mum and dad.

Danny wasn't surprised, of course. *We've all been there.* But it was a conversation I'd wanted to have because I was worried about how anchorless Danny would feel when it happened. I thought that, more than any other parent—including myself—it would hit Danny hard.

'But,' I said, after thoroughly depressing him, 'you'll get him back in his twenties. He'll be your best mate again then.'

Danny laughed.

Now, of course, that is never going to happen. Danny doesn't get to see his son grow any older than fifteen, and Shay has lost not only a friend, but a father.

2018

18 NOVEMBER

Still sickly, me and linda

going for a drive and

chat about missing each

while enjoying some food

19 NOVEMBER

Bean on pregablin

1 300mg ever other Day

its been 4 weeks.

20 NOVEMBER

Danny called to tell me that he could no longer drive. His eyes had been hurting for a while and he was feeling constantly drowsy.

No wonder, I thought, *you're constantly pumping shit into your body.*

I'd gotten to the point where I had little sympathy for him. His life had started to feel like a never-ending tale of woe and, to be frank, I found it depressing. I was going through a very difficult period in my own life, and I didn't need his misery on top of my own.

He told me he'd nearly crashed into the central reservation on the motorway. It should have really shocked me and upset me—but instead, I felt nothing. Just numb. It was as if I had exhausted my supply of Danny-related worry and stress.

Of course, it's one of the many (many!) things I lie awake feeling guilty about. But, back then, I simply felt frustrated.

Piss off, Danny!

2019

DECEMBER

I opened Snapchat and sent another message to Shay.

So pleased you went to school. Well done. Your dad would be proud.

I'd been messaging him every day. The only contact I could establish was via Snapchat, so I used that. I was only on the platform to send silly snaps to my nieces, usually of Lily, but it was a way to keep in touch with him, and I'd take anything I could get.

He always replied, but I got very little else from him. Not that I expected much—he was fifteen and his world had just collapsed. The last thing he needed was his annoying auntie pestering him to discuss his feelings.

So I sent a simple daily message, reminding him that I was there for him, telling him that I loved him, and that, of course, his dad did too.

He'd never have chosen to leave you, Shay.

It was hard to know what to say. I suspected he felt angry, angrier even than the rest of us—after all, your dad should stick around, shouldn't he?

Part of it was that I wanted him to remember, when he looked back on that difficult time, that I was always there—that constant annoying reminder of his dad and how much he loved him. Mainly, though, I hoped that one day the right words might land at exactly the right time.

2018

14 JULY

great Day at the beach
at ST annes with linda

15 JULY

Beach again with
linda Sam + Shay
Boys moaned lots

16 JULY

1 mill

2019

20 NOVEMBER

I'm driving home from Mum's. I borrowed her car, as she has vowed not to leave the house or open her curtains until after the funeral. I worry she'll never leave it or see daylight ever again.

I feel terrible. I abandoned my kids on Monday and left Eddie to it. I've barely spoken to them in days. They need their mum and I need them, but I can't shake the guilt I feel at leaving Mum and Dad.

We stay together during the days but, at night, it really hits home. That's when I feel their sheer need the most—suddenly, I become a carer for my fragile parents.

I'm on the home stretch now. The coastal road feels even more bumpy than usual in Mum's little car. To my right, the ocean looms grey and foreboding, a great hidden world of salt and depth. I turn the volume up on the radio to drown out the sound of clattering boxes in the boot.

'Here's to the ones that we got
 Cheers to the wish you were here, but you're not.'

Goosebumps crawl over my skin. It feels like the song has been sent to me.

Tears fall. This, it seems, is my time to grieve for me. Not for Mum and Dad, not for the family. Not Shay. *Not even you, Danny!* This is for me.

When I get to the school, I park up and fix my tear-stained face in the rear-view mirror. I'm on my last minute, so I dash off to the playground to greet the kids.

79

Please don't cry. Please don't cry. They need their mummy, Alison.

As the doors open, they run out and meet me with beaming smiles and huge hugs. I have missed them so much—crouching there on the tarmac, I want to hold them forever.

I see the concern on Peter's face and he holds my hand tight as we walk back to the car. I'm fighting back tears; it's such a wonderful relief to be back with my kids, but it amplifies the guilt I feel at not being with Mum and Dad. *Who will protect them while I protect you?*

When we finally get home, the kids raid the snack cupboard while I switch on the stereo. I type the lyrics into my phone and press play.

It's Maroon 5's 'Memories'.

I turn the volume up as loud as it will go. I've become so used to listening to music quietly or not at all—either Peter gets overwhelmed or Eddie moans about 'the racket'—but not now. This song is for me; I need to feel it.

The vocalist begins and Peter and Lily stop what they're doing. They know what it's about; why I'm playing it.

Peter comes to me, throwing his arms around my legs, hugging them tight. Lily joins in too. Half her hand remains in her crisp packet and I hear her continuing to snaffle down crisps behind my back. I can't help but smile.

We stand there in my kitchen, holding each other, loving each other.

Memories bring back, memories bring back you.

2008

JUNE

Shortly after Danny left Kelly, he moved into a house with a friend of his. It wasn't too far from Shay, and rent was cheap, so it was a win-win.

It looked like a place for men; not in a plush bachelor-pad type of way, but in a functional, sparse way. It was a far cry from the warm family home he had built with Kelly. Danny's decks took centre-stage, and the inevitable beer cans adorned almost every item of furniture.

It was a Saturday and I'd arranged to see him. I knew he was in a bad place mentally—it had been weeks since he'd seen Shay—and I was determined to spend some time with him. He tried to put me off, but I refused.

A few minutes before arriving, he called and asked me to pick him up some yoghurts. I thought it an odd request, but did so diligently: I pulled into the nearest garage and grabbed a few pots as well as some chocolate to try to cheer him up.

When I arrived, I found he wasn't in the mood to talk. He didn't even offer me a brew. He was distracted and down, and I felt like I couldn't get through.

After twenty minutes of frustrated, crippled conversation, I left. He said he was going to go to bed and sleep off his bad mood.

But something felt off; I couldn't quite put my finger on it. I got back in my car and started driving away but, after a couple of hundred yards, I stopped. Something was wrong.

I must have been sitting there for a while, because the next thing I knew an ambulance flew past me. I didn't need to turn around to see where it was going.

I flew out of my car and down the street, running as fast as my legs would take me. When I got to the driveway, one of the paramedics stopped me while the other took his bag into the house.

'It's my brother!' I cried. 'I know it is!'

The next thing I knew, Danny was being walked down the driveway and into the ambulance. He looked crestfallen when he saw me.

The paramedic—a middle-aged man with grey-speckled hair—explained to his colleague who I was.

'He's okay,' he assured me. 'He's just taken something he shouldn't have. We'll take him up to the hospital; you can follow us if you want.'

Danny looked at me. His sad eyes told me he was sorry.

It turned out he'd crushed a load of paracetamol into one of his freshly purchased yoghurts. He wasn't really intending to end his life, he told me later—he'd just wanted to scare his ex.

I didn't know what to say.

2010

OCTOBER

'Where the bloody hell are you?' I snarled, pushing the phone to my ear.

'Errrrr'—Danny paused, obviously looking around for a clue—'it says five miles to Stansted?'

'Jesus Christ!' I muttered to Eddie, my hand over the phone.

'Danny, I don't know where the hell you are, but you are miles from Bath!'

Eddie fired up Google Maps on the laptop. It was 7 p.m. He'd been due to arrive at six, and was still god knows how many hours away.

Once he'd got his bearings, Eddie took the phone from me and explained where Danny was, reiterating our postcode once again. Meanwhile, I took the lasagne we'd made out of the oven and cut a couple of slices. There was no pointing waiting now.

Two hours later, a tired Danny and Shay turned up at the door.

Danny was in a foul mood, so Eddie handed him a cold beer. He refused to admit that it was his own silly fault, and was mad at the world.

But our attention quickly turned to Shay: gorgeous, funny, tired-yet-manic Shay. He'd walked into the room behind his dad repeating the words, 'Keep right! Keep right!'

Eddie looked at me and burst out laughing. It transpired that Danny had somehow set the destination as somewhere in Luxembourg, so Shay had spent the vast majority of the journey listening to the satnav's robotic voice telling his dad to keep bloody right.

This was to become one of those stories we shared at family gatherings. It still makes me laugh thinking about it now but, at the time, it's fair to say Danny did not see the funny side. Not until he was three or four beers in.

It was Danny and Shay's first visit to our house in Bath since we'd moved at the end of 2007. I had an exciting weekend planned, and was eager to show my big brother and young nephew the city I'd fallen in love with.

We shopped on the Saturday, ate out, and took in the sights. Danny was relaxed and happy—happier than I'd seen him in ages. Just him and his boy.

On Sunday, I suggested a bike ride, much to Shay's disgust.

'Come on, you'll love it!' I told him, playfully grabbing him for a tickle.

He fired me a look that told me to get off. Ah well—we went anyway, thinking we'd cheer him up along the way.

We set off walking through our village and down to the canal. It was a gorgeous sunny day. Danny stopped every five minutes to pick conkers from beneath the many horse chestnut trees. I watched as Danny and Shay sifted through them, trying to find the biggest ones to take home. I reached into my pocket, took out my phone, and began happily snapping away.

We continued down to the canal with pockets bulging with conkers. Eddie went ahead and sorted out the bikes. Danny's had an extension seat for Shay; we thought putting him on a bike on his own might be unwise, as none of us fancied fishing him out of the water. His mood had softened while collecting conkers, but he was fierce again now. As Danny tried to pedal, Shay kept his feet firmly planted on the floor. We'd moved about ten metres in ten minutes, and Danny finally lost his rag.

I was getting irritated in the way you do when it's other people's kids, smugly telling myself that *my* future children would never behave in that way. Little did I know!

Danny threatened Shay with every punishment in the box before finishing with the killing blow: 'Well, you won't be getting an ice cream!'

Suddenly, the lights came on. Shay lunged forward, kicking the gravel beneath his feet, forcing his dad to steady himself. *Turbo power!* he shouted, and the bike shot off down the path.

Eddie and I gaped at one another, laughing, and hurried to catch up. We watched, astounded, as they weaved in and out of dog walkers and fellow cyclists, narrowly missing people's toes. All the while, they shouted observations and encouragements to each other, lost in their own little world.

2019

DECEMBER

For the first few weeks after he died, my husband, kids, and I spent most of our time at Mum and Dad's with the rest of my family. Their home became our new centre of gravity, and my sisters, nieces, Linda, and I were constantly crossing paths.

Greeting and leaving each other with hugs, kisses, and declarations of affection. Taking it in turns to break down; to hold and be held. To look after Mum and Dad.

Seeing your fiercely independent mum allow herself to be taken care of is heart-breaking in itself. I'd never seen her sit down so much before. Everything about Danny had left his body the instant he died; I felt something similar had happened to Mum.

Of course, she was still exactly the same—but, somehow, she was totally different too. Something had snapped, never to be remade.

'No mother should have to bury their child,' she said over and over.

She was right.

My siblings and I were falling over ourselves trying to put our parents back together. But, deep down, we feared it was an impossible task. How do you fix a wound that will never heal?

Returning to work gave most of us a welcome distraction, but we also knew it made Mum and Dad's pain more acute. We knew that, to them, it would seem like we were moving on, but in reality we were simply moving (or limping) forwards.

Our family WhatsApp messages dried up. Our daily calls to check in with each other ceased. If you weren't living it, you'd be forgiven for thinking that, for us, the hard part was over—but we knew it had only just begun.

I began to savour those evenings when I'd get to lie with my son, Peter. His debilitating anxiety made it impossible for him to sleep alone, and the news of his Uncle Danny's death had only made it worse. His worst fear (death!) had hit him hard.

Danny's death had given me an even deeper appreciation for the challenges Peter went through, so I hugged him tighter than ever before. Mainly though, selfishly, I savoured that time because it was quiet time. I could shut out the world and process my grief. I could think about my brother.

What I'd lost. What I'd gained.

1981

SUMMER

I was maybe four years old. I had this giant Fisher-Price treehouse (though, of course, I didn't know it was Fisher-Price back then) that I loved perhaps more than anything—the tree would open up so you could put people inside in the different rooms. It was amazing to four-year-old me.

I remember sitting in the back garden, playing with the figures, minding my own business. Danny came outside—he'd have been about seven—and started messing about. I don't know how precisely (I was four, remember!), but he provoked me, and the next thing I knew I'd sent my beloved treehouse hurtling towards him.

It flew into him and then crashed onto the grass, cracking open, spilling my perfect little people everywhere.

I was devastated and enraged. At him—at myself.

And the little bugger just stood in front of me and laughed.

That's my first memory of him. The first time I recall being aware of the presence of my big brother. But not the last.

Years later, we'd play Dukes of Hazzard with his friend William. I'd pretend to be Daisy, while the boys would be Bo and Luke. We'd wind the windows down on my dad's car and climb in and out, slumping in the seats with our arms thrown casually out the window. Trying so desperately to look cool.

We played with his Action Man figures and my Barbies, but never in a romantic way like I wanted. Instead, they were flung down the stairs on the parachutes Danny and my dad made. Each time, Danny would let out a roar as they soared through the air. When he wasn't looking, I'd make them kiss. He'd have killed me if he'd seen!

We'd watch *Knight Rider* together and, later, *Street Hawk*, which was far better in Danny's eyes (and therefore mine). We'd constantly run around the garden, pretending to chase the bad guys—or, more accurately, he would. I was always trailing behind, desperate to get involved.

I was like the best friend he never knew he had or wanted. To him, I was probably just an ever-present shadow following him around, hanging on his every word.

When you adore your brother in that way it never changes. You get older, get new priorities, but the fundamentals remain the same.

1995

APRIL

When my dad turned fifty, my family and I threw him a huge surprise party. We'd never have gotten away with it if it'd been Mum's birthday, but Dad didn't have a clue.

When Mum suggested they go for a drink at the Navy Club, his local, he just thought she was making an effort for his birthday. He had no idea—you could see that on his face when we flicked the lights on and shouted, *'Surprise!'*

To this day, I think that night was probably the happiest of Mum's life. I'd never seen her laugh so much, never seen her so in love with my dad—with all of us.

Everyone was there. Our huge extended family; so many friends, past and present; Dad's drinking buddies; neighbours; and all six of us together, my family, having the time of our lives. Celebrating Dad.

Danny, Rachael, and I invited our own friends too. Danny was twenty at that time, Rach sixteen, and I had just celebrated my eighteenth. Claire was only eleven, too young to be self-aware in the way Rachael and I were. She dominated the dancefloor with her best friend, Rachel—amazingly, they had a dance routine for every song.

Dad was on top form: making everyone laugh, telling jokes, sharing stories, and singing his heart out to the cheesy tunes. It was perfect.

Meanwhile, I was doing my best to look classy and sophisticated; I was desperate to be noticed by one of Danny's friends who I not-so-secretly had a huge crush on. It was the kind of crush you only experience when you are painfully shy eighteen-year-old.

I was good friends with Danny's then-girlfriend, Julie. She flung me around the dancefloor, encouraging me to let my hair down and dance like no-one was watching. Only, at that moment, Danny was.

I heard him chatting to his friend: 'Just look at her,' he said, motioning towards me with his drink. 'Isn't my sister beautiful?'

I pretended not to notice and carried on dancing, but my heart was bursting with pride. For the first time in my life, I felt that my brother had truly noticed me. For once, I wasn't just the annoying little sister, hanging around and trying to be cool.

He'd said I was beautiful, and I believed he meant it. And those little words meant the absolute world.

2016

OCTOBER

It was one of those crazy busy days. I'd rushed from one meeting to the next, barely drawing breath. I'd not eaten yet, so I took my phone out of my pocket to check the time. I'd missed several calls from Rachael.

I quickly rang her back.

'Hurry up, Rach,' I said as soon as she answered, 'I'm at work.'

'It's Danny,' she said, her voice strained. 'We're really worried.'

Danny was back at my parents' place—partly because it suited him and Shay, and partly because he wanted to be around for my mum.

My dad had been unable to do much since his stroke a few years prior and he'd been growing more and more depressive. He was a builder by trade and his stroke, which had weakened his entire left side, made it almost impossible for him to work. He's tried for a while, bless him, but it only made him feel worse. At the same time, his breathing was becoming laboured, something we'd later find was COPD. Rather than find new ways to live his life, he instead began to withdraw. My once gregarious, always on-the-go dad was spending more and more time inside. This obviously affected my mum, so Danny became her lifeline, something to grasp onto. He was good company and they bumbled along together very well.

At Mum's behest, in an attempt to bring back the happy-go-lucky man she so loved, our parents were on holiday. Cruising—literally. Danny, then, was home alone.

I was living in York—miles away—but my sisters still called me when they were worried about him.

I told Rach I had to go, that I was late.

'He's relapsed, Al,' she said, interrupting me. 'We're really frightened.'

I paused, unable to say anything. Finally, I shook my head. 'Look, I'll have to call you back. I'm really sorry but I'm late. I have to go.'

I rushed off to my meeting, frustrated that my brother was once again a problem I'd have to deal with. What could *I* do? I was miles away and at work.

I plonked my laptop and files down in the office. My colleague, Simon, was on his way out the door; he greeted me and offered me a cup of tea. Nodding my thanks, I began to get everything ready. The screen was just firing up when, at last, I understood what Rachael had told me. *Shit.*

Simon walked back in with a steaming brew.

'I'm so sorry,' I spluttered, scooping up my things, 'I think my brother may have just overdosed on heroin. I have to go.'

I didn't have time to think about the information I'd just over-shared, or what such a bizarre revelation might have done to Simon's impression of me. The words just came out.

As soon as I got outside, I took a deep breath and called Rachael back.

She told me that Claire had suspected for a few days; he'd had itchy skin again, haunted eyes. He was being erratic. By this point, it was easy to spot the signs. She'd not wanted to panic anyone so had kept it to herself—but she'd turned up at the house that day to find the back door wide open and beer cans everywhere. The place was a mess.

She'd gone upstairs and found Danny's door closed. She'd been too scared to enter, so had instead called Rachael, who then called me.

'Someone needs to go in,' I told her, 'and it can't be me—I'm here. Someone has to go in.'

I could hear the urgency in my voice, the fear in hers.

'I can't,' she whispered at last.

She didn't need to say why—it didn't need saying.

After what felt like an age, Claire rang me. She'd persuaded her friend and neighbour to go in and have a look.

And there she found him, alive and well—well, except for the fact that he was absolutely wasted.

He denied it, of course. He protested. He got defensive and angry. But then . . .

He was sorry. He was ashamed. He wouldn't do it again.

Mum and Dad had, of course, worried about leaving him at such a difficult time, but he'd assured them it would never happen again. I truly believe he'd meant what he said.

But, by then, it had become a familiar pattern. Predictable, almost. Looking back, it's clear that day was the perfect storm: a huge amount of stress combined with the perfect opportunity. He was embroiled in a horribly stressful situation concerning Shay. It wouldn't be fair to share the details, but he was faced with an impossible choice:

Option 1) Place Shay in a situation that may harm his mental health.

Option 2) Place Shay in a situation that may harm his welfare.

As always, everything was about his son. The trouble was, there was no support for him, Danny—he couldn't cope.

I watched him try so bloody hard to do the right thing: to show up, to engage. But it was like he was shouting into a storm. As hard as it as to admit, this wasn't a problem I could fix for him.

Danny held a fundamental belief that his son should enjoy equal positive relationships with both of his parents. All his decisions were guided by that principle. Sadly, it turned out to be his undoing.

It was a Catch 22: he was damned if he did and damned if he didn't.

Looking back, I can see why he took the opportunity to shut the world out for a while. And, to be honest, I don't blame him.

2019

DECEMBER

Grief never ends . . . but it changes. It's a passage, not a place to stay.

Grief is not a sign of weakness, nor a lack of faith . . . It is the price of love.

– Unknown

From the outset, my grief was expressed through words; it's always been my way. I write and I write and I write and I write, always hoping to make sense of any given situation by laying it all down on paper. This was no different. The words just kept coming: his eulogy, letters to him, this book(!), Facebook statuses, thank you notes. Pages and pages of raw emotion spilling out; it was all I could do to try to make sense of it all. I was desperate to talk about my brother to anyone who'd listen.

For my mum, it was stillness. I'd always known her as a woman who never stopped; she was always busy, always 100 miles per hour. But, from the moment he died, it all stopped. She stood still. It was unnerving to see; it was as if she didn't know what or how to be in the world without her son.

My dad was different. He was either really, really up or really, really down—there was no in-between. He either brought us to tears as we listened to him break down, Danny's name playing on his lips over and over again, or he worried us by acting like nothing had happened. It was almost like he'd forgotten. Somehow, those periods were the more painful for us to witness.

Rachael was like Mum. Her life was such a whirlwind that even hearing about it made me dizzy. With six children, two grandchildren, a full-time job, and a list of after-school activities as long as your arm, Rachael barely had time to breathe, let alone grieve. She sobbed with the rest of us for the

95

first few days, but quickly switched back to into Functional Rach mode. It was Rachael who dealt with the practicalities—his finances, the funeral logistics, his old stuff—and who soothed her broken kids, helping them come to terms with their loss. However, when I thought about my family's capacity to deal with what had happened, I worried about Rachael the most.

And then Claire. Like me, Claire found comfort in words, but hers weren't on the page—they were in a song. Like Danny, music is the love of her life. So, while I write, she sings. And boy, that girl can sing.

The day after Danny died, Claire sent a video to our sad little WhatsApp group: three sisters, three nieces trying to find some way to make sense of loss.

I pressed play. She was singing:

Tell me what does it look like in heaven?

Is it peaceful, is it free like they say?

Does the sun shine bright forever?

Have your fears and your pain gone away?

It was the most beautiful song I'd ever heard; the words were perfect, her voice incredible. She has always been amazing, but that song was something else. This time, it was personal. And, quite simply, it broke our hearts.

She had captured all that we felt so perfectly and, as she sang, her emotion and sincerity, all that she felt inside, poured out. It was crystal clear from the very first word. She was singing it to Danny.

Only, her biggest fan in the whole wide world wasn't there to hear her sing it.

He'll always hear you, baby sis.

2018

18 APRIL

CT 20 mins level 6

Really Good sweat on

at the gym, not really

a good day at work

For some reason Paul likes

To wind me up. The Fact That I have written it in

here shows it winds me up. enjoying the

Gym But Feel really fat

ive only been back 9 days after 9 odd days off

BE PATIENT

BE HAPPY

2m

2019

22 DECEMBER

He had this really specific way of saying my daughter's name.

L i l y POD. The 'Pod' jumping out like it was going to bite you.

I'm looking through old photographs, and every time I see her beautiful little face, I hear him say it.

Growing up in our family, you were never called by your own name. I think it stemmed from my dad. For no particular reason, I was Banger (Ali Banger), Rach was Rat-shit (Danny made that one up), Claire was Clarence, and Danny was DDM (Claire started calling him Dan-Dan-Mong when she was a baby and it stuck).

Dad uses these all the time. At forty-two, I still walk into the house to be greeted with a 'Hiya Banger' from my dad.

To Mum, we were always Dan-i-el, Alison, Rachael, and Claire. More often than not, we were called each other's names, as parents tend to, but they were never shortened, not by Mum.

Danny's name for my Peter was 'What-What'. Whenever he spoke to or about him, he'd always say the phrase 'You don't do that, do I?' to playfully mock Peter's angelically soft and posh little voice.

I can hear you saying those things in my head. Will I always hear them? I hope so.

The rhythm in someone's voice. Their tone. The little inflections that only they do. These are the tiny things you miss once they are gone.

1999

AUGUST

Dancing

And prancing

Grooving

Keep on moving

Flying

Stop your crying

Choosing

While you cruising.

I was in Cafe Mambo in Ibiza, Spain, when I first heard it. I'd gone on my first girls' holiday with Lisa (who was then Danny's girlfriend) and a mutual friend, Sharon. The place was stunning. We were sat, sipping cocktails and looking out to sea. The beach in front of us was completely packed: hundreds of young, beautiful people waiting to experience the famous Ibiza sunset.

I straightened my long black skirt and sat back. It was relatively early, but we were ready to party. Cafe Del Mar, then Mambo, and on to a club. It was Amnesia tonight, the Ibiza version of Cream. The most incredible song was playing. It was funky, it was cool. I listened to the words.

Music is the answer

To your problems

Keep on moving

Then you can solve them.

I felt the music pulse through me, starting slow and building to the perfect crescendo. The beach revellers, as if in a trance, rocked from side to side. Half-dressed men and women on their feet now, moving.

As soon as the song had finished, I put my drink down on the table and went over to the DJ. Three cocktails in, I was feeling confident.

'What was that song?' I shouted across the speakers.

He mouthed something back but I couldn't hear a thing. I shook my head as if to ask him to say it again. He shouted louder, but I still couldn't hear, so he motioned with his finger for me to wait and disappeared.

A minute later, he returned and handed me a beer mat. On it were the words, *Danny Tenaglia. Music Is the Answer.*

I nodded my thanks and popped it into my purse. Danny's going to love this, I thought. Turning, I began to walk back to my friends but, as I did so, I glanced over at the sheltered sofa closer to the bar. I did a double-take. It couldn't be. Could it? No, surely not.

As I stared, open-mouthed, he began to speak. I glanced around, checking that he was actually talking to me.

'Yes, you!' he shouted, motioning me over. I walked across the room nervously. All my confidence had now disappeared.

I straightened my black halter neck and pulled at the hem of my black skirt.

He motioned for me to sit on the edge of his chair.

'Have you come to fucking arrest me?' he said playfully.

I was speechless. I didn't know what to do or say.

It was Shaun Ryder. Danny's idol.

Oh boy, Danny, I cannot wait to tell you this!

2019

21 NOVEMBER

When it came to planning his dad's funeral, the one thing Shay had an opinion on was the inclusion of Happy Mondays lead singer, Shaun Ryder. Shay suggested asking him to lead the procession and, as the quietly spoken words left his mouth, I watched his mother's eyes brim with tears.

I looked across at my sisters' faces and knew we'd all be thinking the same thing. We have to try to find a way to make this happen.

Danny was the biggest Happy Mondays fan and he idolised Shaun. After first meeting him in Ibiza, I met him again with Danny before a concert in Liverpool. Danny was unable to keep his cool, and immediately started gushing about how incredible he thought Shaun was, who cooly posed for a photo. He looked like he'd been on a two-day bender, not like a man about to perfom in front of thousands of people, but Danny didn't seem to notice. He was just in awe.

A few years later, Danny won a competition to meet Shaun following a gig in the Isle of Man. And, in 2017, he got the opportunity to meet him again.

It was a meet and greet, a regular occurance for Shaun, but Danny arrived at the venue armed with a bottle of a courvoisier brandy for his self-proclaimed 'best mate'. During this meeting, which lasted over thirty minutes, they shared a drink and recounted stories about their love of music and their drug-fuelled escapades.

Danny often spoke of that day and described it as one of the best of his life. He told us how Shaun had treated him like an old friend and how that made him feel like the richest man in the world.

For the briefest of moments, I considered trying to reach out to Shaun and asking him to attend Danny's funeral. I thought that, if we could fufil Shay's one wish, we could somehow fix Danny's broken boy, but I stopped short when I realised how bonkers it would sound.

Instead, I emailed his management. I sent copies of the many pictures Danny had with Shaun and explained what had happened and what Shay had said. I asked if Shaun might consider sending a message to Shay but, even as I typed, I didn't really anticipate a response.

To my surprise, I had a reply within the hour. Anita from his management team was amazing, and promised to see what she could do.

The next day, another message popped into my inbox. Anita told me that Shaun sent his condolences to our family and that he fondly remembered meeting Danny.

There was a video attached, so I hit play. Shaun's bald head immediately came into view. He was sitting in what looked like his living room. My first thought was how ordinary he looked, how ordinary his home looked—just a middle-aged guy sitting on his sofa. He began to speak. He said how sorry he was to hear about Danny's death and how his thoughts were with us all, and then he addressed Shay directly, making my heart sing:

'Your dad was a great bloke, Shay.'

2001

FEBRUARY

Smackhead.

Baghead.

Junkie.

Scum.

Before I'd ever met anyone who suffered from heroin addiction, my knowledge of the drug and the lifestyle was purely based on movies. Well, one movie actually: Danny Boyle's *Trainspotting*.

Heroin addicts were, in my eyes, the scum of the earth. They stole from their families; they neglected themselves. They were the worst of humanity.

I never stopped to wonder what had made these people start using. I never wondered what kind of reality they felt they needed to escape from. These were complex questions, and I had a simple answer: they were just scumbags.

The first time I encountered someone I knew who was embroiled in that world was in my early twenties.

I was walking through Leyland, the Lancashire town I grew up in, when I spotted an old friend from school. I had that lovely warm feeling you get when you bump into someone important from your past unexpectedly. He'd been the first boy to ever kiss me (on the cheek!). My daughter loved hearing the story of how I pretended to be disgusted and then ran upstairs clutching my cheek, deliriously happy.

As I got closer, I realised all was not well. He'd been one of the best-looking boys in my year: a cheeky chappy, everyone's friend. So similar to Danny, actually. Except now, when I saw him up close, it was clear he'd lost his sparkle. He looked pale, thin, scruffy. He looked unwell.

He spotted me and walked up to me, greeting me with a hug.

'Hey Alison!' he exclaimed—and then asked me for some money.

It was like a dagger to the heart. What had happened to my beautiful friend? I was young and naïve, but still, I knew a smackhead when I encountered one. He followed me to a cash point and I handed him some cash. What else could I do? I didn't want to offend him, and was too startled to do anything else.

A few days later, Mum and Dad said he'd turned up at the house asking for me. I wasn't in, so he was turned away.

I've never seen him since, but I think of him often. As I understand it, he's been dependent on drugs for most of his adult life. It's tragic. A terrible waste.

My next and only other encounter, before Danny, was about a year later. My friend Kelly and I were out walking our dogs. She spotted her friend's mum running down a quiet residential street with her purse in her hand, arm in the air. When the lady saw Kelly, she stopped abruptly.

'He's taken from my purse, Kelly!' she cried, allowing herself to fold into Kelly's outstretched arms.

It was so painful to see: a mother realising she had been robbed by her own son. Everything felt wrong then; it was like we were living in a different, horrible world.

So when Danny told me he was using heroin? These memories came flooding back. From his very first emails, I saw the desperation for money, the need to get his fix. So, naturally, I feared for my parents. I knew that the news of him using would break them by itself; they'd not cope with him stealing too.

Thankfully, if you can find a silver lining in any of this horror, it's that Danny never ever stole. He never got so far down the path that he broke his strong moral code.

Small mercies . . .

2019

13 DECEMBER

I'm walking to the train station after work, trying out different responses in my head.

SOMEONE: 'So, do you have any siblings?'

ME: 'Yes, I have a brother and two sisters.'

SOMEONE: 'Cool. How old are they?'

ME: 'Well, actually, my brother's dead.'

No, that doesn't work. Too harsh.

SOMEONE: 'So, do you have any siblings?'

ME: 'Yes, I have two sisters and I also had a brother but he died.'

Cue head tilt.

SOMEONE: 'Oh, I'm so, so sorry . . .'

No that doesn't work either. Too sad.

SOMEONE: 'So, do you have any siblings?'

ME: 'Yes, I have two sisters.'

No, no, no. I will never say that. No!

The question is on my mind as this exact scenario played out earlier today. Thankfully, it was with work colleagues who knew not to ask me, but it won't always be that way.

Who even am I if I'm not one of four? The second eldest; the oldest girl. Such a massive part of my identity has been eradicated, just like that. I realise then that I'm not only grieving for my brother; I'm also grieving for myself.

2016

MARCH

I began to think of myself as having two brothers. There was the Danny I knew and loved and the Danny I was irritated by and often despised. I could distinguish between the two within seconds of answering the phone. I never wanted to get the latter.

One thing I knew about Danny was that my opinion mattered. While I had spent my formative years desperate for his approval, he'd spent his adulthood desperate for mine. It was like we'd swapped places. As his lifestyle had become more wayward, he'd become more reliant on me acknowledging that he was still doing okay. I'd become his little-big sister.

When he first started using, he knew it was wrong and desperately wanted help to get himself clean. As such, he laid himself bare. He was open and honest about his biggest fears because he hoped that by being so he could avoid ever having to face them.

But, once he started relapsing, things changed.

He became withdrawn. His eyes held the tell-tale signs of someone haunted. It was clear as day: I could sift through every single photograph of Danny taken over the last ten years and tell you where he was mentally just by looking at his eyes. But the most obvious thing was the way he spoke. When he called, I could tell, simply by the tone of his voice, whether he was using.

I always, always had his back. But it was becoming harder and harder.

It wasn't because he was stumbling; I had sympathy for that. It was because he lied. The sad reality was that when he was in that place, he didn't want to be helped. Instead, he wanted validation. He wanted to know that it was okay. That he was okay.

His calls would be rambling; he'd go off on incomprehensible tangents about the wrongs people had inflicted upon him (usually people at work), about Mum daring to accuse him, about his ex-calling him good for nothing. Worse, Shay being cross.

I'd have to listen to these long drawn-out tales, with him repeating himself and getting frustrated. They'd always end with a simple question:

'So, what do you think, Al?'

I was the last person he should have called. I wouldn't lie; I had to be honest.

When it came to work, I'd give him another perspective. *Perhaps they weren't victimising you; perhaps there were valid reasons for moving you to another site?*

When it came to Mum, I'd ask, *Is there a reason she's suspicious? It's unlike her to have a go at you for no reason at all.*

And his ex? *Well, what was it you said to her?*

As for Shay, well, that was easier. *Maybe he's just pissed off that you spent the entire weekend in bed.*

I always thought I might talk him around, get him off his high horse, but all I did was wind him up.

He'd get defensive, so I'd get more pig-headed. We'd end up in a huff and end the call. Neither of us would mention the elephant that was clearly in the room, staring wild-eyed at both of us: the sad truth that he was well and truly off his head.

2018

4 FEBRUARY

very itch 7 days straight

close to grabbing me,

wont have a chase soon

2015

NOVEMBER

Like many boys born in the '70s, Danny was a huge *Star Wars* fan. He'd been given a toy Millennium Falcon for Christmas when he was a kid, and was always hungry for anything associated with it.

One of my earliest memories is hearing my dad apologise to another parent after Danny had 'persuaded' the man's child to swap his new model AT-AT Walker for a couple of Danny's old school books. The devastated child and his dad turned up at the house in the early evening. Mum was mortified, so hid herself away in the kitchen.

In 1984, we returned to England from the Isle of Man and discovered many of our childhood toys had been lost in transit, most likely due to my dad's 'enterprising' (cost-cutting) idea to transport our belongings on a fishing trawler.

When *Star Wars* had its later renaissance, Danny's passion was reignited. Still scarred from losing his prized possessions as a child, he bought anything *Star Wars*-related he could get his hands on. Twice.

One was for him and Shay to play with and enjoy. And one was to be kept boxed up, a collection for Shay to keep as an adult.

He had everything: figures, spaceships, walkers, cards. You name it—if it was *Star Wars* related, Danny had it.

So, imagine our sadness and fear when we saw he was selling his entire stash on Facebook. He didn't need to tell us how desperate he was feeling; the 'for sale' posts said it all.

Selling his collection ended up being a double-blow. A 'friend' purchased them as a job lot in Danny's darkest hours, only to re-sell them shortly afterwards and make a huge profit.

Another casualty of Danny's addiction.

2020

5 JANUARY

In hindsight, taking my mum to watch *Little Women* was not the smartest move.

From the moment I sat down, I kept reliving a scene from *Friends*, during which the characters Joey and Rachel swap books and Rachel screams, 'Beth dies!' to a shocked and saddened Joey.

It was too soon to watch other people's grief, even if it was fiction.

As the story began to unfold, I glanced at my mum. Was she thinking what I was thinking? Were we about to lose Danny all over again? I could feel my whole body tense up, tears pricking the backs of my eyes.

It was a beautiful scene at the beach. Fiery protagonist Jo has taken Beth, the shy, sweet one, out for some sea air. In those days, it seemed the thinking was that fresh air in your lungs would fix all your ills. If only it were that simple.

Beth was trying to reason with her big sister—trying to make her understand that she did not fear death. She was trying to help Jo prepare for it.

I felt strangely envious that these two fictional girls had got to share that moment. Jo, of course, refused to accept it, but still, Beth had had the chance to tell her sister that when death came, she'd be okay. She wasn't scared. What a comfort that must have been when the worst happened. I longed to turn back time and have that conversation with my own brother. Did he know? Would he have been okay, knowing the end was coming?

Beth gazed wistfully out at the sea. 'It's like a tide going out. It goes out slowly but it can't be stopped . . .'

Now she was speaking directly to me. She had put into words how I'd felt for years. Danny's life was like that tide; like Beth's. He pushed forwards only to be pulled, a little further each time. Ultimately, like that tide, he would go out.

I'd often pictured him as a cartoon character hanging over a cliff edge, his arm outstretched with us all clinging on to him, pulling him back to the surface. What we didn't know—what we couldn't see—was someone, some*thing*, pulling at his leg, weighing him down.

His life. Our worlds teetering on the edge, never certain who would prevail.

I can't explain how or why I knew we'd lose him, but I did. In the pit of my stomach, I knew. Pulling him back over the edge was never saving him; it was simply buying us time.

The music changed.

I knew we were approaching that scene. I began to cry in anticipation, my tears forcing their way past my eyes. I tried not to make a noise for fear of letting out a heartbroken sob, and contemplated reaching for my mum's hand. No, I thought, not now—I only hoped she wasn't seeing the film in the same way I was.

Jo awoke in the early hours and looked across at Beth's empty bed. She ran downstairs and saw Marmie in the kitchen. She was sitting at the table, her back to the room. She turned as Jo entered, her face telling her all she needed to know.

They ran into each other's arms. Mother and daughter, cradling each other, neither having more strength than the other. Both broken; both bereft.

Mum and I were out in the car park before either one of us spoke.

'It was like watching us,' she said, her voice finally cracking. 'That kitchen scene—it was you and me.'

2019

28 DECEMBER

The big round church was the same as it ever was. Somehow, it had been frozen in time, the world changing around it. I was nine years old again, reciting my line in the Easter play, standing on the beautiful white marble altar:

'Didn't I see you with Peter in the garden?'

I was eleven, sitting in a confessional booth, too shy to talk. An agonising minute passed until, carefully, I silently opened the door and crept out. Of course, I said four 'Hail Mary's before I left!

I was thirty-two, standing in a semicircle with the other godparents, trying to hide my face from the priest. I kept tight-lipped while the others recited the words, 'I believe in the Lord Jesus Christ.'

I was forty-two, attending a mass for my dead brother.

I felt so calm. I began to wonder why I'd spent most of my life hating church, hating Catholicism. I was feeling peaceful; relaxed, even. Maybe, just maybe, I would find comfort in coming here more often. What was it I was feeling? Was I closer to God?

The priest began speaking, a reading from Matthew or someone or other:

'Then Herod, when he saw that he was mocked of the wise men, was exceeding wroth, and sent forth, and slew all the children that were in Bethlehem, and in all the coasts thereof, from two years old and under. . .'

Horrified, I glanced at my son. Fear was written all over his face. I looked around the room, noticing all the religious symbols I'd overlooked on my way in: Jesus pinned to the cross with nails; elderly bearded blokes crying in pain; the Virgin Mary holding out her arms, her face expressionless. There was no warmth here, I thought; only sorrow, sadness, and pain.

Now I remember, I thought, shuddering. *This is not for me.*

Once the service was over, we took the kids to light candles for Uncle Danny. I said a prayer in my head in that hypocritical way ex-Catholic atheists do, just in case.

Dear God, please look after our Danny!

On the way out, I picked up a copy of the church newsletter. I glanced over at the names of the dearly departed and those still in our prayers. Danny's name was on it.

A mass for Daniel

10 a.m. on 28 December

The small chapel

I couldn't help but grin. He'd gotten his name in the church newsletter. Fame at last!

Oh, how he'd laugh at that.

1990

NOVEMBER

'Hurry up, Alison! We're going to be late.'

Mum stood at the front door, buttoning up her fancy coat. It was Sunday morning so, naturally, she was dressed head-to-toe in her best clothes. She looked in the mirror and dusted her hair with hairspray before turning to the door.

Rachael and Claire were shrugging on their coats behind her. Claire straightened for a moment, then bent double once more, trying to throw on her boots as she walked.

'Why's Danny not coming?' I shouted from the landing. I was still half-dressed; I hated going to church.

'He's going to the six o'clock mass instead,' Mum replied snippily, clearly irritated by the further delay and the sight of me in my nightwear.

'Well I'm going to go to that one too,' I said defiantly. How dare he get away with it and not me!

Mum shot me an angry look and huffed because she knew if she argued she'd end up being even later. She ushered the girls out the door and slammed it behind her.

It was a regular Sunday morning in our house. I'm pretty sure my mum always started mass with a few 'Hail Mary's to repent for the cursing she'd done in her head while trying to usher four kids out the door.

Church was Mum's thing; hers was the Catholic family. So out we'd go, every Sunday; no question. It was just what we did.

Except, I always did question. I never got the point of church. Even at a young age, I disagreed with many of the things we were told. Church just made you feel guilty for *everything*, and I didn't understand the appeal of that. Besides, it was boring—watching paint dry levels of boring.

Only my dad got out of going. He didn't believe in God, and didn't approve of religion. My dad was the smartest man I knew, so if he didn't like it, it can't have been right—such was my reasoning at the time!

But you didn't disobey my mum. I was brave, but I wasn't stupid, so at 17:45 that evening, Danny and I began our charade. Mum had made a Sunday roast which we wolfed down quickly, leaving our vegetables because we'd simply run out of time (honestly, Mum!).

It was a beautiful and warm November evening. As soon as we got outside, Danny began to sprint down the street. I struggled behind, pathetically trying to catch up with him.

'Danny!' I shouted, 'wait!'

He stopped abruptly and turned around, shooting me an angry look.

'Be quiet,' he hissed. 'Stay behind me.'

He turned back and hurried on. I stayed the requisite distance behind.

This was the deal. We would go to church together, but I couldn't walk with him. It wasn't ideal, but it was the best he had to offer.

At twelve years old, I was self-aware enough to know I was an irritation. I was too smart for my own good and regularly did or said things to embarrass him or make him feel inadequate. Having your sister critiquing your homework was never going to endear you to her.

But what I had in academic ability, he had in social credibility. In this arena, he got his own back on me in spades.

'Is that your sister behind you?' his mates would call out as we passed.

'Nah,' he'd say dismissively, 'don't know her,' before looking back at me with a glare.

I knew better than to argue.

After forty minutes of weaving up and down Leyland's streets, we finally reached the church. It was a familiar routine: the bells would ring and I'd sneak in and find out who was delivering the service. I'd grab a church newsletter on the way out.

I was allowed to walk beside him on the way home. We had a newsletter to read and facts to recite.

As we walked back into the house, Mum looked at us, her eyebrow raised.

'You're early,' she said, her voice rich with suspicion.

'Yeah, we left after communion,' I answered, feeling confident.

'Who delivered mass?' Mum asked.

'Father Ambrose.'

'Oh. Okay . . .' She was on the back foot now, but not yet satisfied.

'We prayed for Eileen Doherty,' Danny added, a tinge of sadness in his voice.

'Awww. That's nice,' Mum responded, giving him a gentle squeeze on his shoulder.

'God rest her soul,' Danny added quietly, shaking his head slowly.

I suppressed a smile—he was a real pro.

'Any of that chocolate left, Mum?' he said suddenly, perking up.

'Yes, Dan-i-el. I saved you a piece.'

As he scoffed it down, he shot me a wink.

2019

21 DECEMBER

It's the little things that get you. They sneak up on you, catching you when you least expect it.

I'd thought showing my mum and dad the paintings of Danny I'd had commissioned might be painful—but no, that was absolutely fine.

Or perhaps it would be talking to my mum about the collage of Danny she wanted framed—gently asking whether she was sure she wanted a constant reminder of his funeral in her dining room. But no, that was fine too.

It was Claire's son, Ellis. An innocent five-year-old nephew throwing his new teddy into the air and shouting, 'Header Uncle Danny!'

It wasn't so much the fact he'd named his new teddy after his beloved uncle (although, of course, that was lovely)—it was the way he bent his head forward to catch the teddy on the way back down. It was a neat trick—one that someone had lovingly taught him how to do. It had probably taken hours.

And, of course, someone had. Uncle Danny.

I brushed the tears away and ushered the kids—my two, and my sister's eldest three—out of the house. A trip to the park would sort me out.

Of course, it didn't. I couldn't stop watching Ellis, that little kid who would grow up doing so many little things because of Uncle Danny.

Because of you, Danny. Because of you.

2019

MAY

My phone rings again but I ignore it. I grab Peter and Lily's hands and run across the car park, dodging the parked cars and darting in front of those still trying to find a space. Lily complains that I am dragging her, so I slow down a little as we near the entrance. I let go of her hand and take the phone from my pocket.

'Where are you?' Danny asks as I answer.

'I'm here,' I reply, catching sight of the back of his head in the café.

'Okay, whereabouts?' he says, clearly exasperated, 'it's already started.'

We're in Bolton to watch Shay and Sam, Linda's son, play football. We've talked about it for months, but this is the first weekend in what seems like forever that the weather has been on our side and that we're free. I only got confirmation the game was on at nine that morning, so I don't know why he's stressing at me.

'I'm in front of the yellow and black sign,' I tell him, 'where are you?'

I watch as he looks around him. He's scanning every corner of the large entrance area.

'There is no yellow and black sign,' he says.

'Well, I'm here,' I tell him, 'it's where it says "Welcome to Bolton Football Stadium".'

'Al, please tell me you're joking.'

'What?' I ask innocently, sneaking into the café and moving up behind him. Reaching out, I tap him on the head and he spins around, the phone still glued to his face.

He shakes his head and sighs. 'I was going to kill you,' he tells me before turning to the kids. 'Your mum thinks she's funny but she's not.' Grinning, he bends down to pick them up but quickly realises they are too heavy. He settles for a huge hug.

Lily is already eyeing the cakes, so walks her over.

'You can have anything you want,' he tells her, 'but you have to hurry— the match has already started.'

Danny orders coffees and the kids pile cookies, crisps, and cans of pop onto the counter. They learnt at a young age to take advantage when Uncle Danny has his wallet out.

As we reach the football pitch, I spot Linda sat on a bench nearby. She stands to give me a hug, and Danny hands her a coffee.

'Come on, kids,' he says, leading the way to the barrier, 'I'll show you where Shay is.'

They diligently follow him, and I watch as Danny points out at the field. A young man in a white top and blue shorts looks over and waves. I guess it must be Shay.

Danny begins to shout, the way I've only heard him do at the television. It's easy to forget the game used to be his life.

The kids get bored quickly and begin running up and down along the side of the pitch. Linda and I sit nearby, chatting on the benches. She tells me she and Danny have been talking about living together, but they're worried about how difficult it will be for the boys.

Sam and Shay are great friends—they're how Linda and Danny met— but it doesn't mean they'll be content as step-brothers of sorts. Both Danny and Linda want to do right by their boys. Sitting there, listening to Linda's soft voice, I feel happy and sad at the same time. It's been such a long time since I've heard anything about Danny moving forward, and I'm happy he's found someone he wants to take that step with, but I'm sad because it's not an easy decision and, worse, because I know Danny. He won't do anything that he feels will hurt or disrupt Shay.

I look across at the boy I think is Shay. Danny's still shouting:

'Well played!'

'Good pass.'

'Come on!'

It's lovely to see him get so into the game. I expect he's even more into it than Shay, who's never struck me as the sporty type. I suspect, like me, he does things to pacify his dad—but, nevertheless, it's nice to see him on the pitch. I sit back and look between them both. It reminds me of seeing my dad watch Danny play when we were kids. We'd spend every Sunday watching a game—rain, hail, or shine. I used to love watching my dad, even if I wasn't totally convinced he understood the rules.

When the match finishes, we head to KFC for some lunch. Peter and Lily are thrilled at the thought of more time with Uncle Danny and Shay, as well as the promise of more junk food. It's chaotic in the restaurant and we're given the wrong order twice. The first time we let it go, but the second time I notice stress creeping across Danny's face. He'd seemed so good until that point.

'I'm going to go and fucking tell them,' he announces, snatching up Shay's incorrect drink.

'I'm not bothered, Dad,' Shay states, clearly embarrassed. I'm instantly reminded of a similar moment at McDonald's when he was only about eight years old. Danny and I were messing around, being a bit loud, and Shay had shouted at us to stop.

'You're embarrassing me,' he told us, and not in a playful way. It was clear he was mortified. He had the same look now.

'Danny, don't,' I say, taking the drink from his hand. 'We'll make do.'

Shay gives me a shy smile and takes the drink back while Danny settles back into his seat.

We eat our food quickly so we can leave. Danny is keen to get home and relax. It's a good idea—he looks unsettled, and I'm keen to get back home myself. We say a quick goodbye, exchange hugs, and go our separate ways.

'We'll have to do this again!' Danny shouts as I walk towards my car, the kids trailing behind me.

'Definitely!' I shout back.

We never do.

28 NOVEMBER

It took the detective eleven days to return our calls. Rachael and I had left countless messages, and I'd filled in what felt like dozens of reporting forms. We were beyond frustrated.

Finally, late on Thursday afternoon, I got a call from a withheld number.

As if losing Danny wasn't enough to contend with, we'd been inundated with rumours surrounding his death. He'd been left; someone else's body was also there; he'd been moved. There was, apparently, a major cover-up.

We'd had people knocking on the door vowing to sort 'them' out; angry men and women wanting to do right by the jack-the-lad guy they'd known.

I was furious. Did they think we needed more drama, more pain? If any of the horror stories they told were actually true, did they think we needed to know? Could our family take any more shock?

It didn't help that the police had been silent.

All we wanted was some kind of explanation; a debrief on the circumstances surrounding his death, an account of what would happen now. We rang the coroner's office but got little back. Heroin. Antidote. CPR. Likelihood of an inquest. But no timeline, no detail. We were in the dark.

I explained to the detective all of the rumours that had found their way back to us. All of the horrible, grim stories about someone we so desperately loved.

We'd worried the coroner so much with our constant calling that she had asked us to get the low-down from the detective before we went ahead with the funeral. We were beginning to worry about whether it would even go ahead. I couldn't bear the thought of breaking the news to Mum and Dad.

Once I had him on the phone, though, the detective put my mind at ease—at least, as best he could. He talked me through the events as he'd seen them.

Danny had been in a flat with another guy. The other guy had called the ambulance and began doing CPR. The paramedics had been so impressed by his technique that they'd allowed him to continue while they did their thing. This man was clearly distressed; he'd known Danny reasonably well. He'd not seen him for months, he said. He was in shock.

They'd tried for forty minutes but then had called it. Danny couldn't be brought back. He was declared dead.

In just the few short days since Danny's death, talking about my brother being dead had become normal. They were just words, just facts. I went about life as if on auto-pilot, not feeling anything.

The detective assured me he and his colleagues had done a thorough job of reviewing the scene. They'd imagined the worst first and worked backwards. Everything they'd seen and heard had led them to conclude that Danny had died in that flat and that the guy had genuinely tried to save his life.

It was enough for me. Even if there were some holes in that version of events; even if the flustered strangers who turned up at our homes insisted otherwise.

If Danny did take something that ended his life, I believe he did so of his own free will. Still, though—it was comforting to know that someone had tried to save him. That he was with someone who cared enough to try.

'Are you satisfied?' the detective asked. He'd gone back into tick-box mode. He needed my assurance that I was happy so he could confirm it with the coroner.

'Yes,' I replied after a moment, answering on behalf of my family. It suddenly felt like an awful lot of pressure. 'Yes, we're satisfied.'

And I was. I had done the right thing by Danny, and I was happy that his friend, whoever he was, had done the right thing too.

I messaged Shay straight away.

25 DECEMBER

The first Christmas without you.

I think of the things I should have done. Of all the things I tried, and failed, to do.

Pull yourself together, Alison.

2020

6 JANUARY

I'd gained a lot of weight since having my kids. I'd gained some beforehand, but it wasn't until I was firmly post-children that I began tipping the scales in earnest.

Eddie and I were living in Bath, a five-and-a-half-hour drive away from our families. In November 2010, I lost our first baby to a late miscarriage. We were both devastated and grieved for the loss of what might have been as much as we did for the baby that I'd carried. I felt horribly alone, utterly bereft. While Eddie seemed to move on, the loss stayed with me like a rock upon my chest. I couldn't fix it, so I focused all my energy on getting pregnant again. By February, I was pregnant and by March I knew it was twins.

I'd thought getting pregnant would fix things but, in reality, it just made everything worse. I lived in constant fear of losing this new pair; as such, I held back.

I was more than five months pregnant before I began to allow myself to believe that these babies might actually be mine. Under duress from family and friends, I began to plan for a family, to imagine life fast-forwarding from the two of us to the four of us. I began to imagine being a mother.

Despite advice from midwives, I declined all offers to connect with other mothers of twins. I didn't want the 'twin mum' label; I didn't want to be different. I kind of wanted my pregnancy to go by unnoticed, which of course is pretty much impossible given the fact that your tummy swells to the size of a house.

Despite a planned induction at thirty-eight weeks, the birth was traumatic and both Eddie and I thought I was going to die. It turned out to be adrenaline shock from the spinal block I was given, but I feared my children would be brought into the world at the same time my life would end. I could see from the look on Eddie's face that he feared this too.

Back at home, we quickly found our routine. Soon, we were doing everything simultaneously—we diligently fed them, bathed them, and changed them like mirror images of one another, day after day after day after day.

I loved them—at least, I think I did. But I didn't feel that overwhelming, instinctive love that you are told defines parenthood. I knew it was my job to care for them, but the unconditional love came later. I couldn't even say when—all I knew was that something was off from the very beginning.

The kids were chalk and cheese from day one. Peter was needy; he wanted attention and to be held all the time. Lily, though, had her own independent spirit from the second she was born. She wouldn't feed properly so we had to stay in hospital for five days while she got to grips with it. 'Thirty Mil Lil' we'd call her. If we could just get her to swallow down that thirty mil, we could go home and start our new life together. But, as we quickly learnt, Lily does things her way in her own time.

I felt guilt from the earliest days: guilt that Peter got more of my time, guilt that I found it hard, guilt that I didn't enjoy them as much as 'I should'. And so I started to eat to fill the void. Cream cakes—well, *any* cakes. Eat, eat, eat.

Danny was the only person I could really talk to. The compulsion we felt; that absolute need. Danny was the only person I could be honest with because he got it too. Our drugs of choice were different, but the feelings were similar—at least, that's how I felt. We'd find ourselves having over-indulged without even realising how we'd got there.

For me, I knew, it was guilt: guilt that I wasn't the person I'd hoped I'd be. Guilt that I found it harder than I believed I should have.

And Danny? I knew he felt guilty for walking away from Kelly and for leaving Shay.

Nom, nom, nom.

Uppers and downers. Uppers and downers.

Why aren't you here, Danny? I really need to talk to you.

As I tuck into another biscuit without really processing what I'm doing, I think of Danny. I understand why he didn't want to tell the truth about his problems; taking drugs was an escape. It kept him sane. We all have our ways of coping.

7 JANUARY

addict

/ˈadɪkt/

noun

a person who is addicted to a particular substance, typically an illegal drug.

'a former heroin addict'.

druggy

/ˈdrʌgi/

noun

a drug addict or habitual user of drugs.

***

I was beginning to feel a bit frustrated with my family.

It's the beginning of January and we're embracing the New Year with gusto. We've made it through the terrible pain of our first Christmas and New Year without him, and now we have to get practical. There is work to be done.

I turn my attention to the inquest. When is it? Where is it? What do we need to do?

There is a statement we need to submit, so I set about writing it in my lunch hour. It shouldn't take long; it's just the facts, after all. What was he like before his death? What was his state of mind?

I sit down, fingers poised over the keyboard—but the page stays blank.

Normally, words pour out of me, especially when it comes to Danny, but I find my fingers hovering. I begin to tap the desk. Will the family be happy with me saying this? Should I tone that aspect down? Leave that bit out?

Discouraged, I grab my coat and head out for some fresh air. Why is this so damned hard?

It's a beautiful crisp day on campus, far too warm for January. There is an expectant buzz in the air; a hopeful warmth surrounding the new year. A fresh start.

As I walk, I replay conversations in my head.

Mum: 'We're just thankful he didn't really turn into a druggy.'

Rachael: 'I just don't understand why anyone would ever take drugs. I'll never get it.' (Said whilst holding a fag.)

Claire: 'Shay's worried people will think his dad was a smackhead.'

Linda: 'I really don't believe he took anything that night.'

Everywhere I turned, someone was saying something about Danny being different. Our collective lack of understanding was shocking. We wanted to see the best in him and didn't want to tar him with the same brush as the dead-heads we'd until that point associated with drugs.

But the more I thought about it, the more I began to get upset. That 'smackhead' on the street begging for money didn't choose to be that way. They're someone's son or daughter, someone's brother or sister. Why are we putting Danny on a pedestal because he was lucky enough to still have a bit of power over his addiction?

Why is he any different? In fact, why are any of us?

I met my colleague, Sabina, on the square. She noticed I looked a little frazzled, and suggested we go for a coffee. All these thoughts and questions were whirling around in my brain. I didn't want to pigeonhole my brother as some addict, didn't want to associate him with all the horrible connotations that label entailed. But, by not being honest, I was contributing to the problem.

My brother was a drug addict, but he wasn't one of *those* drug addicts. No, he was the good kind.

What the actual fuck!

Danny was the first person to admit that he was addicted to drugs. He was an addict and he knew it. Sometimes he was clean and sometimes he wasn't. Sometimes it was legal, sometimes illegal. But he was always an addict.

Likewise, my sister was addicted to cigarettes, and I, although I hate to admit it, was addicted to food (or, at least, I used food as a crutch). If you stripped away the substances and the law, it boiled down to the same thing: coping mechanisms. Each of us had habits or addictions that contributed to our poor health and that could cause premature death.

The only difference was that Danny's addiction wasn't well understood. Yes, he was the first to die, but what if it was Rachael with lung cancer or me with clogged arteries? Would we be having the same debates? Would we be wrestling with the same sense of shame?

No. Of course we wouldn't.

I was tired of feeling ashamed; tired of feeling that I *should* be ashamed.

Being an addict didn't stop Danny from being a great dad. It didn't stop him playing an active part in our lives. It didn't stop him having a relationship, from having hopes and dreams.

He was lucky to remain at least semi-functional. Not everyone is that lucky.

But he was an addict as much as anyone else. It just hadn't sunk its claws all the way in . . . until, of course, it did.

I shared my hypothesis with my colleague, my thoughts spilling out like verbal diarrhoea. I barely took a breath. I was conscious I was over-sharing, but couldn't help myself.

She nodded along attentively and took a slow sip of her coffee.

'The way I see it,' she began when I finally sputtered out, 'it's like a coping mechanism. We all have them in some form and they're different for each of us.'

'Yes!' I jumped in, allowing her another sip from her cup. 'Like, for me, I'll put my feelings in a box and focus on work and overeat.'

We both laughed. It was painfully true.

'And I shop!' she added, making me laugh. I'd worked with her for almost a year and couldn't remember seeing her in the same outfit twice; she was one of those effortlessly stylish women who could get away with any look she wanted. I envied her—I had to stay in my own style lane, as conservative as it was.

'Exactly,' I continued, 'Danny's go-to just happened to be drugs.'

She nodded slowly. 'But really it's about resilience, isn't it?'

God, we were giving the professors at the university a run for their money at this point.

She went on to recount a story about a couple of friends of hers. Like me, they had a child with anxiety, and they'd sought professional help to support her.

During a workshop, her female friend (the mum) had come to the realisation that she was incredibly resilient. She'd lost her father at a very young age but had got through it relatively unscathed. She handled her daughter's episodes with ease and often managed to keep calm in even the most stressful situations. She wondered if perhaps her early experience—which was, after all, one of the worst things that could happen to a kid—had given her a unique perspective on how to view and handle stress. After all, can things get any worse than the death of your father?

But her husband (the dad) . . . well, he was a nightmare. He got overwhelmed by the slightest thing and, worse, he tended to drink to relax. Car failed the MOT? Drink. Bad day at work? Drink. Daughter feeling anxious? Drink. You get the picture.

'You see?' Sabina explained. 'They both had very different levels of resilience; therefore, they couldn't support their daughter in the same way.'

I thought about me and Danny. A bill coming out of the blue was too much for Danny, as was a phone call that didn't go his way. It would stress him out for days; weeks, sometimes. I, on the other hand, dealt with a stressful job every day. I handled a child with anxiety. I managed all the household tasks.

Our resilience levels were worlds apart, so our dependencies on coping mechanisms were too.

If Danny had been more resilient, maybe he wouldn't have become addicted; maybe he wouldn't have needed a crutch to get by.

Confident we'd put the world to rights, we headed back to the office. *I get it a bit more now*, I thought to myself. *You were never very resilient to begin with.*

I thought back to our childhood. One evening, Mum had returned from parent's evening and had gone up to talk to Danny in his bedroom. I was in bed, pretending to be asleep, but when I heard him crying, my ears pricked up.

'I just want you to try, Dan-i-el,' I heard her say in a soothing voice. I pictured her stroking his hair the way she always did when we were upset; that way you never get too old for.

'You *are* capable. I know you are.'

'I'm not,' he muttered. He was still crying. 'I just can't do it. Mum, I do try. I do. But—'

Mum stayed with him awhile and they talked things through. She calmed him down and, eventually, the tears stopped.

He was clearly gutted that his teachers had reported bad things. He never wanted to let his mum down; her disappointment always hurt and upset him, even more than it did the rest of us.

The next morning, he got up and left for school early. He was out of the house before I was even dressed.

This is it, I expect Mum thought. *He'll make a fresh start now.* Confident that her pep talk had done the trick.

But later that day, Mum got a call from school.

'Daniel's mum?' the teacher asked.

'Yes, speaking,' she responded, probably in her posh voice.

'I'm going to need you to come down to the school. I'm afraid Daniel has just punched another pupil in the face.'

5:30 P.M.

I walked down the hill, letting the light rain break over my face. After such a warm day, it felt refreshing. Liverpool's lights were flickering on across the city and I was on my way home to my kids. It was one of my favourite times.

An advertisement on a bus shelter caught my eye. It was for a zip wire place in North Wales.

Cool, I thought instinctively. *The kids would love that.*

But immediately I felt a pang of sadness; I wouldn't take them. I wouldn't join in.

I'd been trying to lose the baby weight for the last eight years with no success. I'd lose a bit, get in the zone, and then fall off the wagon. The triggers were varied—a stressful day with the kids, maybe, or a complex issue at work. Before I knew it, I'd be stuffing my face, and one chocolate bar or slice of cake always led to another. I'd be so consumed with guilt that the only comfort was to eat more.

My weight meant so many things I wanted to do and experience with the kids passed me by. It made me sad to think about it too much (and when I felt sad, I ate).

How am I any different to Danny, I thought. *How can I judge his choices when I make the wrong ones for myself every single day? Choices that don't just affect me, but the lives my kids lead.*

And really, if I'm truly honest with myself, the only real difference is that Danny didn't have a choice. Drugs controlled him; it hadn't been the other way around for a long time. Eating in response to stress or sadness, though? That comes down to willpower and choice. Chocolate hadn't changed the structure of my brain.

Not like Danny's drugs. Opioids like heroin affect the way your brain works; they trick you into believing that not having it is starving your body of oxygen. It's like you need it just to breathe.

I knew that Danny's drug addiction wasn't about choice—at least, not towards the end. It wasn't as straightforward as that. The further he went down that road, the less in control he became. Opioids made his choices for him.

You need me to breathe, Danny.

He didn't get to choose.

But I do.

Unlike Ewan McGregor's character in *Trainspotting*, I really can choose life—not existence, but to really live.

I quickened my step.

Get it together Alison.

5:35 P.M.

I walked past a homeless man on the corner by the station. The same man I'd seen every evening for nearly a year—hollow-eyed, skinny, the tell-tale signs. The same dirty McDonald's cup tucked between his feet. The same bulging backpack by his side. His arms folded across his bent knees.

I fumbled in my coat pocket and found some loose change. £1.25. Rubbish, but it was the thought that counted, I told myself. I threw it into his cup and he nodded.

I looked at his face and saw him for the first time.

He was someone's son. Maybe someone's brother.

I thought of my money contributing to his fix later that evening. For the first time, I didn't see a disgusting addict; I saw a man able to let out a long, slow breath.

2019

3 DECEMBER

Waking up on the day of your brother's funeral is a surreal experience.

Unlike his death, this was something we'd prepared for. We knew it was going to be full of sadness and tears, and we'd done our best to steel ourselves.

In the two weeks since he'd died, we'd done an incredible amount. It's funny what you consider important in the early days of grief. You begin to make assumptions about what your loved one would have wanted, as if a forty-five-year-old man without any kind of terminal illness would have had a mental plan of how he'd like us to mourn his death or celebrate his life.

We decided Danny would want it to be a celebration; that he'd want some uplifting music. He'd want us to smile, after all.

Just for the record, if I go, I want you to cry like you've never cried before, people.

I had written his eulogy. I'd not given the family a choice. Just like identifying his body, I'd felt it was my duty. Who could tell his story but me?

We all wore something orange, his favourite colour. We'd bought the men bright orange long-sleeved polo shirts (let's blame the grief!) and us ladies wore orange scarves, trainers (Adidas, of course), and bracelets. It's worth noting that all these orange things cost a ridiculous amount of money—anything to make us feel closer to him.

Both my sisters and my nieces went out and got tattoos. I was close to getting one myself; it was only the thought of Danny turning in his grave that stopped me.

Before we knew it, Mum and Dad's house was full. Mum and Dad had never looked so small and lost, so I took charge.

'Come in. Come in,' I'd say, ushering in those who arrived at the door, not always knowing who they were. We'd stopped offering brews when we'd run out of cups.

At 11:50, I kicked everyone out into the street. I hadn't planned it; I'd just had a compulsion to get everyone outside to welcome him home.

Welcome him home, I thought, blinking back tears. I shook my head.

Mum was being propped up by my sisters. She looked like she might crumble beneath them. Dad stood nearby, stoic and sad.

I stood at the front, a guard on the lookout.

'He'll be here any minute,' I shouted cheerily, casting my eye over the line.

There must have been about forty of us. I had no idea where half the people had come from. It was a sea of black and orange.

'He's here!' I shouted as I saw the slow black car turn into the street. 'He's h—' But words failed me.

A tortured sob tore from my throat.

My nephew George reached out and took my hand. It was a gesture that will stay with me forever. I looked at the floor, tears streaming down my face, and smiled.

'It's okay, Auntie Ali,' he said authoritatively.

I kissed his small hand.

I felt the most overwhelming compulsion to run to him. I wanted to hold him in my arms one more time.

Danny. Danny! This can't be real.

Before I had a chance to think, Laura from the funeral home began directing us towards the cars—only, my legs wouldn't work. I felt like I might fall.

Stiff as a board, I began to edge closer to our car, but turned back suddenly. The hearse's back door (boot?) was open, his coffin gazing out at me.

'Can I touch him?' I whispered to the usher.

The man nodded. 'Of course.'

I leaned into the car, spreading both hands over the coffin's cool surface. It was further back than I'd thought, so I felt like I was almost climbing in. I stood on my tiptoes and reached forwards to kiss it.

'I love you so, so much, Danny,' I cried. 'I will do you proud.'

Finally, I tore myself away and limped back to the waiting car. There, I watched as, one by one, my family went to touch him. To say goodbye.

It was heart-breaking yet poignant. He was directly outside our childhood home, poised and ready for his final journey. As desperately sad as it all felt, it was a comfort to know we were going to be with him all the way.

I shook my head again and wiped away the tears before finally climbing into the car.

Get your shit together, Alison. You got this. You have to. I tightened my muscles and sat up straight, concentrating on controlling my breathing. Deep and slow. Deep and slow.

Not content with merely writing the eulogy, I also wanted to read it. The minister we'd chosen was incredible, but I was adamant that Danny's story should be told by us, his family. Grief made me even more impossible than ever before!

In the end I compromised, and Rachael and I agreed to do it together. It was fitting. We'd support each other. Claire's song would be played and Gemma, Danny's god-daughter, would do a reading. All personal. All us. All for Danny.

Getting through that eulogy was all I could think about. As my varied family members settled around me, many of them sobbing, I took deep, measured breaths, trying to focus. Deep and slow. Deep and slow.

The minister said she'd be on stand-by if we found it 'too difficult', but I was determined that wasn't going to happen. I was not going to fail him. This was my job.

I couldn't allow myself to be in the moment, so I didn't pay too much attention when his coffin was walked up the aisle. Deep and slow. Deep and slow. I couldn't let him down; I just couldn't. Deep and slow, Alison. Keep breathing. No thinking. Deep and slow.

When the time came, I walked up to the lectern with Rachael. She began to read and I instinctively reached out for her hand.

'In the days since we lost you,' she began, her voice strong and unwavering, 'we have been so touched and comforted to hear so many stories about you. To know how loved you were by so many people. We hope you knew that, Dan. If you could only look around this room now, your heart would burst with pride. You did this, Danny—only you.

'Every single story and anecdote made us laugh. From wrapping your friend Pete up in Sellotape and popping him in a taxi to telling a goalkeeper you'd kill him if he saved your penalty. Everyone has a story to tell, which reflects who you were at heart: a real character; a boy and a man so full of wit and charm that you were genuinely loved—adored, even.

'So many stories of laughter and banter. So many reflections on your footballing past, your love of music. Oh, how you loved music. And your utter devotion to those you loved—friends and family alike.'

Rachel paused, and I noticed her hands were trembling. She took a deep breath.

Deep and slow, Rach.

'Your friends speak of a man who made them feel a million dollars and who left a lasting impression. Your school and footballing friend Lee Hitchen's post made us laugh and burst with pride in equal measure. He said,

"Without knowing, you taught me that taking a risk is okay. It might get you into bother but it's worth the risk. Calculated risk, I suppose. You floated the risk and I was left calculating. There was a lot of calculating. But you pushed me and I needed that. You showed me how to be scrappy and fight for things. You gave me experiences that were every bit as important as my education. Without knowing, you were instrumental in developing what my outlook on life is today."

'Such was the imprint you made. You shaped so many lives.

'In the last week, we've thought so much about why we are here. Why we are saying goodbye to you at forty-five. Danny, it just doesn't make sense. But then, it isn't goodbye, is it? In our darkest moments, we've shared stories and laughter and held each other, and all the while we felt you were with us. You always were and you always will be. We've listened to so many songs that connect us to you because, and we're shamelessly stealing this from Maroon 5, music brings back memories and the memories bring back you.

'We think you'd like that lyric.

'Shay may have his mother's looks but he has your heart, Dan, and your wit. And we'll treasure him and love him as much as you ever did. All the love and hugs we have for you will be poured into that boy. We'll do you proud, and it goes without saying that he will. He always did, didn't he? Just by being your boy.'

I looked out at the crowd. Many were crying softly, faces nestled in their hands. Others stared as if transfixed, expressionless.

'During the many conversations over the last few days,' Rachel said, 'so many poignant things have stuck in our heads. None more so than Kat's throwaway comment after we were laughing about some silly thing you did. She said, "How did he not know that he was enough?" and the words just choked me. How did you not know?

'Those of us that loved you knew you battled some serious demons. You went down a path you weren't proud of, but you always turned around and came back to us again. Even at the end, we had you back: the real you.

'Why didn't you know you were enough, Danny? Do you know it now? Can you feel it? I hope you can.

'Linda told us just the other day that when you two got together, you told her, "I can't give you a lot, Linda, but I promise to make you laugh twice a day."

'And boy did you.'

Rachael's face broke into a wide smile. There were tears in her eyes, I saw.

'That was so you. Your banter and jokes and quick wit were worth more than pots of gold. Having you in our lives made us the richest people in the entire world. Success isn't defined by money, Danny; it's defined by love. And my god, we had that from you and for you in abundance.

'You were the biggest character with the warmest heart. If there is a person in this room now who doesn't have a story about you that makes them laugh then they must not have had the honour of being your friend. Life with you was never serious for long.

'No-one could be around you and take life too seriously. You wouldn't let them. If any of us got ahead of our station, you'd bring us back to earth.

'Danny. Forever keeping it real, keeping it light.'

With that, Rachael took a long, shuddering breath and stepped back from the podium, shooting me an uncharacteristically shy smile.

Well done, Rach. You did brilliantly. Now my turn.

I stepped forward and took a deep breath.

'Danny, you were your father's son. Two peas in a pod. Our darling, charming, lovable rogues.

'As I speak, I can't think of a single interaction you two had that wasn't a mickey-take. You inherited Dad's quick wit, his ability to tell a story, and his air of fun. Dad felt such pride when you started going out as a teenager; you popping into the con club on your way to the pub dressed head to toe in designer gear, your pony-tailed wingman Sant beside you. He treasures those times; lives for them, even. Us girls never came close to the bond you two had, but we didn't care because we loved you just as much as he did.

'But for all the silliness you got from Dad, you got your warmth from Mum. While Dad taught you how to duck and dive, Mum taught you how to be moral, how to love. One of the most heart-warming tributes we've read in the last few days mentioned your strong moral code, your fierce loyalty to those that mattered to you. That was so much a part of who you were, and that was from your mum. No matter what you did in your life, she had your back. She believed in you. She always will.

'Like Dad, Mum and you had such a special bond. Her beautiful blond and blue-eyed boy. Will we really never see you winding her up in the kitchen again? Mum being mock-offended but giggling away at your silliness—you always made her laugh so much. You could always break her down. Only you, Danny. Only you.

'And then us girls, your three sisters. Each and every one of us looking up to and admiring you in different ways. The protection we felt from you was indescribable; no one could hurt us with you around looking after us, loving us. I know your nieces felt it too. The warm, protecting arms of Uncle Danny will be wrapped around them forever.'

I felt a tremor in my chest, but pushed on—I'd finish this. I had to. I felt Rachael's hand squeeze mine, soft but firm.

'And we can't forget your other nieces and nephews,' I said, standing a little taller and forcing myself to peer out at the massed faces. 'In the days since you've been gone, we've all commented on the silly things our kids have said or done. The silly things you taught them or showed them; the laughter and humour that we know will be with them for generations. Because of you. It's all because of you.

'So, to Linda. Your love. The best cook you've ever known (sorry Mum!).'

My eyes met Linda's for a fleeting moment. She was weeping, but smiling too—sad to say goodbye, but happy to remember.

'Watching you with Linda gave us so much joy. You lit each other up. She came into your life when you needed her and showed you the kind of unconditional love that you gave back. She'll miss the log fires in the middle of summer and the terrible jokes, but she'll forever carry you in her heart.

'But now, Danny, I want to pause for a second . . .'

I looked up and dramatically scanned the room. Despite the terrible ache in my heart, I knew I was getting into my groove. This was the most important public speech I'd given in my life and I was doing it, I was really doing it.

'I want you to imagine we're in a club. The low hum of a beat is in the background. It feels a bit trancey. The dancing has slowed down, and we're all waiting in anticipation. And then the music starts to build up again. We know a crescendo is coming. That sound. Those words. This is that bit, Danny—that bit that used to put the huge smile all over your beautiful face.

'This is Shay.'

I can feel my voice wants to break, but I don't let it.

'Oh boy, where to even begin? Has a father ever loved a son more than you loved Shay? From the second he was born, you adored every ounce of him. Your buddy, your soul, your reason for being.

'It breaks our hearts to think we won't get to see you two bobbing off to the gym together again, hear you laughing together again. All our memories of you are with him; we'll never lose them. Even when Shay wasn't physically with you, he was there. He was such a part of you.

'And we know you cared for his mum and his brother, Ben. The bond that you and Kelly shared with Shay will never be broken. He is the best parts of both of you and he makes us all so proud, no one more so than you. Just like your dad, it was the silly things that made you proud: the jokes he told. His silly sayings. Will any of your family ever be able to open the curtains without thinking, "It's a sunny day, Dad!" in our heads? Oh, how you loved saying that. How you loved him.

'And how he loved you. I could write a book of Danny and Shay stories. Maybe one day I will but, for now, just now, we'll love him. We'll protect him and care for him just as fiercely as you always did. We'll do you proud, Dan. We promise you that.

'I'm going to have to stop soon, Danny, but before I do, I want to share some words from some of your oldest and closest friends.'

I looked up, briefly scanned the crowd, and cleared my throat.

'This is from Dom: "I'll remember him as never looking down on anybody, never being intimidated by anybody, but always looking out for other people, especially his friends."

'And Steve. He captured the essence of you far better than I ever could: "Only Danny, right. Only Danny could inspire such love, his huge heart, his spirit, and his uncompromising love and friendship. I know he is with us; he always has been and always will be. A light so bright wouldn't go out. It burns eternal and it keeps us."'

I looked up and grinned. 'You are the True North, Danny.'

My smile faded as quickly as it had come. 'And now we must let you go, and pour all of our love, hugs, and kisses into your son. We'll keep your memory alive, Danny. We all will.

'It seems fitting that the last words should be to Shay from your idol Shaun Ryder: "Your dad was a great bloke, Shay."

'How right was he? Danny: partner, brother, uncle, step-dad, nephew, cousin, friend, godfather, footballer, superstar DJ, Shaun Ryder's best friend, and the best-looking guy at the gym. But, most importantly, Pete and Pat's son and Shay's dad—the man with the biggest heart and the coolest trainers. You were the very best of the best and we will always carry you in our hearts.

'Fly high, big brother.'

I stepped down and made my way silently back to my seat, dimly aware of Rachael following behind me. Relief washed over me. I didn't dare look up for fear of catching anyone's eye.

We'd bloody done it.

Claire's song began to play immediately, her beautiful, soulful voice booming out of the speakers.

Tell me, what does it look like in heaven?

All at once, the tears burst free. I grabbed Rachael's hand and started to sing, loud and proud. She gave me a smile and joined me in song. Then, hand in hand, we turned and fixed our eyes on his coffin.

We sang our little hearts out for you, Dan.

2019

26 DECEMBER

The hardest part about losing Danny was living with the knowledge that I had failed him.

I felt such incredible guilt. During the last few years of his life, I'd spent more time being angry and disappointed than being empathetic, more energy trying to get him off the phone than keep him on it.

I hated the way he always made me feel guilty. His sly remarks when he called: 'I'm just ringing because you haven't called.'

He always knew how to feed that inner voice that I desperately wanted to suppress: the one that constantly tried to remind me I was letting him down.

My life had become busy and stressful. Peter's anxiety was occupying more and more space in my brain, and I'd uprooted my whole family for a new life because of my job (a big job!). I simply couldn't help Danny; I refused to allow myself to, so the dark version of Danny, the one struggling with drugs and mental health, didn't get much of a look-in.

Despite angrily exclaiming that he was going to end up dead every few months, I was still blindsided when he actually did.

I could have stopped it. I should have saved you!

The guilt was staring me in the face when I announced I'd identify his body. It popped up again when I declared I'd write and read his eulogy. It was there when I abandoned my husband and kids and practically moved in with Mum and Dad.

But most of all it was present when it came to Shay.

I could hear his voice in my head constantly: 'Look after Shay, Al.'

While we all spoke disapprovingly to one another about Danny's flirting with death for much of the last five years, we'd never actually believed it would happen. Danny, we knew, would never leave Shay.

If drugs had become the oxygen Danny needed to breathe, then Shay was the blood that kept his heart pumping. Shay opened Danny's eyes each morning.

It's a sunny day, Dad!

I truly believe that poor kid unknowingly saved his dad from premature death countless times. He saw and heard more than he ever should have; he'd grown up worrying about his parents, pulling them up whenever they were down. Still, he was just a child—he had no idea about the invisible stuff. He didn't know that the mere thought of him was sometimes enough to pull Danny out of a spiralling depression. Didn't know that each and every day hid dad got up and carried on, all because of him.

We were gathered at Claire's house on Boxing Day. She was busying herself in the kitchen, cutting up pizzas into the tiniest pieces to feed nine hungry kids.

I wasn't sure if this was a good idea. It felt wrong to get together without Danny, but his death had taught us the hard way the importance of family, so we'd made the effort. Peter's anxiety was through the roof, so I turned up with Lily, while Eddie and Peter stayed home. Lily was over the moon-she was at last free to do as she pleased without having to constantly worry about her brother.

Oh, the irony!

'Shay's here,' my niece, Becky, announced, throwing her keys on the table and grabbing a handful of food.

Rachael, Claire, and I exchanged looks. Our eyes lit up.

We hadn't seen him since the funeral. We'd all been desperately reaching out, but had got little back. We instinctively wanted to help him heal, but we didn't know how.

He'd agreed to see us on so many occasions in the weeks prior, but had never shown up. Him being in the house was a big deal.

We left Mum and Dad to talk to him in the living room, keen to give him a little space and do the right thing. They needed this; they'd missed him and wanted him as much as we had. They just hadn't had the emotional energy to reach out. If anyone could relate to Shay's pain, it was them.

Claire threw another couple of frozen pizzas in the oven. Rach made a round of brews. It didn't feel right to have a proper drink.

I opened Claire's fridge to retrieve the milk and noticed one of Danny's unopened Coronas on the top shelf. He'd left it 'to drink next time' after her son, Ellis's birthday in early November. I shut the door quickly. I couldn't feel this now.

Danny had spent the year moaning about the injustices he faced at work and the last few months talking about his Christmas bonus. He was adamant he deserved it but convinced he wouldn't get it.

Of course, he did. Maybe the company felt some guilt. Maybe he really had earned it. Either way, a large dollop of extra cash arrived in Danny's account one gloomy December day.

We all agreed Danny would have wanted it to be spent on Shay.

In a bid to make his Christmas experience a little less painful, we bought him his first set of decks and a mixer.

It's what your dad would have wanted, we thought.

It only occurred to me after Mum and Dad had handed them over that we may have made a mistake. Had Shay ever shown any interest in making music? We honestly didn't know. Were we trying to turn him into his dad? Possibly, yes.

It suddenly felt wrong; a bit perverse and inappropriate. But by then, of course, it was too late.

Mum came in to refill her drink, so Rach and I took the opportunity to pounce. Shay was sat on his own, his head down, looking at his phone.

'Hey darling,' we said in unison, sad and solemn smiles plastered across our faces.

He looked startled—of course he did. He'd probably never had this much attention from the family in his entire life.

'Hi, Auntie Ali. Hi, Auntie Rach.'

We began cautiously, worried that once we opened our mouths, all that we wanted to say would come spilling out at once. We were desperate not to overwhelm, but our desperation in itself was clearly a little overwhelming.

We told him that we loved him. That we were here for him. That we understood. Of course, that last one was a lie—neither of us had ever been fifteen and fatherless.

We offered him rooms at our homes, refuge if he should ever need it. He could have money. Time. We were just desperate to convey that he was loved.

Rach was stroking his leg. It was probably the most physical contact she'd had with him for about five years.

'Are you really ok?' she asked tentatively.

'Yeah, I'm fine. Honestly,' he replied, and turned his attention back to his phone. He was fifteen. He was telling us he was done talking.

As I walked away, the tears I'd been holding back came spilling out. I blinked hard, determined not to let Shay see me cry.

Sitting quietly in Claire's conservatory, I watched my family mill about. The kids playing; one of Claire's boys, Tommy stealing the last sliver of pizza after checking no-one was watching; Lily running into the kitchen every two minutes to check that Auntie Claire hadn't opened the toffee cheesecake box without her.

Rachael came over and frowned down at me. 'It's not your job to fix Shay, Alison,' she said.

I let out a loud sob and instantly put my hand over my mouth to suppress it.

How could she have possibly known what was on my mind when I'd not even known it myself?

I thought of the line I'd written in his eulogy: *All the love we had for you will be poured into that boy*. And the messages I'd sent him—one each and every day since he'd lost his dad. The times I'd waited at Mum and Dad's for him to show up only for him to never appear and never explain why.

She was right.

The tears flowed harder and faster than they had for weeks. I realised that I was so consumed with guilt about Danny that I was desperate to make it up to him through Shay.

But Shay was a fifteen-year-old kid, and the only thing I knew about being a fifteen-year-old kid was that it was utterly shit. And that was without losing your dad.

2020

5 JAN

Lily grabbed my phone from my hands and opened Snapchat.

'Come on, Lil, it's bedtime,' I said, reaching across to take it back.

'Oh, just one!' she said, pulling a face and pawing at me with her free arm.

I relented. We could hang fire for a minute or two.

Before I knew it, she had the camera in my face. The filter had placed crazy hats on our heads, huge gold earrings on our ears, and we had eyelashes you'd pay a small fortune for.

'Twinnies!' she exclaimed excitedly.

I had to laugh. At eight years old, there was no mistaking Lily was her mother's daughter. She'd inherited my eyes, my cheekbones, and the family wit.

Weight gain had meant I didn't feel good about the way I looked but I loved the lens through which my daughter saw me. She was proud of our likeness and celebrated it at every opportunity. Her excitement was infectious, so I joined in.

'We're twinnies,' I said into the camera as she expertly held down the record button.

'Yar, we're so alike, aren't we? Yar,' Lily added in her fake American accent, the kind that every kid growing up on a diet of YouTube and Netflix could do better than their own. She flicked her hair from her face and pressed it tightly against mine.

We both giggled and she went to hit send.

After selecting the names of my sisters, nieces, and best friends, she spotted Shay's name. She looked at me cautiously.

'Go on,' I motioned.

She pushed the *send* button.

My phone pinged straight away. Shay's name popped up. Lily eagerly opened the message, her excitement palpable.

Shay's face filled the screen—only, it wasn't exactly Shay's face. It was his trademark hair, but with a giant nose.

We both laughed and Lily immediately began to send more.

But I sat back, realisation smacking me in the face. No wonder he hadn't been responding to my messages. He's fifteen!

The next morning, I put my newfound wisdom to use.

Hope school is ok. I know it's boring but you could be sitting on a train to Liverpool like me.

Within minutes, I had a response.

that's unlucky I'm gonna go school now have a good day at work auntie ali aha

I fought the urge to text back. That'll do, Alison. That'll do.

1984

AUTUMN

When I was about seven years old, I drew a picture of the band King. I loved their song 'Love and Pride', and the highlight of the week was catching them on *Top of the Pops*.

I was in the living room drawing my 'I love King' picture when Danny came in. My picture was going well—in fact, it was perfection: an incredible mountain framed the band members, and 'I love King' was written in bubble writing across a beautiful blue sky.

'What are you doing?' he asked. looking over my shoulder.

Before I could answer, he ripped the paper from my hands.

'Ooohhhh,' he jibed, 'you l-I-u-r-v-v-e King! Whit-hoo!' He stood, dangling the paper above me. 'Alison loves King! Alison loves King!'

'Give it back!' I screamed, jumping up after it.

He ran out of the living room, waving it in the air. He couldn't stop giggling to himself. 'You wanna kiss him! You love him!'

'It's not him!' I protested. 'It's the band! I love the band!'

And it was true! At least, I think it was.

But Danny was having none of it.

Eventually, Mum came down to intervene. I was crying by that point; annoyingly, anger always turned to tears when I was a child. I felt pathetic but I couldn't stop it. Mum shut Danny down immediately and he reluctantly handed back my picture. Once out of her sight, he headed back upstairs, smiling at me as he did so and laughing to himself.

For him, it was a bit of banter that was now over. For me, it was the ultimate humiliation and it led to me vowing to never, ever let my family know I liked any boys ever, ever again. The embarrassment was too much to bear.

It was a vow that plagued my teenage years and led to me keeping my innermost feelings firmly under lock and key.

2001

JUNE

Danny had decided to have a party.

Our cousin Helen's big house in Chorley was the perfect space, and he was embracing his newfound freedom. Chorley was the first time either Danny or I had lived away from home, and when I moved out to a flat in Liverpool, and my cousin and her husband left to set up a new life in Luxembourg, Danny filled the spare rooms with his friends. With his decks taking centre stage in the dining room, a party was the natural next step

'Would you mind if Will did a bit of DJing too?' I asked tentatively, trying to slip his name in like it was the most normal thing in the world, but his ears pricked up.

'Who's Will?'

I squirmed, instantly regretting my words. 'He's just a guy I'm sort of seeing.'

Please leave it there, Danny. I started to blush even though he was at the end of a phone.

'Cool,' he responded, and I breathed a sigh of relief.

'Cool, then.'

The truth was that Will wasn't just 'some guy'. He was *the* guy. And he'd been in my life on-and-off for years.

But I'd have never told Danny that. Not talking about my relationships had been so normal for so long that even dipping in a toe felt like diving in the deep end. Still, I was in my twenties now, and keeping my private life to myself seemed ridiculous.

When the big night arrived, I had relaxed a little and felt comfortable casually introducing Danny and Will. Hopeful my big brother would be cool and like my sort-of-kind-of boyfriend.

Danny was a perfect gent. He helped Will set up his stuff and cracked open a beer for him. I sat back and watched as Will familiarised himself with Danny's set-up. He ran his hand over the black Technics turntables as if scrutinising them, making sure they'd suit his skills.

I should have been pleased. Will was such a big part of my world; I had wanted my brother to like him. I'd often thought they had a lot in common but, as I watched them together, I immediately began to notice the differences. Both were confident, but Danny carried his confidence differently; he had a vulnerability about him. I suspected that is what made him so attractive to women (he was calling them 'women' by this point; once they reached the grand old age of nineteen, he and his friends had pointedly refused to use the term 'girls').

But Will was merely confident; arrogant, even. I could see it the way he interacted with my brother, the way he treated Danny's stuff in *his* house. He had no concept of modesty. You could see he truly believed he was right where he needed to be. I felt a bit embarrassed.

Will pulled his stack of vinyl from his record bag and began working the decks. Danny watched from the sidelines for a minute or two and then left him to it, wandering off to work the room, laughing and joking with friends old and new.

An hour passed before he came to find me. I was chatting to a few friends in the living room.

'I'm going to have to jump on the decks, Al,' he shouted across the noise.

'No problem,' I shouted back. Will had had plenty of time to do his thing.

'I'm sorry, Al, but he's fucking shit!'

I should have been mortified: introducing someone to my brother for the first time was a huge deal. I should have felt protective and saddened, but I didn't.

I just burst out laughing. He was absolutely right.

OCTOBER

After Will, everything got easier. When I introduced him to Chris later that year, I was cool as a cucumber. It wasn't a big deal. Of course I wanted Danny to like him, but I no longer felt I needed his approval. I liked him and that was all that mattered—or so I thought.

But when I saw them chatting together in the club, Danny's eyes twinkling as he laughed, I knew that he did in fact approve. When they turned towards me, Danny's arm casually draped over Chris's shoulder and his other hand outstretched, finger pointing directly at me, I smiled.

And then I thought to myself, *Shit.*

Don't bloody ruin the moment, Dan. Please don't bloody tell him you'll kill him if he hurts me.

2020

9 JANUARY

If there is an upside to grief, it's that you get to be part of the Grief Club, that elusive members-only cult for the perpetually sad and confused. In the months following Danny's death, I realised I suddenly shared a newfound connection with people I'd known forever but never really understood.

There was Jenni. She'd been a member for years—you could even consider her a veteran. She'd lost her dad many years before and each of our conversations were peppered with stories and anecdotes about him, to the extent that I had a mental picture of him in my head. Jenni taught me that somone you love can be even more present after they have died.

There was Alice. She was a relatively new member as she had also lost her dad. Though still finding her feet, she was experienced enough to show me the ropes and warn me it was going to feel like my insides had been scooped out for a very long time.

Then, of course, there was Kelly, my best friend. I could still clearly remember the moment she told me her brother had died and how I wanted to desperately to reach into the phone and put my arms around her. I always knew when Kelly spent time at the club, as she'd seem off or else would post something on social media. I spent a lot of time hanging around outside the Grief Club, waiting for Kelly, but until Danny's death, I wasn't permitted to go inside.

Then there was Sophie. Dear, dear Sophie.

Before I joined the club, I'd thought I knew all there was to know about grief through Sophie's Facebook posts alone. I've always been an empathetic person, which was a double-edged sword; it resulted in me spending a lot of time being sad on other people's behalf. On Sophie's behalf.

I watched her deal with her husband's terminal illness via Facebook. She had two young children, just like I did. I thought I understood her pain.

I saw her fear—and, after her husband's death, her sorrow. I cried for him, for her—for all of them and the lives they wouldn't get the chance to lead.

When she posted the most beautifully crafted words about her loss, I cried again. I cried and cried about a man I had never met, about a lost life I'd never even known.

I felt her pain, I thought. I knew what she was going through.

One evening, a few days after her husband's death, I was driving to the shops while listening to Coldplay, and the song 'Up and Up' came on the stereo. Even though the CD had been in my car for months, I began to listen to the words as if for the first time.

'We're gonna get it, get it together right now

Gonna get it, get it together somehow

Gonna get it, get it together and flower.'

I imagined Sophie's family at her husband's funeral—holding hands tightly, singing to him and to themselves. Willing each other through the pain.

I pulled over and just cried. The sadness, the regret, the might-have-beens were too much to bear.

I feel it too, Sophie.

But on that horrible November morning when my membership card dropped through my letterbox, I realised how absurdly naive I had been.

Feeling sad for someone's loss isn't the same as suffering a loss yourself.

Crying over a man you've never met is not the same as crying for the brother you've known and loved your whole life.

I didn't have a clue. Not the faintest idea of how it actually felt.

Because the thing about Grief Club is that you only get to know what it's like once you are inside it. And once you are in, you aren't ever getting out.

2015

JANUARY

I went into the spare room to change the bedding. Danny had gone home so I wanted to freshen things up for our next guest. As I pulled the duvet cover off the bed, Danny's Shaun Ryder book fell to the floor with a thump.

I quickly kicked it under the bed. I did not want to see that man's face.

Danny had always been a big Happy Mondays fan for as long as I could remember and he was in awe of the man behind the band as much as the music itself.

Shaun epitomised everything Danny wanted to be: an accomplished lyricist, confident, cool—and absolutely minted.

He also spent a fair amount of time off his trolley.

Shaun didn't appear to give a damn about anything, and that's what Danny found so attractive about him. Even his lyrics didn't make any sense—but that, Danny insisted, was part of what made them great.

Ever since Danny was a teenager, everything had been about the Mondays. Everything was about Shaun.

When I went on my first girlie holiday back in 1999, I'd bumped into Shaun Ryder in a bar. At the time, Shaun was splashed all over the British press as he'd gone AWOL, but I'd seen him, arms outstretched, draped over a sofa in San Antonio.

Danny loved hearing me recite the story of how I met Shaun, how he'd accused me of being a policewoman coming to arrest him.

He made me tell that story time and time again.

Once I'd met Shaun *Fucking* Ryder, I became instantly cool.

But even though I admired Danny's devotion to music, I hated the fact he idolised someone like Shaun. After all, the Happy Mondays weren't about clean living; they were about excess. Drugs were a huge part of their world, and they didn't try to hide it. It was part of what made them cool.

And Danny, of course, wanted a piece of that pie.

It's all your fault, Shaun, I thought as I shook the pillows from the pillowcase. Why did he have to idolise someone like you?

1991

MARCH

'You're twistin' my melon, man, you know you talk so hip, man,

You're twistin' my melon, man.'

You could spot our house as soon as you turned down the street. It was a 1960's red-brick semi with Mum's beautiful manicured bushes spilling over the front wall. From the second Danny got home from school, the music went on. Every night, the windows would be wide open and his voice would ring out, reaching several houses down the quiet tree-lined street.

'Call the cops!'

I threw my school bag on the hall floor and went straight into the kitchen. Mum had the door closed and was making tea. Claire and Rachael were out in the back garden, playing on the swing.

I noticed Mum was cooking a Bolognese. It was a fancy tea.

'Dom's here,' she told me, glancing back from the stove and pre-empting my question.

That explains it, I thought.

Dom was Danny's friend from school. He was our headmaster's son— and he and Danny were the most unlikely duo you'd ever meet.

Danny was a gifted footballer. He played for local teams, Leyland and Lancashire, and he'd been signed as a schoolboy for Bolton Wanderers too. We had such high hopes.

Academically, though, he struggled. He was the class clown—he'd make others laugh rather than trying and risking failure. Consequently, he was either thought of fondly by his teachers or utterly despised. There was little in-between.

Dom's dad fell into the former category. Our Headmaster, Mr Clark saw something in Danny and always went the extra mile for him. He gave him more chances than Danny perhaps deserved because he saw through the bravado and careless humour. I truly believe Mr Clark is the only reason Danny stayed at school.

Dom, on the other hand (as you might expect of a headmaster's son), was a model student. He was academic, studious, and a talented musician. He was quiet to Danny's loud and shy to Danny's confident. But, somehow, they were firm friends.

While the boys had first met on the school football team, they'd bonded over music: the Stone Roses, James, and, of course, the Happy Mondays.

When Dom was round, the music was louder and more intense than at any other time. Both boys were desperate to point out a mad lyric or wave their arms in the air to a new sound.

I walked upstairs to get changed. Danny was on the landing, pointing down at me from the top of the stairs. I caught sight of Dom quickly putting his arms down as he spotted me. He sat back on Danny's bed and said an awkward hello.

I closed the door to my room and fished my Walkman out of the drawer. As Madonna's voice began to stream into my ears, I pulled out my schoolbooks. It was homework time.

2020

9 JANUARY

Claire: *What the hell is this?*

A screenshot of Danny's profile page from Facebook. Horrendous profanities listed in brackets after his name.

Rachael and my nieces soon piled in, each sharing their shock and disbelief. Someone must have done this, they all thought.

It was Danny, I typed back. *It's an old profile, he did it years ago.*

It wasn't the first time I'd seen it, but I was slightly surprised it still existed.

Facebook had turned out to be a good indicator of Danny's mental state. If he was posting at two in the morning, you could be pretty confident he was not in a good place. If he was selling stuff, he was probably using again. If he was incoherent and inappropriate, he was most likely off his bleedin' head.

Kelly had alerted me to his social media behaviour years before.

'He's selling an old coat, Al.'

'He's replying to my friends telling them they're beautiful.'

It's amazing how you get a sense of someone's character through a social media account.

Invariably, one of Kelly's messages would trigger a conversation between me and Danny and, nine times out of ten, he'd confess to being in a bad place. It took a while, but we got there in the end.

The first time Kelly alerted me, I'd already been on the case. His status updates had become incoherent. He wasn't making any sense.

Shortly after confronting him about the horrendous words that had been added after his name, he came off the site. He didn't use it again for a long time—months after he moved out of my house in York. When he did so, he created a fresh account.

However, the old remained, stranded in time: a painful record of the downfall of our brother.

Daniel Lee (*?!***** !&>*!***** ?*!*)

2015

MARCH

The nights were beginning to get lighter, but somehow my evening runs were becoming harder, not easier. I'd enjoyed the solitude of winter; I liked the dark mornings and evenings. It wasn't that people couldn't see me run (although I confess, that was a bonus), it was more that the darkness allowed me to be truly alone in my thoughts. I had nothing to take my attention away; it was just me and the road.

Although, of course, my husband had kittens every single time I left the house and didn't relax until I walked back through the door.

Danny and I were several months into our Couch to 5K push. He'd downloaded a copy of the app and was running in Leyland with Shay. I ran on my own in York.

Each night, in a bid to keep each another accountable, we'd text details of our runs to each other. I regularly attached a screenshot of my running app just to prove I wasn't lying. Some nights I suspected he was.

We'd come a long way in a few short months. Danny's counselling sessions were going well and he was beginning to understand how he'd wound up an addict; like me, running gave him the space to process things, and we'd often end up having quite deep chats afterwards.

'The thing is, Al, I don't like to feel my feelings,' he told me one night.

I fought the urge to reply with, *No shit, Sherlock*. It wasn't the time to be flippant; he was opening up.

The counsellor had helped him realise one of his fundamental truths: Danny ran away from any kind of pain. When Mum told him he needed to do better at school, he punched someone in the face. When Bolton released him from the schoolboys programme, he stole my dad's whiskey and got blind drunk. When his marriage fell apart, he turned to drugs.

Some people turn a negative into a positive. Danny turned a negative into a double-negative.

Running gave him space to work through all of this and, although he didn't realise it at the time, it gave him the focus he needed too. We had a big run to train for; he had to put in the miles.

I was feeling better too. I wasn't a natural runner and found it hard, but I was beginning to feel like my old self again—not someone's wife, someone's mum, or even someone's boss—but me again. It felt nice.

I rang him once I was back at the house, revelling in the smug feeling of being done for the day.

'Only two to go. How are you doing?' I asked.

'Not bad, Al, but I couldn't go tonight. I've been let down . . .'

Uh oh. Familiar warning pangs sent shivers across my body.

He told me he'd arranged to run with Shay after school but that Shay had never turned up. It was a minor thing, or should have been, but it always left Danny feeling really deflated.

'Get your trainers on now!' I commanded.

'I can't, Al, not now. Tomorrow, I promise. Not now. No, no. I can't.'

'Now!' I repeated, 'and send me the details when you're done.'

I hung up and switched my phone off before running upstairs for my shower.

By the time I'd said goodnight to the kids and got washed and changed, an hour had passed.

I walked into the kitchen, picked up my phone, and switched it back on.

There was a text.

3.4 miles. Legs fucking killing. Cheers Al

2020

9 JANUARY

I signed up for the Great North Run.

I hadn't run in almost a year. I was heavier and more unfit than I had ever been, but I was going to cross the finish line with his name emblazoned across my chest.

I'm going to do it for you, Danny.

***

Whenever we observed changes in Danny's behaviour, we always assumed the worst. *Once a druggy, always a druggy . . .*

Mum would be the first in his ear. Then Dad, then Claire. And, eventually, it got back to me.

Living so far away, I had to rely on others telling me or Danny's calls to know when he wasn't himself. Sometimes I couldn't bring myself to ask how he was.

When you've put so much energy into helping someone get clean, it's hard not to be personally affronted when they're not.

He'd explain it was the medication. 'Prescribed by a doctor,' he'd make a point of saying, before going on to moan about how we always thought the worst of him and how that was a terrible cross to bear.

It's your own fault, Danny! I'd think angrily as I listened to him ramble on. He'd told so many lies over the years that suspicion came naturally to us; even something as innocuous as 'I'm going to have a shower' would make us question whether he was telling the truth.

The night my Dad found him on the floor of the bathroom. It was a bad reaction to pain medication.

Vomiting each night at Linda's. It was a chest infection he couldn't shake and he'd been given steroids.

That weekend he couldn't get out of bed. Oh that one was flu and he'd been given a sedative.

The list went on and on.

Besides, while Danny could tell you about every single drug in the universe, the rest of us didn't have a clue. We'd pop an ibuprofen when we had a headache, but that was as far as our knowledge went.

I took Danny's diaries from his room shortly after he died, partly to protect Mum and Shay from their contents and partly to satisfy my own curiosity. That night, with Danny at the forefront of my mind, I flicked through his 2019 entries while cooking tea.

I stopped on the 9 January—a year ago exactly.

9 Jan

Went DrS Started

New Antideppresents

SNRIS, Venlafaxine

Sleepapnia Device

Taken back to Runcorn

10 Jan

Me and linda

Took all Decoratinos

down got appointment

For Dr Next Thursday

For Naltraxone

Recerd arrived

Madchester Rave on

General mood

up and down

11 Jan

Records

Pills Record Store day

Pills argentina

last day ever of

Messing my life up

Say good bye to

Tina + carl

Complained To

Ebay about

Madchester rave on

Feel short tembered

a bit angry

4 :)

Shit, I thought. The struggle was real.

As I turned page after page, I found detailed accounts of prescribed medications, dosages, and trials. Danny bemoaned times the drugs hadn't agreed with him and worried about the times they'd agreed with him too much.

I ran my fingers across his familiar handwriting. *Capture your positives, Danny*, I'd told him. *Document how far you have come.*

And here it all was, staring me in the face. His diaries lined up in my kitchen, just waiting to be read. Waiting to be understood.

I began to Google the drugs listed.

Duloxetine . . . Major depressive disorder.

Dihydra . . . Severe pain. Opioid.

Pregabalin . . . Epilepsy and anxiety.

Naltrexone . . . Opiate. Antagonists.

Venlafaxine . . . Major depressive disorder.

Zopiclone . . . Insomnia.

Mirtazapine . . . Anxiety and depression.

The list went on and on. This drug here, that drug there. His world and brain must not have known whether they were coming or going.

So—he'd been telling the truth. All those times he pleaded with me to listen. When he tried to explain. He was addicted to drugs, of that there was no doubt—but it was clearly more complicated than I had ever imagined.

These were things medical professionals had prescribed. These were things he needed to take to simply get through the day.

I closed the diary and put it gently down onto the table. I sank into a nearby kitchen chair and held my head in my hands.

I'm sorry, Danny.

2018

19 JANUARY

He was off work again; signed off for a few weeks by his doctor following a near-death experience on the motorway. It turns out almost crashing into the central reservation because you were nodding off sets a few alarm bells ringing. A month later, he was signed off again following an on-site altercation with his boss.

His prolonged absences were clearly frustrating his work colleagues and it wasn't long before he was being hounded by phone calls and emails asking him to show up for meetings and send documents in.

Danny couldn't handle stress and paperwork at the best of times, but it was clear his co-workers weren't just going to accept him being off for the foreseeable future without explanation.

I was getting almost daily updates from him. *She said this. He said that.* He was increasingly frustrated. But I saw the other side. I managed a team; I knew the difficulties of managing long-term absences; I knew the policies that needed to be complied with and the real-world impact absence could have on the rest of the team.

So, while I tried to offer help and advice, I often ended up pointing out where I thought he'd gone wrong.

'Yes, it is reasonable for them to ask . . .'

'No, you really can't just say that . . .'

He began forwarding me text messages he'd sent to the HR department and his boss, Chris. Incoherent is too soft a word.

One night, after reading his latest flurry, I jumped on the phone.

'Danny,' I began, 'you can't go sending messages like that. You'll end up losing your job.'

He'd wanted to work at Bentley's for years. It was one of the few construction companies that provided perks to the staff. If you were dedicated, you were rewarded. When he'd been offered the job, he'd felt like he finally had it made.

'Lose my job!' he began shouting, 'they *can't* talk to me like that, Alison. They know I have mental health problems—'

I sighed. I didn't have the energy to fight. I could tell he was in no mood to listen to reason. He hadn't called me for advice; he just wanted me to agree. It wasn't worth pointing out that he'd not come across as a man with mental health problems, but instead as aggressive, crazed, and more than a little threatening.

If he'd been on my team, I wouldn't have wanted to go out of my way to help him and to see his point of view. Far from it.

'I'm going to send you something to send to them,' I told him.

I didn't give him an option. I fired up my laptop and typed out a quick email.

Message to: Danny

From: Alison

21:32

Dear Danny,

Send this in its entirety to Sarah. Do it ASAP.

Love you,

Ali x x

Dear Sarah,

I am writing further to the text messages I have sent this week following my discussion with Chris on Monday.

To recap, I spoke to Chris as I had been advised that the work I've been doing on the excavator for the last year should have resulted in a machine driver's wage, rather than the semi-skilled operative's salary I am on. I was advised by many people that I should be classed as a skilled operative, so I wanted to raise this with Chris directly. Unfortunately, the conversation did not go the way I had hoped and Chris refused to acknowledge that I had been and was continuing to be underpaid.

I made myself clear that I was happy working on the excavator and very competent at it, but that I felt my pay should reflect the work I was being asked to do.

As you are aware, I have suffered with my mental health and unfortunately the conversation with Chris took its toll on me and I had to leave the site. I acknowledge that this wasn't the best thing I could have done, but I felt quite overwhelmed at the time. I have since been given a sick note but, as my text messages this week highlight, I am hoping that I can instead take this week as annual leave. I am due to go on holiday with my son shortly and am desperately trying to get the money together to give him his first holiday with me in over ten years. Please can I ask you to reply and advise whether this is going to be possible?

The lack of response to my messages is unfortunately contributing to my anxiety.

I do want a future with the company but it's been feeling recently like my efforts to advance have been in vain. I completely accept that the way I've reacted this week may have left you feeling disappointed in me, but I hope you can appreciate I am a dad battling mental health issues simply trying to earn a good living for my son. You know I work hard and am competent. All I want is to be treated fairly and rewarded for my efforts.

I would be grateful if you could respond to this and let me know where I stand with regard to my holiday request, my work for next week, and my future with Bentley's.

Thanks in advance,

Danny

18 FEBRUARY

STarted Back

at WorK

2019

FEBRUARY

I accepted a new job at the University of Liverpool so Eddie, the kids, and I relocated from York to Birkdale in Southport. After spending our married life in Bath and, later, York, we decided to buy the house of our dreams so that we wouldn't be tempted to relocate again. At least, that's what I promised Eddie.

We'd been in the new house for two weeks when Danny and Linda came to visit. He'd been working weekends so had managed to avoid getting roped into any heavy lifting and, by the time he arrived, the house had already started to feel like a home.

He handed me a beautiful bunch of tulips and a bottle of wine.

'House warming present,' he told me, kissing me on the cheek.

Thanks,' I mouthed to Linda as he passed me.

She smiled.

I showed them around the house. I'd already perfected the tour—start on the second floor, then down to the first, and finish in the basement. We walked into the kitchen.

'Bloody hell, Al,' Danny exclaimed.

I grinned—the kitchen was our *pièce de résistance*, the most beautiful space in our Victorian home.

He gave me a huge hug. 'It's so great, Al. It's gorgeous and so wonderful to have you home.' He hugged me for too long again, and I ducked under his arm to the sound of his cheeky laughter.

175

Linda and Eddie were already talking about all the jobs Eddie wanted to do. Danny set himself down at the kitchen table, and I flicked on the kettle and took some cups out for us.

'So, how are you?' I asked pointedly, fixing my eyes on him.

'Do you know what?' he said, grinning, 'I'm doing okay. Really okay.'

And I believed him—he looked good. There was no wild gaze, no skittishness, no clear desire to be somewhere, anywhere, else—he was happy right where he was. I could see it in his eyes.

Linda came over and sat next to me and picked up her freshly made brew. She began to tell me about the projects she was working on back at the house—the chairs she was upholstering, the wood she was restoring. She sounded so much like Eddie and Mum.

Danny rolled his eyes at me and smiled.

'Listen to these two. Bloody changing rooms.'

She punched him in the arm and he laughed, then threw his arm around her neck and pulled her close so he could kiss her on the head.

You really are okay, I thought as I watched them. *Linda is everything you need.*

For the first time in a long time, I saw my brother content.

I've come home at the right time. Thanks, Linda—for bringing my brother back.

2020

11 JANUARY

A friend recommended *Griefcast*, a podcast by comedians about dealing with death. A bit of death banter on my morning commute, I thought—what's not to love?

It very quickly became a part of my daily routine. Drink coffee. Leave the house. Stick headphones in. *Boom.*

And, sure enough, it did what it said on the tin: it made you laugh. For something about death and grief and all the horror those things entail, it was actually quite funny.

When I'd spoken to my friend about my trouble communicating with Shay, she'd suggested a couple of episodes where people talked about losing their parents as teenagers.

One of these, a guy called Joel, had lost his dad at fifteen, and the presenter, Cariad, had too. It was perfect. I sat back in my seat on the crowded train, staring out the window at the world whipping by.

Joel explained how going back to school following his father's death had felt. He'd wanted to go unnoticed, he said—he knew the kids knew, but he didn't want the fuss. And, thankfully, he didn't get it. Turns out fifteen-year-old kids are too self-involved to really notice, let alone care.

It made me feel sad for Shay. Green fields stretched on outside and, as the train thundered through them, I wiped the tears from my eyes. My poor darling Shay—back in school, surrounded by people, and yet so alone.

Joel went on to talk about another boy in his year who'd been off for six weeks before returning to school with a dead dad. Joel had known, but not paid much attention. He described it as just another adolescent fact, like knowing someone lived in a bungalow.

I laughed out loud, immediately transported back to my own teenage years. I remembered standing at the lockers as Joanne returned to class; her dad had died too and she'd been off for a while. And, as Joel described, we just walked on by. Sure, her friends paid attention, I'm sure (I hope!), but for the majority of us it was just another thing we knew about that girl. I totally got where Joel was coming from.

He went on to describe his six weeks off: a shit-load of time to master his Sega Mega Drive. I got that too.

After all, what are you supposed to do with grief at fifteen?

All this time I'd spent worrying that Shay felt like I did, or perhaps even worse, when maybe, just maybe, he wasn't worrying at all.

Maybe when he said he'd been playing games in his room, he'd actually been playing games in his room.

Images of him sobbing into his pillow every night suddenly faded from my mind. He was a kid. He was fifteen. You didn't care about anybody else when you were fifteen.

Of course, that's not to say I suddenly believed Shay didn't care at all. But I knew that Joel was right—he wouldn't be feeling it like we were. His brain wasn't mature enough for that yet.

I felt like a lightbulb had been switched on.

Joel went on to say how much harder it had been in his twenties. That's when it really sunk in.

It'll come, Shay. And we'll be right here waiting to support you when it does.

12 JANUARY

When someone you love dies after battling mental illness for so long, it colours your perspective going forwards.

For my parents and sisters, so many memories were tainted by Danny's seemingly endless struggle. I couldn't remember when we'd last casually talked about him doing simply this or that; it was always whether he was in a good place or not.

I didn't realise it at the time, but we were always subconsciously waiting for that next relapse, never quite believing that the nightmare was truly over.

For my teenage nieces, it was very different. Gemma, Hannah, and Becky had enjoyed very different relationships with their aunts and uncles than their younger cousins. For a long time, it had just been them and us and, as Danny, Claire, and I were without children of our own, they got spoiled rotten.

As they grew into independent young women, however, they developed different relationships with each of us. Just like their younger cousins, they all adored their Uncle Dan—whether it was going out for a beer with him or jumping on the bikes at the spinning class, the girls all loved his company.

They saw him in a different light than we did, and I envied that—they didn't need to worry about what he might do or what he might become. He was just Uncle Dan. They got to love him, no questions asked.

As they became involved in relationships of their own, I watched them introduce Danny to their partners in the same way I had, each hoping he would approve and each being thrilled when he did. Their boyfriends looked up to Danny, it was clear to see, but to Danny, they were equal—just a bunch of lads who enjoyed a beer and a chat about the footie. But he always made it clear: *you hurt my girls and you'll have me to answer to.* Rather than freak them out, it made the lads respect him more. They were in awe of him, just like their girlfriends.

I envied the way they all saw Danny. Without the constant worry and the pain, they saw the Danny we all knew and loved. I'd not allowed myself to see that Danny for a long, long time.

14 JANUARY

They say grief comes in waves. While that's true, sometimes it feels less like a wave and more like a punch in the face.

It's a regular Sunday morning in our house. The kids are making a ridiculous amount of noise and mess and Eddie and I are discussing how we're going to transform another room in our Victorian house. We've been in for almost a year but it's still our favourite thing to do. Gradually, room by room, we're transforming our home (or rather he is; we have the big ideas together, but he does all the work!).

He's pulling off the skirting underneath the modern fireplace we both hate, desperate to return it to its former glory. As the cheap wood is ripped away, huge pieces of breezeblock come into view. Big slabs of grey make their way up the wall. Sandwiched between the timeless red bricks are paper towels stuffed between the joins. Yet another piece of shoddy workmanship he laments.

He begins to talk about how he'll take it out, making way for the original fireplace, and starts to question himself, reminding himself of the things he'll need to think about.

But I've stopped listening. I'm just looking at the breezeblock and the task in front of him and all I can think is, *Eddie, you just need Danny.*

Eddie is a craftsman. There is nothing he can't make from wood. He has the vision, skill, and patience to create something beautiful from raw materials, but brickwork is not his thing. Sure, he could learn it, of that I have no doubt, but Danny would be able to jump right in.

Like my dad before him, Danny became a bricklayer. After years of labouring on construction sites, he began to go to college in the evenings to learn the skill. His work on our parents' driveway is now the lasting legacy of his skill; the daily reminder of how much he could achieve when he put his mind to it.

Eddie's still speaking, but my mind is elsewhere. I hurriedly excuse myself and go down to the kitchen. I want to prepare our evening meal so we can all go out for a walk.

I switch on the speaker and open YouTube on my phone. I quickly find what I'm looking for: *Graham Park and Pete Tong—The Cream Sessions.* Perfect.

As my body chops chicken and vegetables, my mind flies back to the Park Hall in Charnock Richard, to Cream in Liverpool, to the Hacienda in Manchester.

Dancin'

And prancin'

Groovin'

Keep on movin'

Flyin'

Stop your cryin'

Choosin'

While you cruisin'

I was with Danny. We were surrounded by our friends. We were dancing. And laughing. And feeling. And beaming.

I moved as I sliced, casually throwing my vegetables into the pan in time with the beat. To my family, I had just taken myself off to prepare tea; little did they know that I had disappeared to be with Danny.

I glanced at him across the room as I danced with my friends.

He had his arm slung casually over his girlfriend's neck, his friends surrounding him.

He came to find me on the dance floor as 'Brothers and Sisters' began to play.

I was blissfully happy.

Peter's screams brought me back down to earth.

'Mum! Mum!' he screamed from the third floor of the house.

Lily followed: 'Mum! Mum! Muuuuum!'

By the time they reached me in the kitchen, they were breathless. I met them at the bottom of the stairs.

'It's Rabbie,' Peter shouted excitedly as he waved his childhood soother in his face.

I joined in the excitement, delighted to see a familiar face again. Rabbie was Peter's rabbit teddy, a comforter he had slept with since he was a baby. Unlike Lily with Duckie, he hadn't outgrown it. We'd lost count of the number of nights we'd spent turning the house upside down, hunting for Rabbie so that Peter could go to sleep.

At eighteen months old, Peter had clutched Rabbie as we left our home in Bath to relocate to York and, at seven, he'd still held him firmly in his hands when we moved into our new home in Birkdale. It had been months since we'd seen him and, although Peter was managing without him, he frequently talked about how upset he was about Rabbie being lost. Eddie and I were too; it's impossible to invest so much time in something and not be upset when it disappears.

I embraced both kids. Rabbie was suffocated between us all as we began jumping up and down in excitement. I picked Rabbie from Peter's hands and kissed what was left of its face, then I bent to kiss his head and give him another squeeze. The relief and happiness on his face were infectious.

'All my boys are together again!' I proclaimed as I held them—but the words tasted like ash on my tongue. I'd never have *all my boys* together ever again.

1999

31 DECEMBER

The most anticipated night of the entire century and we'd somehow ended up in Yates's Wine Lodge in Preston. My friends and I had spent months discussing grand plans for the big event but had failed to put anything in motion, and so, like thousands of others, we'd turned up on Preston's busiest street. Young people were already spilling out of bars, clearly intoxicated, as we headed through the large double doors.

Danny's friends had ended up in the same place and I immediately spotted him standing three-deep at the bar.

'Get us Bacardi and Cokes, Dan!' I shouted over the sea of heads. 'Doubles!'

His bright blond hair meant you could always find him. It was one of the best things about being on a night out with him—that and knowing he would punch someone's lights out if they upset you.

The pub was rammed and we were all sandwiched together. Hundreds of sweaty bodies bobbing along to the music, getting more and more drunk.

Danny returned with our drinks and spotted his friend, Andrew. He held his arms out so we could prise our drinks from his hands without him losing grip of his. Andrew and several other men came to join us, and Danny and his mates began to chat with them. My friends and I turned our attention back to the crowds and resumed dancing, slowly sipping our rum through our straws.

I glanced at the digital screen on the wall. The brightly coloured intersecting circles that had been moving all night were suddenly replaced with words and numbers.

Just then, I felt a strong arm around my neck.

I turned around to see my friend Kris. He immediately began drunkenly shouting in my face: *'Ten! Nine!'*

I could smell the beer on his breath. He was so close I could practically taste it.

Shit, I thought. *This must be it.*

'Eight! Seven!' I joined in, reaching across to get Danny's attention. I caught his arm.

'Seven! Six! Five!'

We were all at it now. Danny had thrown his arm around Andrew and Andrew around the guy next to him.

'Four! Three!'

We were in a semi-circle, glasses swishing around our necks. Beaming smiles on our faces.

This was really it.

'Two! One!'

And there we were: the year 2000.

'Happy New Year!' we screeched, throwing our arms around each other.

I moved away from everyone, waiting to hear the familiar intro to 'Auld Lang Syne'. Seconds passed—the long moment stretching on. I glanced around. One by one, we all did.

Something was off.

Why weren't the rest of the crowd celebrating? It was the year 2000 for heaven's sake! An entirely new millennium. We wouldn't live to see anything like this ever again.

I glanced down at my watch and looked back at the group, my eyes settling at last on Kris's sheepish face.

It was ten past bloody ten!

2000

1 JANUARY

It was two o'clock in the morning when we arrived home. Parties continued up and down the street, but our house was in darkness.

Mum and Dad must still be at Auntie Jane's, I thought as I stumbled in, finding the curtains all wide open.

After prematurely celebrating the New Year, the actual event had been an anti-climax. My friend and I arrived home with Danny and his then-girlfriend, Emma.

Danny dived into the kitchen and went straight to the fridge. He'd developed a taste for champagne, so he took out one bottle of Moet and one of Chandon. I got four glasses from the cupboard and he filled them up.

Before I knew it, he was upstairs firing up the decks, so we all followed and crammed ourselves into his little box room. The music was soon pumping, and he opened the blinds and windows.

'Happy New Year!' he shouted outside.

'Happy New Year!' we joined in.

We sat on the edge of his bed: three drunken girls, all sipping champagne, all bobbing along with the music.

I flung my head back—it was my way of testing how drunk I was. If everything was spinning, I knew I was in trouble—but, this time, I was okay. I topped up my glass.

'Play that one I bought you, Dan,' I instructed as he turned his attention to his record stash.

He fished it out and put it on the turntable. It was Martin Luther King's famous 'I Have a Dream' speech.

He found another record to work into it and, as Martin's voice boomed out of the speakers, so did a low hum, a soft beat, perfectly complementary to the gravity and pace of Dr King's words.

We moved our heads and tapped our feet, captivated by the power of the speech and how wonderful it sounded mixed into a dance record. It was exactly how I'd imagined it'd sound when I'd bought it for Danny—I knew he'd do it justice.

It was the beginning of a new century. We were four young people sitting in a little box room listening to Martin Luther King.

I have a dream today!

I was a young woman in awe of her big brother.

The new millennium closed its fingers around us.

'Free at last! Free at last! Thank God almighty, we're free at last!'

2020

10 JANUARY

I was beginning to get addicted to the Griefcast. Every day I'd learn something thanks to the collective wisdom of the bereaved and laugh to myself about the absurdity of death. It was therapeutic, and getting all the grief chatter out of the way on my train journey allowed me to focus at work.

I was listening to Dr Kathryn Mannix chat with Cariad, the presenter; they were talking about dying rather than death. It wasn't quite what I had gone to the Griefcast looking for, but I figured I might learn a thing or two. My own mortality had never been something I'd really thought about.

She spoke like a true counsellor, her voice soft and soothing. I thought that if I was going to die imminently, hers would be the voice I'd like to deliver the news. She had that wonderful ability to let meaningful words hang for a second before moving on. It was strangely calming.

As a former palliative care professional, she knew a lot about death. Together, Kathryn and Cariad shared anecdotes and facts as if playing a spiritual game of ping pong. I searched in my bag for a notepad, eager to write it all down.

One of the most interesting things she talked Cariad through was the reality of what happens to your body when you die. How, tragic accidents aside, your body gently shuts down when it's your time to go. She spoke about breathing and unconsciousness, and how the latter happened so that the former could stop. And, all the while, as I listened to their conversation drown out the rhythmic clacking of the train, I was thinking about my dad.

He had a degenerative disease called COPD which affected his lungs. Year after year, we'd watched him get sicker and sicker. He found it increasingly difficult to do the one thing he needed to do more than anything else in the world: breathe.

He didn't talk about his death, but we knew he thought about it a lot. We'd grown up around a man who'd never let anything bother him. He'd once appeared invincible and carefree, but it all changed when it came to COPD. He was sick—and he knew it.

Mum had told us he'd spent a lot of time researching how COPD caused you to die (or 'pop your clogs' as Dad always said. Cheery!). I'd always found this horribly morbid, but listening to Kathryn gave me a different perspective. After a few short minutes, I began to think of it as absurd to not prepare for our bodies to change as we get ready to die.

She shattered two myths for me: the first was that we don't leave this world gasping for air and clutching our hearts in the way you often see in the movies; rather, our bodies slip into unconsciousness as we prepare to die. *Makes sense*, I thought, reflecting on my own painful experience of childbirth versus the 'two pushes and they're out' version I'd seen in countless Hollywood films. Loved ones often see this pre-death unconsciousness as a deep sleep, but in fact the dying person often slips in and out before the end.

She went on to explain that during unconsciousness, a dying person often simply stops breathing. The body makes the decision to stop, not the conscious brain. I loved the idea of that. It comforted me to think that my dad's death might be like that—a kind of gentle drifting off that you never wake up from. I was certain this wasn't what he envisaged for himself. Like me, Dad liked a good drama—I imagined him reading the absolute worst-case scenario and worrying himself silly.

Kathryn made it clear that all this didn't mean that unpleasant and painful things never happen as the body approaches death, but it was nonetheless reassuring to know our bodies take control when it's finally time to go.

God, if you're listening, I know I say I don't believe in you and, let's be honest, I'm not sure if I do, but please don't take my dad. Not yet, and not for a long, long time.

And then she spoke about morphine.

I instantly thought about my Uncle John and how I'd seen him lying unconscious in his bed one evening, dying of cancer following a long battle with COPD. We'd heard the next morning how he'd 'slipped away' during the night.

'He'd been given some morphine,' I'd been told gently.

That's what they do to send them on their way, right? Give them an extra-large dose when they know that time is nearly up.

Except that's not what they do, Kathryn explained. Apparently, morphine simply took away the pain, allowing the body to fall into an unconscious state so that it might finally die.

So the drug didn't kill you—it just took away the noise so your body could do what it needed to do. Who knew?

My thoughts turned to Danny. What if heroin took away his pain and allowed him to die? Aside from sounding like a nice literal way of viewing his death, it also felt like the perfect metaphor too. What if that last drug simply gave his body permission to let go?

I knew it would be months before we'd have the inquest. Months before we'd be put through the turmoil of combing over the circumstances relating to his death all over again.

But, I thought to myself, if it does turn out to be a heroin overdose, I can handle it. It is going to be okay.

2019

19 NOVEMBER

Nobody wanted to believe it was heroin. *He just wouldn't have done that*, they all said.

I felt like I was watching my family from afar. I felt like I was letting him down by assuming the worst. Why was I the only one who believed it was? But I couldn't stop thinking about the way he had described it: '*It's fuckin' euphoria, Al.*'

I realised I didn't just *think* it was heroin. I *wanted* it to be.

2020

13 JANUARY

The worst thing about grief is that you are constantly discovering a new worst thing about grief.

Today was . . . well, it was another instance of 'the new normal'—a bog-standard grief day.

Wake up: think of Danny.

Get ready: think of Danny.

Walk to train: think of Danny.

Sit on train: write about Danny.

You get the drift.

I arrive home to find Lily at the door. She's bouncing up and down behind the frosted glass as I try to turn the key in the lock. When I finally get it open, she flings herself at me, uncharacteristically affectionate. I struggle free so I can put my bag on the floor to hug her properly. She's still bouncing like an excited little puppy. Someone must be here—it's like she's desperate to reveal the surprise.

And for a moment—the briefest moment—my brain tells me it's Danny. Danny's here! Oh my god, he's here! It entered and exited my brain quicker than a flash of lightning, but it was there nonetheless. And even though it was the tiniest moment in an otherwise busy day, it still has the power to knock me sideways.

I walk into the living room and see Peter reading to his dad. There's no-one else. I look back at Lily, who's now eagerly clutching her reading book and her homework planner, ready to guide me downstairs to the kitchen. I realise that the reason she's so excited is simply that I'm home to read with her.

I make myself a quick coffee and we plonk ourselves down on the big grey chair in the kitchen, just the two of us. She balances herself on the arm of my chair so I can drink while she reads.

She begins to entertain me with her story about a walrus trying to fit in with his friends. I sit back and watch her. I love listening to and watching her read; she reminds me so much of myself—like me, she takes great delight in giving all the characters different accents and bringing them to life with her voice. I watch her tiny little hands turn the page and notice her fingernails.

Sometime between me leaving her at breakfast and me arriving home, she painted her nails the exact same shade I painted mine the night before. She always notices little things like that. I feet a sudden rush of love for my daughter; I put my coffee down and pull her off the arm of the chair so she's sitting directly on my knee. My beautiful, sassy, funny little Lil.

I see you.

2019

9 NOVEMBER

Once he'd finished Rhonda Byrne's *The Secret*, Danny began to take the idea that positive thinking brought you positive things very seriously.

He recognised that he had become so consumed with sadness and the avoidance of pain that he'd stopped seeing the good in the world. He'd call me and tell me about a plant he'd noticed that morning, or a bird in a tree. Tiny, little things that I would roll my eyes at, but I always humoured him, I always listened—I knew that learning to pay attention to the world was a big deal, for Danny and for anyone else.

Each morning, he'd force himself to focus on one positive thing. It was always Shay—that went without saying—but he also began noticing and thinking about new things.

It became infectious, and a part of his character we grew to know and love.

'Oh yeah, Dan, that leaf really is a beautiful colour, and yes, isn't it wonderful how it grows and thrives,' we'd say as we exchanged sarcastic looks with each other behind his back in the kitchen.

He also began to journal, capturing his moods and feelings in diaries. It gave him an evidence base to prove to himself how far he'd come. It also gave me ideas for his Christmas gifts, because I always like to choose something myself—I *hated* getting requests! Danny had pestered me to buy him a Happy Mondays rare vinyl for his birthday one year and I was so annoyed at the frequency with which he nagged that I stubbornly refused. It became a battle of wills between us. He was determined I was going to give in and I was determined he wouldn't win. But journals and books about positivity that he needed rather than wanted? Well, I would buy him those all day long.

A couple of weeks before he died, he had a poignant conversation with Linda. He explained that drugs created a fog in his brain and that he viewed the world in black and white. He described it quite literally, insisting he couldn't see any colour. It had made her feel enormously sad.

A few weeks later, he had this same conversation with Gemma. Danny and Gemma had a wonderful bond; she was a wise old owl, and understood her uncle better than most. When she faced her own mental health battles at sixteen, Uncle Danny was the only one that really 'got' her and, consequently, she 'got' him. Both knew exactly what it was to fake a smile when you were crying inside and they talked often and openly about their mental health. When she began to get her life back on track, no one was more proud of her than Danny. He truly noticed her. Gemma couldn't walk into a room without him commenting on how beautiful she looked. He saw the whole of her, which made his words all the more special.

He'd noticed a phone box, he told her. It was red—standing tall in the middle of Leyland. And it stuck in his mind because it was red, red!

She was overwhelmed. The fog was lifting. He was coming back to us.

It's a sunny day, Dad!

2000

OCTOBER

Mum used to think it was Stella. I used to think it was cocaine. Whichever of us was right, Danny became a pain in the arse during nights out.

I don't remember when it changed but, all of a sudden, I began to dread being with him when we were out. The more he drank (snorted!), the less I did. Consequently, he'd be off his face while I was stone-cold sober.

Like a meerkat, I was always on the lookout for danger. Waiting for someone to look at him the wrong way or bump into him. Then it would all kick-off.

We'd been out at the Railway pub in Leyland and he was wasted that I decided it was time to head home. A group of us began walking down the hill from the station when we spotted a youngish lad walking alone in our direction. He glanced at us and then crossed to the other side. Danny shouted something at him and the guy replied with a confident, 'Fuck off, you dick!'

Danny began to cross the road, his chest puffed out like a peacock.

'Don't, Danny,' I shouted, 'leave it, please. Let's just get home.'

He ignored me and began to square up to the guy. Our friends joined me and together we pleaded with him to walk away.

But he was off on one, full of aggression and fixing for a fight. To his credit, the guy gave as good as he got, but their voices were getting louder and louder. It was becoming a scene.

Conscious we were in the middle of the street and that things could turn nasty at any second, I ran across the road in my heels and grabbed Danny's arm.

'Come on!' I yelled at him.

He shook me off.

Then I grabbed it again and pulled, almost taking him off his feet. 'We're going home!' I commanded, pulling him further away. I fixed him with an 'I'm not asking, I'm telling' stare I'd picked up from my mum.

The guy took the opportunity to walk off and our friends crossed over to join us. We continued on down the street, the altercation forgotten by everyone but me.

I shouldn't have to do this, Danny!

2020

4 JANUARY

Shay is hurting.

I keep thinking that if Danny could have seen into the future and witnessed all the pain he'd cause, he would have gotten the help he'd needed. It is hard not to feel angry when you see a fifteen-year-old kid that you love so desperately lost.

We keep telling him his dad wouldn't have left him, that it wasn't his choice, but I can't blame him for not believing it. Sometimes I struggle to believe it myself.

But every time I let anger seep into my brain, I think about Danny's personal library. He used to talk to us about his books all the time—he read everything he could about addiction and the brain, and learnt all about neural pathways. He wanted us to understand too, but we were dismissive, thinking these books were contributing to his problem.

Why didn't I listen to you, Danny?

He tried to sell them on Facebook once and my mum went crazy. She worried people would think he was some kind of drug addict and asked him to take the ad down.

Why did you have to die for us to get it?

I want to read those books now. I want to know what he knew; to fully understand.

11 JANUARY

My legs are screaming. My heart is thumping. My lungs are working on overdrive.

I open the app on my phone and press *Done*.

My first run is in the bag.

14 JANUARY

This is what I do. I am shopping and I see him—well, someone who kind of looks like him. Sometimes it's the back of the head, the shoulders, or the walk, but this time it's the eyes. Long blond eyelashes, fine lines at the corners, deep blue—just like he had. I squint my eyes and turn this person into him. Hello Danny! He's walking and talking again. He's grabbing some shopping. I hold my gaze for as long as I can before this person feels my eyes on them and looks back at me, breaking the spell.

Once that spell is broken, I feel that familiar clot in the back of my throat. The tears want to come but I push them back. I'm in a supermarket. *Not now, Alison. Shopping to do.*

I realise I do this a lot—as often as I can. It hurts more. It's torture, really, but for a few seconds I get him back and realise it's a punishment I am willing to take. Back in the car, I take two Belgian buns out of the cellophane and stuff them into my face before I turn on the ignition. I find a cloth to wipe my sticky hands and fold the wrapper up so tightly that it just about fits into my handbag.

15 JANUARY

Hi Danny, how are you doing?

I've been writing about you non-stop for weeks, but it's only just occurred to me to try writing to you. So I'm giving it a whirl—finding my feet, as it were.

I talk to you in my head all the time. Can you hear me? If so, please don't turn up at the end of my bed to let me know. Send a gush of wind through the room or make something fall off a shelf or something, but if you scare me in the middle of the night, I'll bloody kill you.

Sorry, shit joke. I can't stop, Danny. You know how funny I am (or not!) when I am on a roll.

So, what is there to say? We miss you, obviously. I think about you every single day. I know you'd like that. Remember all those times you made me feel guilty for not calling you? Well, you have well and truly made up for that now. I'd say you occupy about 90 percent of my free time. It's not all sad, don't worry, but there are enough tears in there to remind you that I care.

And I do. Trust me.

It's still hard to believe and accept that you are gone. Even as I write this, I'm looking around the train carriage trying to find people that look like you. I want to remember your shape, your hair, your face, your smell.

Okay, I'm crying now. See! Told you I cared.

Mum and Dad are doing okay. I mean, they're sad, of course, and they miss you terribly, but they are getting up and moving forward every day. Dad's taken it hard. He misses the chats and the banter. I don't think anyone has told him he's a fat bastard since you've been gone. The laughter is missing from their house. Could you bring it back please? Thank you.

Mum's pleased her yoghurts remain in the fridge.

Sorry, shit joke again. Honestly, Dan, I can't stop!

Seriously though, Mum is okay. She's trying to keep herself busy because she's worried she'll crumble if she stops—so far, so good.

You're currently on the mantelpiece. Do you know that? I find it a bit weird, but they both like having you home. Dad probably talks more to you now than he ever did. Every cloud and all that.

I'm on fire tonight!

I'm worried about Shay though. Sorry, Dan, I don't want to burden you with worry, but we're finding it hard to get through. He stayed at Mum and Dad's last week, which was great, but he hasn't been back since. He's not opening up, not even to his mum, so we feel like we're getting it all wrong. How do we speak to him, Dan? Sorry to ask for advice at a time like this, but what should we do? Any tips would be greatly appreciated.

On a happier note, my kids are doing well. We've finally found a bit of help for Peter, which is a positive. I'm not holding my breath that it'll have much impact, but it's a start. I know you didn't rate therapy that much, but it's all we've got, so we're giving it a go.

Lil's the same as ever. Still doing her art. Playing with Rem and Rizz. Keeping us all sane. She really is beautiful, Dan. In the last few months she has really blossomed. I wish you could see her now.

As for me, I'm okay, I think. Work is going well and I've lots of exciting things to keep my mind occupied during the day. I'm so relieved I moved, Danny. Imagine if I'd been in York when you went? It doesn't bear thinking about.

Anyway, we've really all pulled together. You'd be very proud, but none of us could have gotten through it alone.

I'm writing a book. Do you know that? It started out as a way to process my grief (get me sounding all posh), but it's actually turned into a kind of therapy about you. I'm using your diaries—I hope you don't mind—and sharing our stories. I hope you don't mind that either. Not that you can do anything about it. Ha! There I go again.

I guess I just want (hope!) for something good to come out of your death. Because for the life of me, Danny, I can't see anything good now.

I hope that changes.

Miss and love you more than you'll ever know.

Love always,

Your Al x x x

PS I'll buy you that Monday's record if you come back!

17 JANUARY

Two months. In fact, less than two months—and yet the world has moved on and everyone expects me to be okay.

I get it. I look okay. I sound okay. I am able to function. But guess what, world? *I am not okay!*

I'm in a meeting with Ian at work. We finish half an hour late, and I should be rushing home. I'm halfway out the door when he drops the question: 'How are you? I mean, really?'

I know it's sincere, so I walk back in the room.

The politically correct answer is 'I'm okay.' Or, 'I'm okay, just getting by.' Or even, 'I'm taking each day as it comes.' I know the script; I've heard others follow it so many times before.

Except, well, I don't do scripts. I've been over-sharing since 1977, and I'm not about to stop now.

So poor Ian gets it. He gets the *not okay!* I've been storing up for weeks. If he's going to have the god-damn audacity to show real genuine concern then he deserves everything he gets.

Ten minutes in and he's had it all: the sadness, the pain, the masked feelings, the writing. I'm on a roll—it's all coming out, so why not go for broke?

I drop the H bomb.

I pause for a second, letting it sink in. We're directors. This is a university. We don't talk about stuff like this.

I wait for the look of horror to spread across his face. I glance at his feet to see if they are shifting uncomfortably. But nothing happens. Instead, he just looks sad. And then says:

'Something similar happened in my family too.'

He tells me his story. And I try to listen, I really try, but in my head I'm screaming. This is why I say too much; this is why I overshare! Memories of a talk I'd given at work a few years before flooded my mind during which I'd reflected on ten lessons I had learnt in my career. It was the lesson rooted in my experience of post-natal depression, though, really struck a chord with my audience—I explained how someone can look like they have it all together on the surface, but really be clinging on for dear life underneath. I spoke to colleagues and friends, people who had known my professional persona for years and who had assumed I had my shit under control.

The incredible response I got floored me, but it also made me sad. Why aren't people more honest about this stuff? My talk wasn't praised because what I'd been through was remarkable, but for its honesty.

The experience just made me more passionate about openness, about admitting that mental health struggles are faced by *us* and not *them*. Everyone can champion 'talking' and 'sharing', particularly when it comes to men, but so few stick their hand in the air and say 'It happened to me too.'

I wanted to hug Ian. He'd immediately made me see the power of Danny's story. By being open and honest, I'd enabled him to open up too. Maybe, just maybe, we could help families see their loved ones who had suffered with mental health and addiction in a different light. Maybe we could learn to understand who they truly were.

What if Danny's story could help release people from the shame of drug addiction? Wouldn't that be nice?

I thought about celebrities who had hit the headlines.

Ant McPartlin. *Hi, my name is Ant. I have battled alcoholism and addictions to prescription drugs.* Oh Ant, you poor thing. Go straight to rehab. Dec needs you!

And Matthew Perry. *Hi, my name is Matthew and I am addicted to paracetamol.* Addicted to paracetamol? Who knew that was a thing? Sorry, Matthew, our thoughts are with you. Stay strong but get to rehab.

And Elizabeth Taylor. *Hi, my name is Liz and I am a functioning alcoholic.* Woah. We'd never have known. You are so talented *and* beautiful. I mean, you look okay, but perhaps get yourself into rehab and get checked out.

And Danny. *Hi, my name is Danny and I am addicted to opioids, namely heroin.* Wait, what?! *Call the cops!*

Something had to change.

I'll never lie about you, Danny. I won't contribute to the problem. I'll show people who you really were, who you really are. I promise you that.

2010

SUMMER

I began to hate him when he'd had a drink. When I saw those wild eyes I'd do my best to avoid him, but it only made things worse.

'What's up, Al?' he'd say, throwing his arm lazily around my shoulder.

'Nothing,' I'd reply, 'I'm good.' My brain would be on overdrive, trying to think of ways to get away. I'd look for a distraction, someone else to talk to or something to do.

He'd fix me with a stare. His eyes would be dark and intense, his pupils wide and crazy. 'Don't be boring, Al.'

Oh, here we go, here it is. I'd take a sip of my drink and tell him, taking great care to keep my voice even, that I was having a good time. I'd say what I needed to say so that he'd move on and leave me alone. All the while, I'd be thinking about the one thing I didn't dare say: *I cannot bear the sight of you when you are drunk.*

I used to wonder if it was just that I'd grown up and left him behind. He was like the perpetual Peter Pan, I thought—was he so different to the Danny I'd known in my teens and early twenties? Was he so different when he was drunk, or had life changed me? I couldn't remember the last time I'd truly let my hair down with my family. I was constantly on guard. Did you make me that way, Danny? Or did I just grow up and get, well, boring?

I hated the way he made me feel: on edge, unable to relax, self-conscious. But mostly I hated him for stealing the best version of my brother. This Danny was not one I could bring myself to love.

2020

16 JANUARY

We finally had a support meeting booked to discuss Peter. I'd sent a series of highly charged emails in the midst of my grief in December and they'd seemingly done the trick.

This is it, I thought. *Finally, we'll be taken seriously. We're on the path to getting him the support he needs.*

They asked for a synopsis but, somehow, everything came spilling out. I'd rehearsed the narrative so many times in my head, desperate for the right people to pay attention—I owed it to my whole family to cover it all, to convey the enormity of living with an eight-year-old with extreme anxiety and the impact that had on the family. The women were warm and understanding and I felt, for the first time in a long time, that I wasn't alone.

We discussed strategies and support for Peter but for all of us too. I wanted to cry—the idea that we mattered too was foreign to me. I couldn't remember the last time I'd truly thought about my own needs. I brushed the thought away quickly. *That's what you do, right?*

But I was at pains to explain the impact on Lily. I explained the relationship she had with her twin brother, how she looked after him, how she would cover for him and how she always, *always* put his needs above her own.

'I worry that she doesn't feel important. Like her needs and feelings don't matter. Like it's all about him.'

I had a strange out-of-body moment. Had I just described myself? The parallels between Lily's relationship with Peter and mine with Danny were so stark.

I thought back to my early twenties. I'd been in full-time work and financially independent. Danny had gone to Tenerife to make it as a DJ. We were so proud. His big break!

The things he got up to and his stories kept us entertained on a daily basis. He was living the high life. He had a regular spot at a place called The Crow and I was planning to go and visit him with some friends later that summer.

Danny was an exceptional DJ. He had a huge talent, but he was no MC. When a new manager took over The Crow and asked Danny to warm up the crowd, have some banter, he wanted to crawl under a rock. He was the most charming and witty guy in his comfort zone, but forcing banter when he was in the spotlight was absolutely not his thing.

But he had no choice, so he downed a couple of vodkas and decided he'd have a go.

It was early evening and the pub was very quiet when two girls walked in.

'All right girls! Where are you from?' Danny shouted from behind the DJ booth.

'Wigan!' they replied immediately.

A long moment passed, and the girls looked at him expectantly. Later, he'd tell us the thoughts that had raced through his head: *Oh my god. What now? What the hell do I say now? Think, Danny, think, think, think!*

'Good,' he replied.

Good? Good? Fucking good?

He put on a record quickly, putting his head down to hide his red face.

The next morning, he called me to relay the story.

'I'm not doing that shit, Al, it's painful. I'm coming home.'

And with that, his Tenerife dream was over. He was coming home and I would have to organise it and pay for it. He didn't have to ask and I didn't have to offer. It was understood that I would sort it out.

That's the first time I remember having to dive in and fix things for Danny. After that, it just became the norm.

I thought back to Lil. *My* Lil. At that moment, I vowed to teach her that she is important too. We'll spend our lives supporting her brother—we all will. But we'll teach him how to fix himself. And I'll teach her that loving him doesn't mean putting his needs above her own.

It's not your job to fix your brother, Lil.

18 JANUARY

Three sisters get together to drink coffee and discuss their dead brother's finances. Just an ordinary Saturday night, hey?

It had been two months to the day since we'd lost him, but that milestone remained unspoken. The significance of the date had popped into my head several times but I didn't let it linger. We had practical things to discuss.

From the second we'd been given the news about Danny, our instincts had kicked in and told us to protect Mum and Dad. We didn't discuss it, but all our actions were carefully calculated so as to protect our parents from any further distress. In an instant, the tide had turned on our relationship: they were no longer our protectors, our carers—we were theirs. We couldn't give them Danny back, but we could perhaps shield them from further pain.

Mum and Dad explained their wishes for his funeral, but we handled the practicalities—and that included ensuring all the right people were paid.

Rach sorted out Danny's paperwork, making sure that accounts were closed down and debts understood. Claire dealt with his work, securing his final paycheque and ensuring the relevant paperwork was filed and signed. And I got the joy of liaising with the undertakers and being the go-to person for all things funeral.

Like little mice, we went away and did our thing and then came back together to share our progress. It was the most we had communicated as a threesome in years (maybe ever?), and it was strangely nice. We were all grieving, all completely and utterly up the wall, but I felt that the three of us understood one another in a way no one else did. Our relationships with Danny had all been different, but he'd always been a part of our four. No one else understood what it felt like to have that piece missing, not in the same way.

Guiding our decisions about Danny were three guiding principles:

1. Protect Mum and Dad from having to deal with anything.

2. Do the right thing by Shay.

3. Try to do what Danny would have wanted.

When you are faced with your brother's death at forty-five and it's the first death you've experienced, you think emotionally, not logically. At least, we did. We sat together, frantically Googling words like 'probate' and 'estate' and 'interstate', trying to get our heads around what it all meant.

Rach, who was sitting in front of the fire in my kitchen, looked pissed off. Her head was fixed to her phone. Her lips were tightly pursed, like she was about to say something but trying to stop herself. She was unsuccessful.

'I'm pissed off,' she announced. 'All we've tried to do is the right thing. Everything was for the right reasons and now I feel like it's all wrong.'

She had tears in her eyes—frustration, anger, but also sadness written all over her face.

And she was right.

I'd been quoting Google like it was gospel, like my fifteen minutes using Safari were akin to a law degree. Each time I'd discover something new, I'd announce it as fact. I was like a teacher schooling my children.

'The thing is,' I'd declared not moments before, 'Shay is the beneficiary but it depends on whether it goes to the beneficiary or the estate.'

'But isn't Shay the beneficiary of the estate?' Rach asked.

'Ah yes,' I'd say, on a roll, 'but if it goes directly to the beneficiary then it bypasses the estate.'

Getting our head around the legal jargon was tough. As well as frazzling our brains, it hurt to be talking about our brother in this way. It had been two months and we were already there—talking about his life as a collection of debts and assets.

We realised that we'd been getting things wrong. The bonus Danny had received for Christmas was rightly Shay's (the beneficiary's), and we had used it to buy Shay a Christmas present from his dad. Not our wisest move—in the eyes of the law, everything Danny left behind was a part of his 'estate'.

I thought back to the days after he'd died; how I'd bravely gone in his room and folded his clothes away. They were bone dry on the maiden beside his bed, as if he'd expected to come home and put them away. I couldn't bear looking at them.

I folded them and put them away in his drawers. Every drawer I opened was immaculate, every item of clothing folded perfectly. I half-expected him to walk in and tell me I was doing it all wrong. I giggled to myself. Oh, how you'd hate me snooping around your room, Danny!

The very last thing on the maiden was a faded t-shirt. It had been dark blue once, but was now closer to grey. It had a hole in it—not like Danny at all. I spread it out in front of me and began to fold the arms together when I realised what it was. Across the chest was emblazoned *Great North Run Finisher 2015*. I held it close and soaked up the smell. It was fabric conditioner, not Danny, but it was still him. Tears fell, soaking the fabric as I let my feelings take over.

You've left this for me, haven't you? I thought. I truly believe he had.

I folded it up and left the room, slipping the t-shirt into my overnight bag before heading back downstairs. Mum was in the kitchen. She looked up as I entered, and I told her what I'd done. She nodded. 'He'd want you to have it,' she said, and I knew she was right.

But now, thinking about estates and beneficiaries and doing the right thing, I began to feel like I'd done something wrong.

Shay was Danny's beneficiary, not me, not us—we had no legal right to make decisions on Danny's behalf. It hurt to think we had mistakenly assumed we could.

It seems there is no place for emotion and instinct when someone dies.

20 JANUARY

I'm on the train, writing. All I do is write, write, write. I'm eager to capture my memories and stories, but worried they'll disappear from my head.

I feel like I am nearing the end of a complex jigsaw puzzle. I'm piecing together the fragments of his life and our lives alike. I'm getting close to that point where I'll be able to sit back and gaze at something beautiful, something that only makes sense when every hole has been filled, every gap eradicated.

As the train arrives, I tuck my phone into my pocket and push my headphones into my ears. I listen to Claire's song as I stand on the escalator, letting thoughts of and love for Danny pour through my veins. It really is the most beautiful song.

When I get to the barriers, I reach into my pocket to play it again. And again, and again, and again—all the way up the hill. And, like a perfect metaphor, the song ends as I reach the top. This has become my daily routine, and I ask myself what I will do with myself when it's over. And my brain quickly delivers the answer.

Grieve.

When it's over. When I'm done. That is when I have to let him go.

I don't want to let you go, Danny!

I was waiting for a room to become free for a meeting, so I picked up my phone absentmindedly. I had a missed call and a voicemail from an unknown caller.

'I'd better check who this is,' I said to my colleague before dashing back into my office and closing the door. 'Give me two secs'

I dialled voicemail, expecting to hear a message from the kids' school. But it wasn't school—it was the coroner. The toxicology results were in, the voice said, could I call her back?

I popped my head out the door again.

'I'm so sorry, but there is just something I need to take care of. Please start without me.'

I had to know.

I clicked my office door shut again, picked up my phone, and dialled the coroner's number. As I waited for an answer, I grabbed a piece of paper from a pile on my desk and flipped it over. I picked up a pen. I was ready.

I'd emailed the office earlier that day with a copy of our statement and asked for an update and, when Fiona from the coroners office picked up, she said that, as chance would have it, she'd literally just had the toxicology results land on her desk. By this point, we had spoken so often that I considered her a friend.

She began reading the report to me but it was all jargon. Words like 'toxicity' and 'concentration' flew straight over my head. But then she said three words I understood far too well: 'Morphine from heroin'.

There it was. Heroin. I let it wash over me for a second. She was still talking—there were still words, but that was the only one I'd needed to hear.

For months I had wondered how that word would make me feel. Would I break down in tears? Would I be angry and shout? Would I even scream out loud? *Noooooooooooooo, Danny! It can't be! It can't be!*

But nothing happened. I felt nothing: not anger, not sadness, not surprise. Nothing. I just noted it down on my paper. My work life on one side, my personal on the other.

She went on to explain that they had also found cocaine.

And diazepam.

And pregabalin.

And alcohol.

I had the bizarre urge to make a joke that one was quite enough, but stopped myself. It wasn't the time.

Jesus, Danny. What a cocktail!

The heroin was in lower quantities than would usually cause death, but a number of factors worsened his situation—namely all the extra drugs and booze (yes, that would do it!) and the fact he had most likely not used heroin for some time.

At least we can be (fairly) confident that you were honest about that.

So it was as I predicted. He'd not been using until that last moment. It was his 'one last time'.

He'd been given an antidote by someone he was with and another by the paramedic. These, apparently, had not helped, but they'd not

211

contributed to his death either. Low toxicity. There were the words I didn't understand again.

The ambulance was called at 23:47 and arrived at 23:52. He was pronounced dead at 12:30 a.m. on Monday 18 November 2019.

So there we had it: the news we had been waiting for. It was confirmed. Heroin. I didn't care about all the other stuff. It was heroin—that was all we needed to know.

I put the phone down and processed all that I had been told.

Then, feeling nothing, I went back to work.

Oh, hang on. I do feel something. My chest is tight. My breathing is shallow yet laboured. I feel hot like my blood is pumping faster and harder than usual.

I feel anger.

All of this. All of this could have been avoided. He could have prevented this pain. He could have gone home.

I'm tired of being the one trying to justify his actions. I'm done with being the person that figures it all out. I want to love him so, so much, but right now I hate him for what he has done to my family.

It was never my job to save you, Danny. You should have saved yourself!

The coroner advised that we'd be either persons of interest or persons with an interest at the inquest—I couldn't remember which. Either way, we'd get to put our questions to the coroner and he/she could use them to gather witnesses.

I began to note some down on the way home.

Why?

Why did you do it?

Why did you promise Shay you wouldn't touch it again and break that promise?

How are we supposed to convince him you loved him now?

How is he supposed to believe that you loved him at all?

Why?

Why did you tell Mum you'd left it all behind?

Why remove all traces of that life from your room?

Why let her believe she had you back?

Why?

Why did you get dressed up that day?

Why did you make us feel that it was a fresh start and that you were on the up?

Why, Danny, can you answer that, please? Why?

Why did you go there? What did you want?

Why take so much?

Why take anything at all?

Why? Please help us understand this, Danny. Why?

Why weren't we enough?

Why didn't you feel enough?

Talk to us, Danny. Why? Why? Why?

21 JANUARY

I shouldn't have Googled his name.

There it was in black and white, under 'inquest openings'. His name in full. In stark capitals.

It stung. The name my mum and dad had lovingly chosen for their son. Mum had wanted to name him Lee, but Dad was insistent he should be Daniel—so they compromised with Daniel Lee and threw a Christopher in for good measure.

I thought about the hours they must have spent debating it. The love poured into getting it just right. They'd been through a heartbreaking miscarriage and then a traumatic stillbirth, so their beautiful blond-haired blue-eyed boy was so yearned for, so wanted.

And now his name was on a website, at the bottom of a long list.

Not my Danny, but their little boy.

2015

JUNE

'How about *Sharknado*?' Danny suggests.

'Oh yeah, *Sharknado*!' Shay joins in excitedly.

'Bugger off,' I tell them, grinning, 'I'm not falling for that!'

They're giggling now.

'Honestly, Al, it's real—' Danny begins.

'It's about a tornado,' Shay takes over, 'but with sharks in it.'

They both fall about laughing, but I remain stony-faced. It makes them laugh even more.

We're in the living room in my house in York. They've come to visit for a weekend and, with my kids in bed, we're settling down to watch a movie. Eddie's in the kitchen getting some snacks together.

Danny straightens his face. 'Look, we can just watch the original *Sharknado*. We can do *Sharknado 2* and *3* another time.'

'Yeah! The first one is definitely the best. Oh Dad, I love it when—'

More giggles.

'Oh, Auntie Ali, we have to watch the first one. Come on, Auntie Ali, you'll love it.'

I raise my eyebrows at Shay, the little bugger. I'm not going to do it; I'm not putting 'Sharknado' into the Netflix search so that those two can fall about laughing even more. I've been there too many times before. In fact, every time these two are together I'm subjected to a wind-up.

Eddie returns with bowls of crisps, which distracts them. They both dig in and fill their hands. I take the opportunity to quickly select a movie and hit play. I turn up the volume, signalling it's not up for debate.

As the opening credits roll, they continue to quietly chat about *Sharknado*. I can hear them saying I'll regret it for the rest of my life. They're still giggling as they talk about their favourite bits, shooting me mock-angry looks whenever I catch their eyes. They could be mistaken for a pair of school kids rather than father and son. The sight of them makes my heart burst.

A few years later, I'm scrolling through Netflix again, trying to find something for the kids to watch—and, suddenly, there it is in front of me.

Sharknado.

I scroll on.

Sharknado. Sharknado 2: The Second One. Sharknado 3: Oh Hell No! Sharnado 4, 5, and *6!*

I pick up the phone and text Danny.

Just stumbled across bloody Sharknado *on Netflix.*

I have a reply within seconds.

Told you! It was so good they made it six times! You're going to love it Al!

2020

21 JANUARY

I called Linda to update her on the toxicology results. She was saddened but, like me, she'd expected it. She sounded calm and composed.

The reality of knowing the cause of his death, truly knowing, was beginning to sink in. It wasn't emotional pain—I couldn't cry—but every fibre of my body hurt. Even lifting the phone to call Linda felt a strain. I wanted to crawl into bed and never get up.

In typical Linda fashion, she immediately asked how everybody else was doing.

'How has Shay taken it?' she asked sadly.

I confessed that he hadn't been told yet; we were still working out how. Claire had told Kelly, but she was letting it sink in before speaking to Shay.

How do we convince him you loved him, Danny?

I couldn't stop thinking about Shay. In the days after Danny's death, as the rumours about how he died had begun to swirl, Shay had stayed resolute. His dad wouldn't have taken drugs—he'd promised him he wouldn't.

He'd told us they'd spoken about drug use while at the gym, how Danny had vowed he'd never go back there again. Shay had believed him. I envied him for that kind of trust—the blind sort you only seem to have while you're a kid. *He said he wouldn't, so he won't.* Oh, how I wish I had that kind of faith in Danny.

But, as time went on, Shay changed. He began to accept that it had been drugs that had killed his dad, that Danny's promise had been broken. It was

217

then that the self-torment began— for in the same conversation that Danny had vowed never to touch drugs again, Shay had told him he'd never speak to him again if he did.

Shay went over and over that conversation in his head until he shared it with Gemma on Boxing Day.

'What if he took too much on purpose because of what I said?' he asked her quietly, avoiding her eyes.

She told us those words made her want to cry out in pain.

Oh Danny, your poor darling boy! It would devastate you to know how he felt.

I told Linda we'd be careful with Shay. We had to help him understand that his dad's death wasn't his fault—and we wanted him to understand that it wasn't his dad's either. Danny wanted to be with Shay—around for Shay—more than anything else in the world. We had to help Shay see that.

'And how are you?' I asked, already knowing the answer.

She sounded so sad and worn down. We had all lost someone we desperately loved, but Linda had lost her soulmate. They'd planned to grow old together. I had lost a huge connection to my past, a part of my identity, but Linda had lost her future.

It didn't really matter to her how he'd died. What mattered were the sadness, the torment, and the injustice she felt. She'd had her future mapped out—and now she faced it alone.

23 JANUARY

I was hours away from a career-defining moment: sharing the first iteration of the university brand with the Vice-Chancellor. It was either going to be really positive (hoorah, she loves me!) or really difficult (get your coat, Alison . . .). Okay, I'm being dramatic, but suffice to say I felt a lot was riding on it.

And yet I'd spent half an hour staring at a picture of my brother on my laptop. I'd traced his entire face, including his bright white eyebrows, with the cursor. Try as I might, I couldn't shake Danny from my head.

Danny, Danny, Danny, Danny.

It had been over two months. I was supposed to be back in the game, but my head hadn't got the memo. I was stuck like a broken record, replaying thoughts of Danny over and over in my mind. Some days, it just didn't feel real. Consciously I knew he was dead, but subconsciously there was a part of my brain that liked to disagree, telling me, nah—you'll see him again.

I liked that part the best.

I was acutely aware that I was not really in a good place. I was gaining weight; I wasn't talking because it hurt to talk; I was either working too much or unable to concentrate; I was not being as present for my kids as I knew I should—they felt it and that made it hurt even more; and I was merely functioning with my husband, changing the subject when he asked if I wanted to talk. It was easier to be alone in my head, to keep everything inside rather than admit I felt like I was spiralling out of control.

When I was alone, I talked to Danny. I just let it all flow out. The one thing that really caught in my throat was hearing myself say the words, 'You hurt me too'—because he did. *You did, Danny.* He hurt me so much.

And I was trying so desperately to fix everyone else.

The time came to deliver my presentation, to get back in the zone. I greeted my colleagues from the agency with a warm smile and we exchanged niceties as we walked towards the Vice-Chancellor's office. I carried on—just as I always have, just as I always will.

2019

29 SEPTEMBER

I'd had to change the kids' birthday plans at the last minute due to the weather. We were supposed to have a party with their friends on the Saturday and visits from the family on Sunday, but the rain meant I had to merge the two events and move it all inside. My sister's kids were delighted; they got to enjoy the bouncy castle and got a party bag each—but for Danny and Shay, it wasn't so simple.

Danny couldn't handle disruption—last-minute changes always stressed him out. And then there was Shay, who wouldn't attend a kids' party.

Danny and I exchanged texts for most of the afternoon. He wanted to know the specific times and arrangements, which was difficult as things were in a state of flux. In the end, we agreed he'd just come up with Linda the following weekend.

He arrived with cards *(Why oh why did I throw them away?)* and money for the kids. They were delighted.

Peter jumped on him immediately. 'But when are we going to the football match, Uncle Danny?'

Danny looked at me, his eyes pleading with me to help.

I jumped in. 'Well, Uncle Danny's already taken to you to see Shay at the football stadium, hasn't he?'

Danny shot me a relieved look, but Peter wasn't convinced. 'Yeah, but you said we were going to see Man United.'

Danny's face fell as he received a harsh reminder of why you don't say something to a kid that you don't really intend and cannot afford to do.

I give up, I thought. *You get yourself out of this one.*

'One day,' Danny responded, 'soon, pal.'

'Oh, Peter,' Lily interrupted confidently, 'it's never going to happen, you know that, don't you? Grown-ups always say things they don't mean!'

Peter looked crestfallen as we all began to laugh at Lily. She was absolutely right, only not for the reasons she thought.

The kids ran wild in the garden while we sat outside at the top of the garden. Danny lit up a cigarette. I looked over at him, ready to reprimand.

'Tomorrow!' he said. 'I'm giving up again tomorrow.'

Before I got a chance to follow up, he cast his eyes to the fondant fancy in my hand.

'Tomorrow,' I said, laughing. 'Fair play, you bugger.'

It was nice to see him and Linda on their own. He listened intently as Eddie spoke about the grand plans he had for the house, and then he told us about his own work and the hopes he and Linda had. Shay, and Linda's son, Sam, were both up to mischief at school, and Danny was trying to get Shay into the gym with him to keep him focused and out of trouble. It sounded like it was doing the trick, and Danny was looking and sounding better for it too.

It was one of those nothing-special days, but it's everything to me—it was the very last time he came to my house. It was the last time he drank tea from one of my cups, sat on my step, spoke to my husband—the last time he stepped into my world.

2018

25 JANUARY

Message to: Alison

From: Danny

16:49

Naltrexone read up and see what you think please x

Naltrexone

Generic name: naltrexone (oral) (nal-TREX-own)

Brand name: *ReVia*

Naltrexone blocks the effects of opioid medication, including pain relief and feelings of well-being, that that can lead to opioid abuse. An opioid is sometimes called a narcotic. Naltrexone is used as part of a treatment program for drug or alcohol dependence.

I'm racking my brain, trying to remember whether I looked into back when he asked me to. He started speaking about it in late 2017—I remember. It was an option; a possibility; a way of ensuring he didn't relapse. Could I look into it? Could I tell him what I thought?

Did I do it, Danny? Did I help you in the way that you asked?

I vaguely remember. The problem I had with it was simple: why did he need something like this if he was okay? After all, he was insistent he was okay.

But now, in the cold light of day, I can see it: he *knew* he was on the brink of addiction. He was desperately trying to protect himself—and everyone he loved—from the grip it was getting on him.

To him, what I thought about it mattered. But, at the time, I was too tired, too worn down to really care. It was just another drug, another jar of snake oil.

> Naltrexone is used to prevent relapse in people who become dependent on opioid medicine and then stop using it. Naltrexone can help keep you from feeling a 'need' to use the opioid.

I wish I'd spent more time researching, trying to understand.

> Naltrexone is not a cure for drug addiction or alcoholism.

He started taking it but it didn't last too long. He said it made him feel numb to everything. It wasn't worth it, he said.

2017

13 SEPTEMBER

Few days gone bye

Holiday to Wales With Shay is

my only real good memory

need to start back at the gym

18 OCTOBER

it's all out in the open now

20 OCTOBER

He told Mum. Everything. *Everything.*

His history with drugs; his dependency on them; the cocktails; the times he'd almost overdosed—all of it.

She was truly and utterly heartbroken.

I mean, she'd known. She'd known that he struggled. She'd even known he took more of his prescription drugs than he should have. But she hadn't *really* known, not properly. How could she have?

Mum was raised a Catholic. She had strong morals; she was good. She got married and had kids and spent her life raising a family. She baked. She sewed. She planned holidays and ironed uniforms and kept our house nice and made sure we all ate some vegetables. The most Mum knew about drugs was what she'd seen on *Coronation Street*.

I was angry with him for not preparing her or for letting her dip a toe in first, but he was angry with her because she'd reacted in the only way she knew how; the way anybody who hadn't lived in a world where drugs were normal would. It was predictable, really, because she loved him and wanted him to be happy and healthy beyond anything else. But it was the worst possible outcome for him.

Mum was disappointed.

It doesn't matter how old you get; disappointing your mother is still the most devastating blow. If nightmares ever gain a face, it'll be your mother looking straight at you, tilting her head to the side, and slowly releasing those crushing words:

'I'm not angry—'

Long pause.

'I'm disappointed'

Shudder.

I spoke to her shortly after their conversation. He'd shared too much, and she was overwhelmed—you could hear it in her tiny voice. She felt like she'd never known him at all. Mum couldn't understand how abusing drugs could ever have even been an option; she'd been raised in a world where you simply shook things off and carried on.

I listened to her and soothed her until her voice became normal again. Then, I did my job: I gave her her boy back. I helped her understand why he'd done the things he'd done. I helped her see the battles he'd faced and understand what he'd been trying to do by sharing the truth with her. I explained his logic—that maybe, just maybe, if he was truly honest—if he told her *everything*—there could be no going back. Maybe he thought she had to know to save him from himself.

After an hour and thirty minutes, she was in a better place—bruised, but not broken. She still didn't understand, but she was closer to accepting. She was less disappointed and more saddened. It was progress, I suppose.

But as soon as I'd hung up on Mum, Danny called me in a fit of rage. He couldn't understand how she could have been anything but pleased and relieved. He'd finally, *finally* told the truth, and for what? To be made to feel like he should have kept his mouth shut?

No, *no*—fuck that!

He couldn't see the other side—he'd never been able to. It was all or nothing.

And when he felt like that, I worried what he'd do.

21 OCTOBER

going to start working every other wkend

23 OCTOBER

Stared Back at The gym

5 mins Running

30 mins gym

Asked for Pay rise

Vitamin D

I m Boldenone

24 OCTOBER

(1 week today)

26 OCTOBER

Exercise had done Danny a world of good, and when he called that day he sounded happier and more content than he had in days.

'I think I swap one addiction for another, Al,' he told me as he emptied his gym stuff into the washing machine.

'I think you do, Dan,' I replied absentmindedly as I shepherded the kids into the bath. He had a habit of calling when I was either feeding, bathing, or putting the kids to bed, and I always felt like he thought I was trying to get him off the phone as I juggled our conversation and the twins.

I tucked the phone under my chin as I got them undressed and then stood outside the room so I could hear myself think as they began playing.

'Sorry Dan, I was just getting the kids in the bath,' I told him, turning my attention back to him properly. 'I think you have an addictive personality and that it's both good and bad. You know this. Exercise is a good addiction; when you are in the zone, you are brilliant—so I'm glad you're back at the gym. You sound in a much better place.'

'I am. I really am.'

'How's Mum?' I asked, knowing full well how she was as I'd spoken to her the night before.

'She's better. We've talked a lot this week. We're good. I know it's a lot for her to take in.'

And I was pleased to hear him say that, because Mum had told me the same. After the initial shock, she'd spent time talking to him about his drug use and, although she didn't really understand, she was trying. It seemed like she'd finally reached a place of acceptance. What upset me was that she privately blamed herself. She asked herself where she had gone wrong, what she had done to lead her child to think drugs were the answer, and it broke my heart. Danny and I had grown up in a different world to Mum; drugs had been a rite of passage for us in the 90s. It was the rave scene, indie music—pill-popping was as prevalent as drinking. Danny was no different from anyone else, it was just that he'd not stopped. When most of our generation moved on and settled down, Danny and his diminishing circle of old friends carried on.

Uppers and downers. Uppers and downers.

When did it stop being fun? When did drugs change from being about partying and fun to just a mundane way of life?

2020

23 JANUARY

Claire had seen a medium. She called me at work, incredibly excited, and told me about it. She'd communicated with him, she said. The medium had known too much for it to have been fake.

I was sceptical—I've never trusted people like that. If you ask me, we all have ways of conveying too much and we always forgot the things we didn't need to hear.

'I've got a John? A Michael? James? Don? Dan? Daniel?'

'Yes, yes! That's me, he's here for me!'

Still, it was clear that Claire had gotten a great deal of comfort from her mystical encounter. I didn't want to deflate her—after all, we were all looking for any connection to him we could find, so I let her be.

I knew my own connection was writing. I was trying to tie endless memories and stories into the puzzle that was his life—no, *our* lives, together. I knew my family thought I was bonkers too, so I wasn't about to criticise Claire.

Well, not too much anyway.

She'd told me Danny was trying to communicate by sending a sign through a lamp. Even though she believed it, we both laughed at the sheer absurdity of it. We'd seen the movie *Ghost* after all, and this certainly sounded a bit mad!

Later that night, still giggling at the thought of it, I sent her a text with a single lamp emoji. *Bugger off* was her swift reply. She told me I wouldn't think it was so funny when he came to see me at the end of my bed.

That shut me up.

The next day, the memory of Claire's medium fresh in my mind, I played a song that took me back to Danny. It was Danny Tenaglia's 'Music is the Answer'. It reminded me of happy times, of Danny's elation when he'd first heard it, and of the many, many times we'd listened to it over the years.

But hearing it after his death made me feel suddenly overwhelmed. I picked up my phone and typed out a message to Claire.

I feel like he's talking to me, I told her. *I can't explain it but I do.*

She text me back, telling me I'd made her cry and that she'd Googled the song in question. Then, she called.

'Alison,' she began, 'I know you're not going to believe this, but the last thing that medium said to me was that Danny's taking a baseball cap off and putting it on your head. It didn't mean anything to me at the time, but I just Googled that song and I shit you not, it's a silhouette of a guy dancing and guess what he's wearing?'

A moment's silence.

'A baseball cap!' she exclaimed.

As she was talking, I'd pressed play on the video in question, and there it was.

Okay, I felt a bit weird now. The song was a sign, and now this? I felt like Danny was confirming that I'd got it right, that it was okay. He'd sent me a message.

What the hell am I doing falling for this shit?

It was a strange feeling. I wanted to believe, but the rational part of my brain was resisting. But how could I explain how I'd felt listening to that song? I'd heard his voice talking to me. Felt such a rush of warmth and love.

I began to type, keen to capture all that I was feeling, but I was quickly distracted. I went cold.

I picked up the phone immediately and sent a text to Claire.

Oh my god, I kid you not. I am sat in my kitchen and my lamp just flickered on and off!

24 JANUARY

Services to Hooton have been suspended due to a person being struck by a train.

Liverpool Central Station, early morning.

I stare down at the platform. Is this really the best we can do to announce that somebody has lost their life? I rattle through all the words in my head—tragic, sadly, unfortunately . . .

We have got to do better than this. This is someone's loved one.

It makes me furious.

I've had two conversations with two different people on two consecutive days about the same thing: what it is to be content.

The two people are women from two parts of my life, personal and professional, but they're so similar. I've known them both for under a year, but we have that familiar, easy way of talking that I normally only enjoy with life-long friends.

I'm in a very emotional place. Grief has hit me like a truck (again), Claire's medium experience is making me question my beliefs, and I'm feeling overwhelmed because I've stumbled across the reason for all my writing. I feel more connected to Danny than ever before, but the closer I get to him, the further I feel from my family. Well, my immediate family. Eddie, to be precise.

And these two incredible women are talking to me about what it means to be content. Truth be told, I envy them. I envy them so much because they are exactly where I want to be. Right where they should be.

They're divorced, both of them, and they've been through some horrendous pain. But I see them now, having passed out the other side. They are positive, radiant, and free.

Helen challenges me first. I feel like she sees right through me.

I tell her I don't know if I am enough for Eddie. She immediately throws it back to me.

'Is Eddie enough for you?'

I catch my breath in my throat. I am taken off guard. It's not a question I have ever asked myself. My eyes fill with tears.

Eddie and I are a team. I have loved him since the moment we met. He is a good, kind man. He's the most talented and creative person I know. When we laugh, there is nowhere else I'd rather be. But is he enough?

I keep looking to him to make me feel enough, but now I'm being asked to consider whether he is enough for me.

'I love him so much,' I tell her.

'That's not what I asked.' She narrows her eyes and fixes me with her gaze.

Her eyes are bright and beautiful. *I wish I looked as shiny and happy as you,* I think. *I wish I felt that.*

Is Eddie the reason I feel so discontented?

The next morning, Sabina and I end up having the same conversation at work. I can't even remember why we started talking about it, but soon she too is telling me that she's content. She's feeling better than she has in years, she says; she's right where she wants to be.

I sigh. How I wish I felt the same. In the pit of my stomach, I feel off-kilter, unnerved, as if I'm on the brink of a drastic change.

I think about these two divorced women and the positivity they convey. Is Eddie holding me back? Is my marriage the root of my unease?

It's too painful to even consider. I can't go there. I won't.

'The thing is,' Sabina begins, interrupting my thoughts, 'if you had millions of pounds, if money released you from the confines of the life you currently have, you have to ask yourself: where would you choose to be?'

I just peer at her blankly.

'I'd be right where I am,' she said confidently, and I can tell she means it.

We go back to work, heads down, emails firing left, right, and centre. Our busy day has begun. I welcome the distraction.

I'm on my walk home when I allow myself to pick that train of thought up again. I mull the conversation over. *Where would I be?*

I think of all the holidays I want to go on; the travelling I feel I'm supposed to do. The romantic dinners and weekends I should be enjoying. The country mansion, the fresh air. The freedom. I think of being told how amazing I am. How bloody incredible and beautiful and talented. And I soak it all up, letting it wash over me.

What do I need to be? What will make me feel enough?

And then I think of my house. *Our* house. The house I've spent years saving for. The beautiful location sandwiched between both of our families. I picture Eddie sorting out tea in the kitchen; my kids on the sofa, arguing with each other about what they want to watch on TV. The coats and bags strewn across the floor. The chaos that will greet me when I walk inside.

I turn the key in the lock, kiss the kids a quick hello, and head straight to the kitchen. Eddie has his headphones in and an iPad in his hand. I take the buds out of his ears, kiss his cheek, and wrap my arms around his waist. He returns my embrace.

'What's this?' he asks, surprised.

'You'll think this sounds mad, but I need to say it.'

He nods, a concerned look on his face.

'If I had millions of pounds, if I had all the options in the world, this is exactly where I'd want to be. Right here, with you.'

He hugs me tightly and rubs my back before letting me go.

As he pulls away, he gives me one of his trademark smiles, showing the dimple in his left cheek.

'Okay, don't kill me,' he says, 'but I wasn't expecting you back yet, so I haven't made you any tea.'

I shake my head. That's my bloody Eddie.

Later, as we eat together at our kitchen table, my thoughts turn again to Danny. Like me, I know he carried the weight of feeling that he wasn't enough. Had he been in the same position as me? Had he just needed to ask himself honestly what he really wanted, where he really needed to be?

If I could ask him now, what would he say?

I immediately know; he would answer without hesitation.

Danny would just be hanging out with his kid.

25 JANUARY

Mum and I are going to see *Strictly Come Dancing* in Manchester, and we've decided to take Lil along too.

It's her first time at a big arena and she wakes me by bursting into mine and Eddie's bedroom and jumping on the bed, singing, *'Du du du du du du derrrrrr. Du du du du du.'*

I manage to give her a squeeze before she dashes off, announcing she's desperate for a pee.

I'm excited: a whole day with my favourite girls. The first big show for Lil and a day away from everything for Mum.

Strictly was one of the first things she mentioned after Danny died. In the strange way you do when you lose someone, she announced all the things she felt she could and couldn't possibly do. Rose's christening? No, she couldn't face it. It was weeks away, but I got it—too raw. Christmas? Well, none of us would cope well with that. *Strictly?* Well, probably not— she planned for a sad January. But Helen's wedding in late spring? Oh, absolutely. She'd be happy again by then.

I came back to *Strictly*: 'Let's just see nearer the time, hey Mum?'

She reluctantly agreed, as if agreeing to even discuss it in the future was somehow betraying her son. But now the time has come, it's clear she needs it—and, now that she feels like she's been given permission, she's even excited.

I booked lunch (we all shared a love for good cafes) and arranged trains. Lil has already planned her outfit, and it truly is the mother of all outfits. We're good to go.

As I start to get ready, I think about Danny and worry about how we'll feel doing something so special and (hopefully) fun. I immediately think of one of Peter's anxiety books, *The Worry Monster*—it's about how you carry your worries around with you in a bag. Naturally, the more worries you pack away, the heavier the bag gets and the more it drags you down.

This perfectly describes how I feel about grief and about Danny. I carry him everywhere with me. He's more present in my life in death than he ever was when he was alive. He's in my bag (sorry, Dan! I'll make it an Adidas one just for you), weighing me down but present, comforting almost.

After he died, I told Mum to think of dealing with Danny's death as moving forward rather than moving on. I said we had to somehow make it manageable. *Just get up. Just breathe. Just get sunshine on your face. And look at the sky.*

Today, though, I'll give her some new advice.

I'll tell her she's carrying him with her in her bag. And he'll be watching her, hoping to see her smile.

26 JANUARY

I woke up next to Lil at Mum and Dad's house. It was my great-nephew Teddy's second birthday, so we were all getting together to celebrate. His mum, Gemma had pulled out all the stops and Mum had made Teddy the most beautiful jungle cake.

We rose up late as Lil had enjoyed a late night—she'd got to play on the iPad until 10:30 while I'd sat chatting and drinking wine with Mum and Dad.

We'd slept in Danny's bed. I'd found it strangely comforting, and I knew he'd be okay with it. I thought about the times he'd not given up his bed for us when Eddie and I had come to stay. It had bugged me at the time, as we'd had to sleep on sofas and floors. *Thanks for making up for it now, Dan.*

I left his room pristine, just the way he always had it, and took a final long look around. Everything was just as he'd left it, only now it was thick with dust. My parents refused to move anything, and it clearly wasn't getting cleaned. It made me sad. The only room in Mum's house where she didn't feel she could go in with her duster. The thick dust was the only reminder that he was no longer there.

Before I left, I opened his wardrobe. I fished out his books from the back of his shelf and popped them into my bag. I was sure no one would mind me borrowing them; I was going to give them back, after all, but there was something I had to do.

I walked downstairs and grabbed myself a coffee before joining Mum in the living room.

'How did you sleep?' she asked, clearly worried I'd have found sleeping in Danny's bed unnerving.

'Okay,' I replied, and I meant it, 'what about you?'

'I didn't sleep at all,' Mum said, and I knew she hadn't. Her face looked tired and grey.

Mum didn't sleep well at the best of times, but it had gotten worse since we'd lost Danny. It pained me to see her looking so frail.

'I just kept thinking about that bungalow,' she announced, 'it was going over and over in my head.' She sounded a little brighter. Excited almost.

The bungalow was our latest thing. After getting together to discuss Danny's affairs the week before, Rach, Claire, and I had agreed to talk to Mum and Dad about moving. It was something they had talked about for years: downsizing, finding somewhere more suitable for Dad, trying to free up some money to live a more comfortable life.

They'd never done it because of Danny. They'd not wanted to leave him without a home or force him to move out. Now they were free of that obligation, but still we feared they'd never move because of Danny. After all, how could they possibly leave that house? That room that was and only ever would be his?

But Dad seemed to be growing weaker and weaker by the day. Rachael was convinced he had given up on life since losing his son.

'He just wants to be with Danny,' she said sadly, and I couldn't help but agree.

So we resolved to broach the bungalow subject again, and this time Mum agreed to look. In fact, she'd not only agreed; she was positively *happy* about it.

I'd found one that I thought looked perfect. It had the kerb appeal I knew was important to Mum, and inside it looked like a cottage. Of course, you can never be too sure with photographs, but I had a good feeling about it nonetheless.

I'd shown it to her before we got the train to watch *Strictly* and she'd talked about it a lot that day. It was gratifying to see her in a positive headspace again.

'So, are you looking forward to viewing it?' I asked. Claire was due to take her the following day at 10:30.

'Yes,' she said, 'but I'm worried about your dad.'

I'd known this was coming. We were all worried about how he'd handle a move so soon after losing Danny, but we couldn't see an alternative. Dad was unwell, really unwell, and his mood had never climbed back since losing his son. The house was no good for him; he couldn't walk upstairs and he had to pee in a bucket in the back garden during the day. They either needed to spend a lot of money adapting the house, or they needed a new home.

And then, of course, we had to consider the unthinkable. How would Mum cope if she didn't have Dad? Danny's bedroom comforted and scared her in equal measure; It was a reminder of the son she had lost and the pain he had suffered. She openly told us she wouldn't live in the house if she ever ended up on her own.

Mum and Dad had stayed up late last night, long after Lil and I had gone to bed. Mum told me the next day that Dad had said he didn't think he had long left—just months, in fact.

No, he was neither a doctor nor a fortune teller, but it had upset Mum.

'I feel like he is just giving up,' Mum said.

'I know,' I agreed. I didn't want to cause any more pain, but we all felt it. We felt Dad was slipping away in front of our eyes.

'Rach thinks he just wants to be with Danny,' I told her, and immediately wished I hadn't.

She looked incredibly sad. Broken. 'But that is so incredibly selfish,' she spat, tears in her eyes.

And it was—for a million reasons. He was preparing to leave her on her own to grieve for their son and her husband; to deal with the house and all the stuff of life (so much stuff!) without him.

'But Mum,' I began, 'I don't think Dad thinks he is being selfish at all. I think Dad feels he holds you back.'

I knew I was right. I watched my wonderful parents night after night; my mum running around like a madwoman while my dad sat in his chair, struggling to draw breath. I listened to my mum on the phone lamenting all the things she couldn't do. She wanted to go to cafes, for drives and holidays, and just live her life. But my dad had neither the will nor the ability.

No, I didn't believe my dad was being selfish at all. Yes, he wanted a pint with his boy again—but, even more than that, he wanted to see his wife free again.

237

As I thought these thoughts and tried to comfort my mum, tried to make her feel positive about the bungalow and all it could represent again, I couldn't shake the selfish thoughts from my own mind: *Please, God. Please do not take my dad. I am not ready to lose another person I love.*

***

Mum gave me a gift bag for Teddy's present. I'd totally forgotten to buy wrapping paper and we were now in a rush.

I popped everything in and tied the strings tight. Lil walked into the kitchen and, like a guided missile, immediately homed in on it.

'Awww, it's like the card Uncle Danny got me!' she announced.

It was. The gift bag was covered in peas and had the words *two peas in a pod* written across it.

'I know Lil,' I said, 'I remember.' He'd given it to her a week late and it had been left in the letter stand on the shelf in our hall, not on the fireplace with the others.

'He wrote "don't stop playing with the rats!"' she giggled.

'And Mummy threw it away,' I said.

Eddie had joined us in the room and I noticed his ears prick up.

'I threw it away,' I said again, 'I didn't know it would be the last one you'd ever get.'

I felt Eddie's eyes on me. He was waiting for the tears to fall, I knew— but they didn't.

'I've thought about that card a lot, Lil,' I went on, 'I'll regret throwing it away for the rest of my life.'

'Really?' she asked, incredulous. Her face betrayed her thoughts: *It was just a card, Mum!*

'Yes, really,' I confirmed.

Little did she know that I saw that green card, with its round, perfect peas, every single time I walked through the front door.

I take Danny's books out of my bag and set them on the kitchen table beside my laptop.

- *Once an Addict* – Barry Woodward

- *The King of Methlehem* – Mark Lindquist

- *Tweak: Growing up on Methamphetamines* – Nic Sheff

- *The Rewired Brain* – Dr Ski Chilton

- *Lithium for Medea* – Kate Braverman

- *Painkiller Addict: From Wreckage to Redemption: My True Story* – Cathryn Kemp

- *The Krays: The Prison Years* – David Meikle and Kate Beal Blyth

And, of course,

- *High Life 'n' Low Down Dirty: The Thrills and Spills of Shaun Ryder* – Lisa Verrico

I'm learning a lot about the different ways in which we deal with death.

Claire is now an advocate of mediums. She's convinced that Danny communicated with her and she's now reading a book written by the medium she saw, desperate to hear from or see Danny again.

I think she's secretly jealous that I got the weird thing with the lamp!

I take the mickey out of her, but have to confess that I'm a little spooked. I'm sending random pictures to our WhatsApp group; cats that keep wandering into my garden that I'm convinced are Danny reincarnated and bottles of Corona that I spot out and about. Suddenly everything feels like a sign! I'm a walking contradiction, but I don't care.

While Claire looks to connect with Danny's spirit, I try to connect with Danny's soul. I have felt from the moment he died that he is everywhere.

Not in a physical form—sorry, Claire, I just don't buy him sitting in heaven eating a bowl of cornflakes—but in a more abstract one.

I'm trying to connect with the meaning of his existence. What was he here for? What did we learn from him? What did he leave us with? I'm writing endlessly about him and our life together. About grief. About me.

I'm ignoring my kids, who are currently jumping on my bed in my high heels, each of them brandishing steel poles.

I'm thinking about something I saw on Facebook years ago. A colleague's wife had lost a good friend and she started a post entitled 'Because of You'. She wrote about all the ways her friend had shaped her world, all the things that would always take her back to him. I'd watched as their other friends followed suit. So many beautiful memories—all because of you.

My kids are getting louder and louder. The clothes I'd piled, ready to put away, are now strewn across the floor. But I have to get this down.

So, Danny, because of you:

- It will always be Man United over Liverpool despite the latter being close to my heart

- I'll put peanut butter *and* butter on my toast

- I'll talk openly and passionately about mental health and drug addiction, particularly the latter. I'll challenge the stereotypes.

- I'll consider it a privilege to put my kids to bed every night because I know how much you missed doing that with Shay.

- I will find meaning in lyrics and pass those meanings on to others.

- I'll believe that I am beautiful, because you said it and I know you wouldn't lie about something like that.

- I will listen to music every day for the rest of my days.

- I will complete this book and tell your story. *Our* story.

- I will read about and understand addiction so that I can help other people understand it too.

- I will hug our family until they feel uncomfortable. Especially our niece, Hannah because she hates it.

- I will appreciate the beauty in everything around me.

- I will tell myself 'It's a sunny day!' each and every day for the rest of my days.

2001

FEBRUARY

I'd not long ago moved to Liverpool when some friends came to stay for a club night at Nation, the home of Cream. It was darker and deeper than the house nights I usually enjoyed, and I felt out of my depth from the moment we arrived.

We popped our pills and headed for the dancefloor. It still felt a massive deal to be here; to live in this city that was such a Mecca for dance. I hadn't been there long, hadn't really got into my groove, when I spotted an old friend on the dancefloor. She had been a huge part of my life but we'd lost touch when she started university and I hadn't seen her in years. She was instantly recognisable but at the same time entirely different. Her face was hanging loose; her jaw protruded; her eyes were wide. She was being led around the room by her boyfriend, but she looked lost and vacant.

Despite the drugs inside me wanting to push me forward, wanting me to feel, I pushed back hard. This wasn't where I should be. It suddenly felt like a different world—one that I didn't want to inhabit.

And right there, with an illegal substance still pumping through my blood, I vowed never to touch drugs ever again.

And I didn't. I grew out of them.

Meanwhile, Danny was in Chorley, growing into them.

It was no longer ecstasy; it was cocaine. It was no longer big clubs; it was house parties. It wasn't dancing; it was feeling.

Uppers and downers. Uppers and downers.

MAY

With Danny's new lifestyle came new friends. They had fancy cars and designer labels. He wanted a piece of it; the expensive champagne, the exquisite brandy. He wanted the very best of the very best.

I could see him changing in front of my eyes. I knew he was different, but I couldn't put my finger on it.

DECEMBER

By now, he was a man I barely recognised. His friends had always been my friends—but no longer. For the first time in our adult lives, I felt like we were growing apart.

While I was planning to travel the world, he was reading books by Howard Marks, desperate to figure out how he could be Leyland's answer to Mr Nice.

We kept in touch—we always did—but it was getting harder and harder to reach him, both literally and metaphorically. He had moved in with Kelly and her son, Ben. I'd see him as often as we could, but he was moving on with his new family and I was building a new life for myself, in Liverpool.

I felt like I was losing him.

2010

25 DECEMBER

Eddie and I were at my mum and dad's for Christmas. We'd just finished our dinner and were clearing the plates when Danny walked in.

He was with his friend Rick. They were blind drunk and Rick was carrying a stereo on his shoulder like a teenager. They were singing along to a song by Johnny Cash. They were laughing and joking, but everything about them oozed sadness. Danny greeted me and Eddie with a warm smile and a big hug, but I could see the pain in his pin pricked eyes.

It was Christmas Day. He wasn't with Shay.

Rick was in the same boat: already deep into drugs—deeper than Danny ever got. The shadow of the man we'd once known.

I urged them to stay with us. I wanted to give them coffee and play games. They needed to know they were loved.

But Danny refused. He picked up the stereo, threw his arm around Rick, and together they went off on their merry way, the sound of Johnny Cash carrying them all the way down the street.

2016

18 OCTOBER

I was leading a massive restructure at work. Almost fifty people were considered 'at risk' of redundancy and my job was to liaise with every single on them. I knew that the new structure would provide opportunities for them, but it didn't make the situation any less stressful. Change and uncertainty will make even the strongest people feel off balance.

The individual meetings to discuss people's roles were often fraught with anger and frustration. I knew it was hitting them hard—they had families, mortgages, and commitments, and they no longer knew precisely where they were or what they'd be doing. I understood.

While my job was to listen, to advise, and to move us forward, I couldn't help but feel emotionally involved. When someone spoke to me with resentment and rage, I understood it came from a place of fear and worry. I felt it. I felt the pain and I took their worries home with me every night. It was hard.

My colleagues in the project team became my emotional support. After I'd taken verbal lashings from the individuals at risk, they were there to comfort me. 'I worry I feel too emotionally involved,' I'd tell them after a particularly challenging meeting.

'We'd worry if you weren't,' Sara would say. These colleagues gave me the power to keep going when I felt like it was all getting too hard.

One afternoon, after a very difficult conversation with someone who was very anxious about the coming changes, I put my head in my hands.

I was with Geoff. Throughout the process I'd got to know him reasonably well. He was a similar age to me and had a similar dry humour.

I'd found him a bit rude at first, but had quickly realised that it was simply his style.

'Oh Geoff,' I moaned, 'if only these people knew I was human too. I don't want to disrupt people's lives. I'm really trying to do the right thing.'

He fed me the HR lines about process and transparency and assured me I was getting it right. Then, he said, 'How are things with your brother?'

Geoff had gone through some family issues of his own. His father was seriously ill, and every now and then he'd come into the office looking as drained as I felt.

I told him I was tired, too tired, and that I couldn't take much more. I said I couldn't deal with being lied to and constantly feeling let down.

'One day,' he said wisely, 'one day you'll just be done. He will make you reach a point where you can do no more. You'll put your shield up and he won't break it down.'

'Hmmm,' I said, unconvinced.

'It happens,' he continued, 'because people have to save themselves. You realise you can't do it for them, however much you try.'

How I longed to have that shield, but I couldn't imagine it would ever happen. I could never turn my back on Danny, no matter how hard it was to face him.

But Geoff had planted a seed; a seed that showed me there was another way. Could I ever just give up?

26 OCTOBER

Work was hard. I'd had to meet someone I liked and respected and comb over the reasons why they hadn't got the role they'd applied for. It broke my heart—I'd hoped they'd get it too, but I wasn't allowed to say. I had to listen and advise and attempt to keep them cool, nudge them toward possible next steps, and try to ensure they remained engaged in the process.

I just wanted to go home, pour myself a large glass of wine, and collapse on the sofa. However, it was my night to collect the kids from the after-school club, which meant a detour to Spar to grab them a snack and something to make for tea. Lily had asked for two packets of sweets and

I'd refused, so she'd stomped off down the aisle with a face like thunder. Already weary, I plonked the basket by the till and began to make small talk with the woman behind the counter. I turned to see that Lil had returned, her pockets bulging.

'What's that?' I asked, pointing at her coat. Her face turned bright red and she began to walk away backwards. I quickly grabbed her and yanked the items from her pockets. The sweets!

Bloody hell. I made a huge show of her in front of the shop assistant, ensured all the sweets were returned to the shelves, and marched her and a confused Peter out of the shop, leaving the items I had intended to purchase on the counter.

I lectured them all the way home, partly because Lily needed to know that stealing was *not* acceptable and partly, if I'm honest, because I was in an awful mood. I couldn't handle work, shop-lifting, and the thought of what I had to do that evening—I needed rest. I needed some peace.

When we got home, I fed the kids fish fingers, bathed them, read with them, and then settled back down in front of my laptop.

I text Danny. *Call me when you're ready. The kids are in bed.*

I opened up a fresh document and began to write. I knew the basics; I could get a head start.

He'd relapsed again, but he was out the other side. He wanted to sort everything out; he was going to clear up everything with regards to Shay, he said, and put some order back in his life. I had to help, of course. I knew that if I didn't, it wouldn't happen, so we'd arranged to go through it all on the phone so I could write it all down and present his case as it were. We then had an appointment to get some legal advice on Saturday. I was driving to his flat from York. It was a plan and it had made him feel positive again, yet as usual I had to do all the leg-work. I felt that all of Danny's initiatives relied on me in some way.

I waited twenty minutes before trying to call. I'd downloaded everything I knew from my brain but I needed his input.

He didn't answer.

'Danny, it's me. We arranged to speak at seven. It's now twenty past. I have made a start but can you call me ASAP? I'm tired and I need to get this done.'

I text again at 7:40

Danny. I need you to call. It's getting late. Can you let me know one way or the other?

I amended the formatting. I tidied up what I had, but I needed him. I couldn't put words into his mouth—not this time.

I called again at 8:15. My head was in my hands. I was worn out, emotionally and physically.

Danny. It's a piss-take now. You promised. RING ME!!!

Eddie brought me a cup of tea and put his hands on my shoulders.

'You okay?' he asked, knowing that I wasn't.

I shook my head, shaking his hands away.

'I just have to get this done,' I said grumpily, frustrated at Danny but taking it out on him. He backed away, smiling softly, and I reached for his hand to apologise. This was a familiar routine.

I text again at nine.

I'm switching off the laptop. I tried. I'm so cross at you. Don't ring me now. I am going to bed.

I walked over to Eddie, who was lying on the sofa, and allowed myself to be folded into his outstretched arms. He didn't ask. He didn't need to.

28 OCTOBER

I didn't even want to answer the phone.

'Hello,' I said quietly, hoping my mood would be conveyed through that one word alone.

'Al, I'm so, so sorry. It's just—' Danny began.

'I don't want to hear it,' I interrupted.

Geoff was right. You *could* reach that point

I was done.

2020

27 JANUARY

I'd been thinking about it all day so, as soon as I had the kids tucked up in bed, I came downstairs, made coffee, and picked up my wedding picture.

I opened the back of the frame and carefully took out the envelope entitled *2015 good things.*

Danny's distinctive handwriting spilt out in front of me—and with it, flashbacks from our childhood.

'You're writing a note, not a novel,' I laughed as I watched him painstakingly press his pen into the paper. He always held his hand above the pen and pressed down hard, a look of deep concentration on his face. I'd once got a card from Danny that had simply said, *To Alison, from Danny,* and it had always amused me because I knew the effort he must have put into writing it.

I spread out his envelope so I could read it properly.

I thought back to how we must have looked that night as we wrote our cosmic orders and burnt the lists of things we wanted to leave behind in 2014. Eddie must have thought we were bonkers—and, to be fair, Danny would have thought the same a year before. But that night he embraced it with gusto. He was determined to make it work.

Danny had wanted to free himself from his relationship with Kelly, his ex-wife. There was still so much hostility between them, but they needed to stay in touch for Shay's sake. He asked the universe to make their relationship functional and calm; he was done with intensity and anger.

He'd wanted to say goodbye to anyone who was part of the world he was trying to free himself from.

He'd simply wanted to wake up the next day and start anew.

2015 Danny 11:57 2014

Stay drug free. Alcohol?

Meet new girlfriend. Possibly oriental

Learn a new trick or two legal

Bass fighting?

Move into new flat

Some new friends. Positive ones.

Good will and health to family and friends.

Reading it back made me sad, but it also made me smile. In the midst of all he was going through, he still found mentioned us—and his Nicole Scherzinger-style future girlfriend of course! I thought about how, if he was here, I'd be reprimanding him for using the word 'oriental'.

I'm going to let that one go, Danny. Under the circumstances it only seems fair.

I held his envelope up to my lips and kissed it before picking up mine.

Alison

I want to be fit and healthy again by June 2015

I want my family to continue to be healthy and happy all year

I want Danny to have moved on with a positive new life by March 2015

I want to be doing more active things with my children in the summer of 2015

I thought back to March 2015 and realised that the universe (or perhaps Danny) had delivered. By March, he'd been in a good place: he was working, back at the gym, drug-free. He was reconnecting with good friends from his past. He was spending quality time with Shay. They were running together, training for the Great North Run.

And I was better than I'd been in years—training with him, losing weight, finally released from worrying about Danny. The worst had happened, or so I'd thought—if you'd asked me then, I'd have said yes, he'd reached an all-time low, but he'd turned back. I'd *helped* him turn back. Now he was free.

If only we could have frozen time in 2015.

Sadness began to creep over me as I thought of these brighter days and of how crushing it had been when he went dark again, but I quickly shook it off. Our cosmic orders were for 2015. He died in 2019. He'd fought a hard battle for five long years. I told myself off for thinking about all we had lost and how it had all unravelled. Instead, I thought of those five precious years and all that we'd been given: the treasured memories, the laughs, and the life lessons (so many!). Our cosmic order didn't save him, but they bought us some time.

I popped our envelopes back into the main envelope and picked up a pen. Before I placed them back behind the frame, in the secret space that only he and I knew, I wrote on the back.

27 January 2020 – Alison

I want to have published our story by December 2020.

PS I love you, Dan. X

28 JANUARY

I can think of my dead brother for an entire day, but as soon as someone else mentions him, I feel the same shock as I did when I first heard he'd died.

Eddie and I had been having a lot of deep and meaningful conversations recently (instigated by me—obviously!). I had to feel more connected to him—I was feeling alone, bereft. He listened intently and, when I finished, began to explain why he had been behaving the way he had.

251

'I'm just trying to do the right thing,' he told me, 'I'm so conscious that your brother has just died.'

And all of a sudden, I didn't want to talk about me and him anymore.

You're never coming back, are you Danny?

***

We have a date for the inquest: 16 April 2020.

The court has assigned only two hours for us to reach a conclusion about his death. I'm perversely looking forward to it—two hours of pure unadulterated Danny. Officials and loved ones coming together to put the pieces together: it's the least he deserves.

I'm consistently told the coroner is only concerned with answering four questions:

- *Who* the deceased was.
- *When* and *where* he died.
- The medical *cause* of his death.
- *How* he came to his death.

I've submitted questions on behalf of the family, but I know most will get knocked back. We want to know his trains of thought, what he took and when—and why (*why?!*) heroin. That's the big one. Why go back to black (or brown as I'm told it's called on the street)?

I've a growing list of questions in my own head too. Did they have music on? What was it? What was he talking about? What were his last words?

Did he know? Please tell me he didn't know!

I want to believe he was listening to something really cool. I want to picture him feeling relaxed and happy before gradually slipping away. I want him to be smiling—euphoric, even—and then for things to just stop. No panic. No spluttering. Just suddenly, silently gone.

But as I think about my perfect vision of the most imperfect situation, I realise I am not prepared for the inquest at all. It's not two hours to enjoy Danny; it's the two hours it took for him to die.

1988

JUNE

'You have to bloody run!' Danny shouts as I stroll over to pick up the bright green ball. It's Wimbledon season and we're out on the tennis court at school. Mum's at home, swooning over Pat Cash, so we thought we'd get out of the house.

I've played tennis once before in PE class, and spent months begging Mum and Dad for my own Slazenger racket. It's a thing of beauty, with pink edging and a shiny case, but spent the last few months propped against a wall in my bedroom. I'm glad to finally put it to use, and swing it around proudly as I go, my mum's squash shorts and a crisp white t-shirt completing the look.

'C'mon Alison! You have to run for it!'

I may look the part but, much to Danny's annoyance, I don't act it.

It's a gorgeous summer evening. School has finished for the day and it feels like years until bedtime. When Danny suggested a game, I jumped at the chance—any excuse to hang out with him.

The football season was over so he had energy he needed to release. But as he stood across from me on the courts, patiently waiting for me to once again collect the ball, he's quickly realising he won't get to release any of it.

I've never been sure whether I'm just innately rubbish at sport or whether I've never really tried. But, either way, I'm a terrible opponent.

After ten minutes of frustration, he tosses the ball in the air and, his arm arcing a perfect circle, whacks it. I see it come hurtling through the air in my direction. I lift my racket feebly but it's no use, it's too fast. I'm in the wrong place. I'm pathetic.

Before I know it, the ball hits my shoulder with such force I fall to the ground. I scramble up quickly, not wanting him to see the tears forming in my eyes.

He fixes me with a stare, a cocky 'what did you expect?' look on his smug little face.

I want to punch him. So bad.

A noise disturbs us and we both look towards the edge of the court. More kids from our street are joining us. Danny waves his racket at them in greeting, a smile breaking over his face. Maybe now he'll get a decent game. I see my chance.

I lift my arm in the air and release the ball—it's the first time I've hit it all day. I swing fast and hard, unleashing all the anger and embarrassment in one serve.

He's still looking at the kids as the ball arcs towards him. He turns ever so slightly as the ball begins to make its way down—and it lands smack-bang in the middle of his forehead.

Bingo!

My self-satisfaction soon turns to fear.

He throws his racket on the floor and comes after me, fury written across his face. I dart out of the courts and start sprinting across the fields, faster and faster with every step. I don't stop until I reach the safety of the kitchen, where my startled mum awaits. I'm confident that I can convince her to tell him off rather than me.

I might be rubbish at tennis, but at least I can run!

2020

18 JANUARY

Danny had talked about taking Shay abroad for as long as we could remember, but it had yet to happen. He was either not in work, working too much, or in a bad place.

When Rach asked him to go with her and her family, we were all relieved. We knew she'd make it happen and they'd all have an amazing time. The holiday gave Danny something to focus on and a new lease on life.

When they returned, they were all so happy, so full of beans. We listened to the endless stories, endured them falling about giggling and sharing private jokes that you 'just had to be there' to get.

Do you want some Fanta with that banter?

Apparently, Danny had been the first in the pool every day, and would spend the next several hours trying to gather players for a game of water polo, only to playfully kick off when his goals were disallowed. Then there were the evenings spent singing karaoke with Becky (while stone-cold sober!) and chatting up ladies at the bar.

They'd all had the time of their lives, and it sounded as if they'd really bonded with one another.

Rach brushed over the one horrible night they'd had on arrival, the one where Danny had clearly been off his head. She didn't dwell on the horror of racing her family across an unfamiliar town to respond to Danny's SOS, only for him to laugh in their faces, telling them he'd only wanted to see if they cared.

They did. And, more importantly, Shay did.

She only briefly described the look of sadness on Shay's face. How a poor kid, excited about his first holiday with his dad and family, had looked crestfallen but at the same time unsurprised.

But she did tell me, often, about how she'd fallen in love with Shay. They all had. They'd got to know him better than they ever had before, and had discovered he was funny, kind: the best bits of his mum and dad.

Claire and Rach had come to my house to talk about Danny's finances. As I made yet another coffee, Rach picked up Danny's diaries from my shelf. I watched her casually flick through them, trying to find anything that might help.

She stopped on August 2017—the pages were crammed with text. It was unusual for him to write so much.

She looked at me, her face pale and sad. 'This was the day before our holiday, Ali,' she said. 'It's breaking my heart. He was so, so sad. Why didn't he say? Why didn't I know?'

I could see the memories of her holiday racing through her mind. All those happy days, all that fun suddenly tainted by the revelation that her brother had been in a dark, dark place.

'None of us knew,' I told her, handing her the coffee cup. 'None of us really knew at all.'

I picked up the diary from the floor and glanced over the page Rachael had been reading. It wasn't really a surprise; after all, I'd pored over Danny's diaries for hours. Still, one thing jumped out at me, something I hadn't noticed before: he mentioned a best friend dying. Strange—how could he have had a best friend that I didn't even know about?

2018

1 AUGUST

Worried about my son.

Best friend is in intensive care, if his heart stops again, they will not start it.

Don't seem to be getting any further up the housing ladder

150 odd days off heroin. Don't want it again but even more scared about hurting my family and also my dad is getting no better and still not getting on with Kelly

2 AUGUST

My sister worried and wants me to stay in York for a few days

Sicknote for work

Get repeat prescriptions as mine won't last till my hols. Some tramadol pain killers to last to the 15 August

And some diazepam for flying and to help me get through my best friends inevitable death

2020

30 JANUARY

Our WhatsApp messages are full of concern for Mum. My nieces (Rachael's kids) are worried she's becoming increasingly withdrawn, and it's certainly true that she seems smaller and frailer than ever before. She's keeping herself busy, but with things that take her further away from us: sorting clothes, decluttering rooms—anything that keeps her active and her mind away from her son.

Mum has always been glamorous and active, and has never shown any sign of slowing down or getting older. Now, though, I'm painfully aware that she's vulnerable, no matter how hard she tries to hide it. The sadness is always there, right behind her eyes.

She is exactly the same but also entirely different. Another shit thing about grief: the fact that when your parents lose a child, you lose your parents too. Mum always used to say that the worst thing in the world would be burying your own child, and now she's done it. She has to wake up every day and remember it; play it over and over again in her head.

For some reason, hearing her say his name hurts more than anything. *Dan-i-el. Dan-i-el.* That distinct way only she says it, because it was her son—it's reserved for her and that special relationship they had. To all of us he was Danny, 'Our Danny', even to my dad. But to Mum, he was always *Dan-i-el.* Hearing her say it out loud totally and utterly breaks my heart.

Someone is coming to reclaim Danny's car and the girls are worried it'll be too much for her. The car is a symbol of all he wanted and all he lost. It's a black sporty Golf; It looks the business, but for as long as I can remember it's been sat in the drive. Shortly after bringing it home, he announced he'd careened into the central reservation and, before we knew it, he'd surrendered his driver's license. The car just sat there from then on, gathering dust. He never got to drive it again.

I want it gone. It's a painful reminder of him and, to me at least, it holds no sentimental value. But to my mum it's another piece of her boy that's being taken away.

I ring her.

Dad answers and chats to me for five minutes before passing me to Mum. Of all the things that have changed since we lost Danny, this is one of the loveliest and most painful. Dad has always been terrible on the phone; we've always joked at how quickly he can manage to pass us over to Mum, how rude he can be when you ask him a question only to realise he's already walked away, and how he decides to end a conversation by simply hanging up without warning.

Now, though, he talks. He asks how you are. He shares news about his day. He wants to know about yours. It's both wonderful and tragic.

'Hey, are you okay?' I ask Mum.

'I'm fine, Alison,' she responds.

'I know it must be hard, Mum,' I tell her. 'Have they taken it yet?'

'It is hard, Alison.' I can hear her crying. I keep talking and let her cry—she needs it. The girls have been texting her all morning, but she's pushed them away, trying to be strong. She needs to let go.

It's just a stupid bloody car. We barely even saw him drive it—but I know that Mum watched him bring it home. I understood the pride she'd have felt as he turned into the drive and how, for her, it symbolised him being on the up. And he had been—at that moment, he really had been.

That is the horrible thing about loving an addict: the simplest of moments become such a big deal. It was never just a car to Danny, or even to Mum. It was a symbol of him getting his life together and moving on.

So I tell my mum to cry and to give herself permission to feel. I tell her to sit down, even though she worries that if she sits down she'll never get up again, and to allow herself to be sad for a while. I tell her what to do in the same way I instruct my kids, and she responds in the same way they do: firstly by protesting, and then by accepting. Mum was always right. Mum knew best. Except this time, I wasn't her mum—she was mine.

***

Things I can do while crying:

1. Cook burgers. Not hand-made (I'm not superwoman!), but still.

2. Chair a meeting (it's amazing what a deep breath, a shake of the head, and rub of the hands can disguise).

3. Navigate my way through a busy train station.

4. Put a week's worth of recycling into the recycling bin while chatting to the neighbour.

5. Listen to my kids read at bedtime.

Things I can't do without crying:

1. Talk to my mum.

2. Cuddle my dad.

3. Look at pictures of Danny.

4. Listen to Claire's song.

5. Think about Shay.

Things I absolutely won't allow myself to do for fear of having a breakdown:

1. Listen to his voice.

31 JANUARY

I can't stop thinking about how painfully ironic it is that Danny couldn't forgive himself for leaving Shay, even though he didn't, only to actually leave Shay by punishing himself with heroin.

Everything changed for Danny when he walked away from his marriage because he felt like he was walking away from Shay. He ached when he wasn't around his boy. He found everything too difficult.

6 p.m. was *The Simpsons* time—'I should be watching this with Shay.' 7 p.m. was bath time—'I should be bathing Shay.' 7:30 p.m.: 'I should be putting Shay to bed.' Every hour of every day was a painful reminder of the life he'd left behind. He saw Shay most weekends, but the gaps in between became unbearable.

Uppers and downers. Uppers and downers.

We first noticed changes to his sleep schedule. He'd be awake all night and would sleep all day. If he wasn't seeing Shay, he'd be in bed. He just didn't want to be present in the world without his son. It was as though he wanted to turn the lights off until he got to see Shay again.

He began to talk about Valium and diazepam in the same way we'd discuss having a coffee or tea. It was so unfamiliar to the rest of us that we let it wash over our heads. We'd always known he was different—so what if drugs weren't just for parties? Of course, we didn't know the extent to which he relied upon them.

We pleaded with him to get some formal arrangements in place with his ex-wife so he could make concrete plans with Shay, but he would never do it, always believing it was better to try to remain civil than to go through the courts. Sometimes it worked—sometimes he'd have Shay for long periods and it was all rosy—but sometimes it didn't. It was during those times that he'd go dark. And it then became a vicious cycle: he'd get to the point, through drinking and taking drugs, where he was no longer fit to look after Shay, so the poor kid would be let down. And the cycle would begin again.

It hurt us because we couldn't do much to help. Even our company was difficult because we had our own growing families that just made him feel worse. He loved his nieces and nephews, adored them, but he never felt right being with kids if he couldn't be with his own. It coloured every relationship he tried to have; he simply wouldn't allow himself to spend time with other children if Shay wasn't around.

If I had to pinpoint the one moment it all started to go wrong, I'd choose the moment he left Shay. Only, he never left him, not really—he left Kelly. Danny was more present for Shay than any father I've ever known, but he couldn't see that—he didn't allow himself to. And so he turned to drugs, which made the pain just go away.

2020

6 FEBRUARY

I stood outside my office, salty teardrops mingling with the cold rain that lashed down on Liverpool. The coroner had called me with the date of the inquest and to warn me that the questions I'd submitted were likely to go unanswered. It all felt ridiculously dramatic, like a cheesy old movie— woman weeps into phone while some robot-like individual on the end of the line explains the legalities and technicalities of death. Okay, so she wasn't exactly robot-like, that's unfair, but she had the air of someone who delivers this kind of news as a job. The emotion was missing. Danny was a case and I was a 'person of interest', nothing more.

I'd expected it, of course, but still—the news hurt.

All the questions now destined for the bin were the ones we desperately wanted answers to. *Why had he ended up there? What did he ask for? What was his mental state? What did he say?* Anything that took us closer to the *why*. Instead, the poor woman on the phone was matter-of-factly explaining that the inquest couldn't give us that. It was designed to explain how Danny had died, nothing more. The *why* would go unanswered.

And I sobbed to her in that pouring rain (okay, it was light, but who doesn't love pathetic fallacy?) because the one person who could have given us what we wanted, what we needed, wasn't around to tell us.

It just made me miss him even more than I already did, which was a lot. That morning I had cried at an Oasis song, and Danny didn't even like Oasis! It was no longer memories that took me to Danny; it was *anything*.

The call from the coroner unleashed another wave of grief, another few days of debilitating sadness that made me cry in the office, struggle while walking to school, and unable to sleep.

God damn you, Danny, for interfering with my life!

***

Before I know it, it's my working from home day so I'm sat in my basement kitchen with my laptop on my kitchen table. I finish a particularly intense work call and get up to stretch my legs. I look out the window into the still-dead garden and begin to talk to him. Totally unplanned. Just me chatting to my dead brother.

It starts quite nice, quite jovial even, but quickly descends into anger. I'm so bloody angry with him for leaving me like this. There's sadness in my belly that's purely his fault—there's a gaping hole in my heart.

I'm angry because he isn't there for me to call, to tell him how angry I am. I find myself staring at my lamp, the one that had seemed to flicker just a week before, hoping against my better judgement that he'll reach out to me in some way again. I stare at the doorway, hoping a vision of him might waltz in and apologise for being such a dick. And then I'm picturing him. His eyes, his head. His blond hair all over his arms.

The phone rings. Work. My next call.

7 FEBRUARY

There is a picture of him on Facebook. He's with Shay. Both are looking at the camera while Shay pretends to punch his dad. It's not their faces I look at; it's their arms. Danny is crouched down and his arm is wrapped tightly around Shay's waist, while Shay's is around his dad's neck. It would have meant nothing at the time—just a normal thing for a dad and son to do—but now it makes me cry. That closeness, that bond that only those two shared, is now broken. Sure, we can shower Shay with memories and love, but it's not the same. Nothing will ever be the same for him, that adorable kid my brother loved so much. Nothing will ever be the same again.

9 FEBRUARY

Eddie and I had enjoyed a rare night out. I drank prosecco; we ate fine food; we shared stories with our friends and ran home laughing in the pouring rain.

I awoke feeling dehydrated and with crazy curly hair, but I was content. The kids were amusing themselves and my mum, who'd babysat, was sitting in the kitchen with a cup of tea.

'How's Dad?' I asked, realising that despite having been around her for the last twenty-four hours, I hadn't asked about my father. Talk of Danny was all-consuming when we were together—it was easy to forget about everyone else.

Mum took a long sigh. He was getting worse, she told me. His breathing was getting more laboured and he was sleeping a lot more. She felt like she was almost forcing him to get out of bed each day. And on top of everything else, he was increasingly depressed. Like us, he was consumed by thoughts of Danny, and desperately wished he could have his son back.

My mood soured as I listened. She looked beaten and sad. My darling mum. My wonderful dad. What has happened to my bloody beautiful family? The content feeling I had enjoyed only minutes earlier was by then a distant memory. Once again I felt broken, and it seemed unlikely that I would ever find a fix.

10 FEBRUARY

I placed both my feet on the scales and looked down towards the ground. Yes, just as I'd thought. I jumped off quickly and placed the scales back beside the bathroom cabinet before the kids could barge in.

I picked up my phone and added my weight to my app. The graph immediately shot up. I was half a stone heavier than I'd ever been before.

I imagine most overweight people have a 'safe zone' weight range, a state where you're still obese by normal standards but okay 'as long as I don't go over this'. Well, I certainly had mine, and for the first time in my life I was beyond it. By seven pounds. Exactly two stone heavier than the month Danny had died. I quickly did the calculations in my head—it was a gain of 2.3 pounds a week. I suddenly felt sick.

I'm eating my feelings. I know this.

I thought back to the conversation I'd had with Mum a day earlier. I'd cried (again) and told her how I understood more about Danny's addiction now; how I wished I'd made the effort to understand when he was still alive. I explained the things he'd tried to get me to read, to review, because he'd so wanted me to have the knowledge he had. I admitted to her that on almost every occasion I'd declined or, worse still, pretended I would and yet never did. It was just another stick to beat myself with.

And then I spoke about my own weight, my own battles with food, and how Danny had understood. He'd told me he thought we were the same. When we talked about compulsions; about doing something without processing it first; about being so, so good and then so, so bad in the blink of an eye—well, it felt like we were battling the same demons.

'He'd have wanted you to get yourself well,' Mum told me as she watched me cry, picking at the last of the kids' Jelly Babies. 'You can do this for him now, Alison.'

Oh Mum, how I love you caring about me so much when you are in so much pain.

And I knew she was right. Danny hadn't just chatted to me about my problems with food because he could relate; no, he'd wanted to help me too.

When I'd managed to lose enough weight for it to be noticeable in the past, he'd always been the first to congratulate me—he'd always been quick to tell me how great I looked and how proud he was. Of course, I believed him—I knew he meant it. Just as I could read Danny, he could read me—he knew what my weight meant for my mental health. When he said I looked great, he knew I was in a better place, and that made him happy.

As I sat on the train to work, my trousers uncomfortably nipping my waist, I began to think about my struggles and my life.

It was easy to understand why Danny had become dependent on drugs. His marriage had failed and he felt tremendous guilt about leaving his son. His torment was plain to see.

For me though, what? My life looked rosy, even to me. I'd travelled extensively in my twenties. Partied hard. I had a great career. My own home. I'd met Eddie at thirty and in him found my soulmate. We'd moved around the country, living in some of the UK's most beautiful cities. We'd collected extra friends in each new place. And then we'd married and been blessed with two children: a boy and a girl. It's the stuff of fairy tales.

Except, stop. Rewind.

Before Peter and Lily, there was Sleepy Baby—the baby we'd seen on the screen but who never seemed to move much. The twelve-week scan where we weren't offered a picture. Telling my work colleagues the exciting news one day only to be at the early pregnancy clinic the next.

The green jumper I had on. The beads I held as they moved the monitor away from my view. The way the woman told me there was no heartbeat. The tears falling steadily, one by one, from Eddie's eyes. The waiting room where we were told to let nature take its course.

And then nature did, days later. The agonising pain. Feeling my body expel something, someone, I desperately loved.

My body had failed me. Failed us.

And as I look back, I see that this is where it all began. An extra Hobnob here. A piece of cake there. Food made the pain a little easier to bear.

The only thing I'd been able to think about with any clarity was getting pregnant again. That was the only way, I thought, of filling the dark hole inside my heart. But I soon learnt that loving another child doesn't take the pain of loss away.

As I struggled with being a new parent, as I battled post-natal depression because I simply wouldn't admit to anyone that I found it hard, food became my solace. My crutch.

Sugar. Sugar. All the sugar.

Uppers and downers. Uppers and downers.

I stared out the window at the Liverpool skyline and thought about all those years I'd spent battling my weight. I thought of the food I had eaten when I'd been sad, happy, stressed, scared. What had begun as a way to cope with pain had turned into a way to cope with life. I thought of Danny. Our mindsets had been the same: compulsion, addiction. A means of escape.

I have to beat this, I resolved as my train pulled into the station.

I know I couldn't fix you. But I can fix myself.

2020

12 FEBRUARY

I have a new worst thing about grief. It's the gift that keeps on giving!

I opened up to my best friend. After several weeks of replying with the thumbs-up emoji whenever she asked me how I'm doing, I let it all out.

I'm hurting, I tell her. I miss him so god-damned much. I hurt for Shay. I hurt for Mum and Dad and I hurt for me. It's too hard.

And I don't know what I expect her to say; she lost a brother, after all. She gets it. But whatever I expected, it wasn't this: 'Immediate grief is different from long-term grief.'

'So it gets worse?' I asked her, already knowing what her response would be.

Long-term grief, acceptance, the reality. That's the hard bit. Immediate grief is the sweetener that draws you in. Long-term grief sticks around *forever.*

And it's when she says this that I realise I can't handle this new reality. I am a fixer—always have been, always will be.

And so I'm writing a book to sort everything out in my head. Mum and Dad will soon be moving into a new home so they can start afresh. I'm trying to find some therapy for Shay. This has to end; we have to move on.

And yet my best friend, the woman I trust with my life, is telling me this is just the beginning. At that, I want to throw myself on the floor and throw a full-blown tantrum. *It can't be!*

I cry a lot that night, more than I have in weeks. Eddie doesn't know what to say so he makes me coffee and agrees to leave me alone. I don't want to talk. Talking can't fix this—he knows that as much as I do. I can sense his relief.

And so I cry alone. I take a break to watch *Cold Feet* on ITV, and then I cry some more.

When I finally crawl into bed, feeling tired and drained, I flick through my social channels. There is a message from Shay. It's a picture of his face on a sausage and it simultaneously makes me laugh and cry because underneath it he's written *Missing him lots*.

I think of how much harder it will get for him. How much he'll miss. The birthdays, anniversaries, and celebrations that will be hard for the rest of his life. I want to throw a tantrum again. It's all so horribly unfair. *I have to fix this*, I think. *I have to find a way.*

2017

NOVEMBER

Every fibre of my being told me it was drugs. Instinct, awareness, common sense—call it what you want. Yet he denied it all the same.

'But you're showing all the signs, Dan,' was met with a detailed description of the ailments that were affecting his speech, his skin, and his sleep.

'I'll never shake this off, will I?' he'd say. He'd be angry and upset. He made you feel like he was an ex-convict who had served his time but could never catch a break.

And yet, you knew. I always knew. I knew which Danny I was getting simply by the tone of his voice or the look in his eyes and, while I wanted to accept him warts and all, drugs or no drugs, I couldn't allow myself to. I knew my Danny, the brother I desperately loved, was worth so much more.

I have to find a way to fix you.

2020

16 FEBRUARY

'I'd like to be a rapper, but I can't rap.'

I'm lying in bed, giggling, replaying the conversation I had with Shay earlier that evening. After hours of talking to him about his dad and his feelings, I turned the conversation to school. I asked him how he was getting on and what he wanted to do once he leaves, painfully aware that it was hardly an ideal time to have to make decisions about his future.

He told me he was rubbish at everything, that he was thick. My heart was on the verge of breaking when he started telling me about music. He admitted he wasn't any good on the decks, not like his dad, but he did have an interest in making music and that music was rap.

'I'd like to be a rapper,' he told me, and I leapt on the most positive thing he'd said all evening. My mind began to go into overdrive and I started to mentally catalogue all the courses he could take, the equipment he'd need, the connections I could introduce him to. And then he followed up with, 'but I can't rap.'

We both fell about laughing. It was so wonderful to see the smile break across his face, that familiar giggle that I hadn't seen in so long. It was the Shay I knew and loved and the one I'd feared we'd lost. I immediately thought of Danny laughing too. He'd always considered Shay-isms just about the funniest things going—he could dine out for months on something silly Shay had said.

It was a lovely evening. Sad, poignant, but also relaxed. I thought of how proud Danny would have been if he could have seen us, how pleased he'd be knowing I took the time to chat to his boy and how happy he'd be to see him smile. But I didn't do it for Danny; I did it for me. I worried we were losing Shay, that he was pulling away from us and sinking.

Yet seeing him that night made me realise who he really was. Not Danny's boy, but Shay—kind, caring, slightly shy, incredibly funny Shay. I will giggle about his rapping comment for the rest of my days.

17 FEBRUARY

It felt like we were planning the funeral all over again. When I arrived at Mum's, I found the kitchen full of flowers—a sea of orange, only fake, not real. Gemma and Mum had gone to town and had brought back a box of goodies to rival any party-hire company. Only, it wasn't a party they were planning—it was the internment of Danny's ashes.

I'd had to look that up; I'd not known what to call it. The funeral after the funeral? My family talked of laying him to rest and I had to fight the urge to tell them that we'd already done that. His ashes meant nothing to me. We'd said our goodbyes back in December. But I bit my tongue because it was important to Mum and Dad, and therefore it was important to me. It wasn't the day to take the piss. They were preparing to say goodbye to their son—again.

Everyone turned up wearing orange, ready to give him another good send-off, but I refused to get involved. Call it stubbornness, call it denial; all I know is that I just didn't want to feel the day was anything other than a practical finale. The ashes had to go somewhere, after all—Mum and Dad wanted a place to visit.

But I quickly realised I was alone in my view. Claire arrived already in tears. Rachael followed suit. They both kissed his box, desperate to say a last goodbye. I picked it up from the fireplace and popped it in a gift bag emblazoned with the funeral home's name, chuckling at the fact the funeral home had taken the opportunity to brand the cardboard bags—*The perfect size for your loved one's ashes!*

Everyone looked at me as though removing the box from the mantelpiece was some kind of ceremony in itself. All I knew was that they had to be moved from A to B. Claire picked up the now-heavy bag and began walking to her car. 'Danny's coming with me,' she shouted on her way to the door.

Rachael followed suit: 'Claire's taking Danny,' she announced to the busy room.

I tried not to laugh. I knew no one would join me; I was clearly the only one who didn't feel the gravity of the occasion. But for me, the idea that Danny was in that box felt absurd. I wanted to scream at everyone, *Danny's gone!* Why does no one see that but me? He's not here anymore!

Most of us walked to the cemetery. Dad went ahead on his scooter. It was the first time I'd seen him use it in months, and I was painfully aware that his haste was so he could have a crafty fag before Mum arrived. It was something we were all choosing to overlook. It made his physical condition worse and it would probably shorten his life, but the sad reality was we knew he no longer felt life was worth living. Dad hadn't just lost his spark—it was worse than that. He was a shadow of the man we'd once known.

The kids led the way. My nephew George was singing and dancing around, and my kids followed close behind him, mesmerised by their older cousin. Rach linked arms with my mum—one of us did whenever we went out together now. Unlike Dad, Mum still got out a lot, but she seemed slower now, smaller. We protected her like she'd suddenly become a frail old lady, though she was still only sixty-nine.

We walked past the flat where Danny had died. It stood out like a shining beacon at the top of my parents' street, and each of us glanced up into its the upper windows. No one said anything.

When we arrived, we headed over to our plot, his plot. There was a hole in the ground for his box. A man from the funeral home stood respectfully to the left as we all filed around the space. My thoughts turned to my miscarriage before I'd had the twins, to the tiny box Eddie and I had buried in the churchyard near our house. I thought about how I'd thought losing my unborn baby had been the most terrible pain I'd ever experienced. And yet it didn't even compare to now, to this loss. Danny's death was bigger, more intense than anything I could have imagined. He'd been a huge part of me. He still is.

I remained calm, emotionless, and even quite relaxed—that is, until I saw the headstone. It was a chunky marble square with my brother's name etched into it. All at once, shit got real. This piece of stone would remain in this churchyard for generations. A reminder of a life lost. Danny.

I held on to Peter, knowing he'd be feeling anxious in a graveyard but mainly because I wanted to distract myself. I didn't want to cry—it wasn't his funeral. I wouldn't cry. Not today.

I looked across at my mum, sisters, and Gemma, all holding each other, tears flowing down their faces. My dad sitting on his scooter, looking lost. Still though, I wouldn't allow the tears to flow. Shay stood in the background, biting his fingernails. I knew he felt as awkward as I did. It should mean something, but it didn't; or maybe we simply refused to let it.

Later that evening, back at home, I handed the kids to Eddie and announced I was going for a lie-down. I didn't want to talk and felt physically and emotionally drained. I just wanted to be alone.

In bed, I thought about Danny and how he'd have laughed at the fuss everyone had made today. How he'd have teased us getting all spooked when a black cat came and sat by us as we decorated his plot. How he'd have been sad seeing everyone upset again. And how he'd have been gutted to miss out on the meal we had afterwards: a pub lunch with the family and a nice cold pint. That was one of his favourite things to do.

But still the tears didn't flow. Instead, I just felt angry.

You did this to us, Danny. It's all down to you!

18 FEBRUARY

Caroline Flack died over the weekend and I am channelling my anger into thinking about it. I'm not angry with her—on the contrary, I'm terribly sad—but I feel angry with the world.

She was a TV presenter, beautiful and vivacious, but had clearly struggled with her mental health. She was hounded by the media and tormented by vicious online trolls. In the end, she ended her life and, perhaps without knowing or realising it, completely changed the lives of her loved ones. I can't stop thinking about her family and the journey they're now on. The regret, the guilt, and the unbearable pain. Danny didn't take his own life, not in the same way, but he did self-destruct. We couldn't love him back from the brink and that is an incredibly hard truth to bear.

I'm thinking about her on my journey into work, reflecting on how it seems the entire world is now behind a campaign to call everyone else out—to blame the media, the trolls, the people who read and share gossip. And I don't disagree; we're all culpable, after all. We all play our part.

But I feel angry because the one thing people aren't saying is the one thing that needs to be said. Every single one of us suffering is silence has a hand in her downfall too. The one thing I know about mental health struggles is that looking out at everyone else's seemingly perfect lives makes it all even harder.

So many people, or their loved ones, suffer in some way at least some of the time. I don't care who they are or what they do. How many people can honestly say have not been impacted by mental ill health? I can feel the anger burning up inside me, so I take out my phone and write a post on Facebook:

> Our mental health is a part of our overall health. While the majority of the world stays silent or, worse, puts up a front, the people who have fallen into the deepest, darkest places will continue to feel alone.

> We shouldn't just be telling others to talk and posting platitudes. We should be shouting our own stories from the rooftops. We should be telling them, 'Me too!' We should be open about our coping mechanisms and find new ones together.

> My brother died in November. Since then I cry almost every day. My family has been ripped apart. We'll never be the same again. I feel lost.

> I miss him. I am sad for him. I am sad that he was so unwell, and sad that he battled with depression and drug addiction for so much of his adult life. I'm sad that he thought his struggles were different, worse somehow. I am sad because they weren't. He was an ordinary guy. Like Caroline, he just didn't see that. He thought he was alone.

> It's not their mental health problems. It's ours.

> Stop hiding. Start sharing.

I put the phone back into my bag. I can't post it today; people will think I'm mad. Yes, I sigh, I'm a part of the problem.

2010

22 OCTOBER

Message to: Alison

From: Danny

16:17

hi alison hope all is well in the tum tum,time is marching on which is good. just a couple of ideas for the web sit i clean windows traditional style i would also like on there that i clean conservatory roofs and clean gutters on a domestic or commercial basis. i think cleaning conservatory roofs is very rare so if i could expose this through your brilliance i could make some money out of the richer people,maybe get contracts to clean every year.a design logo wold be more important tan the company name,maybe ed could help with his style of stick man standing dangerously cleaning windows or conservatorys, my window round only really pays if its local, but cleaning the roofs i would be prepared to travel wider a field as i believe there is more money to be made.i love the coulor orange and yellow. my window round is still building but is not yet substanible for me so i need to be attracting more work. i hope this helps and i hope you get a minute.love danny

2013

10 FEBRUARY

Message to: Alison

From: Danny

10:57

outstanding balance £1,192.77. self employed really bad year 2012 not helped bye seriuos deppression, plus a car crash on the 1,st november which has made work even harder,still wiating to see if i should recieve sick pay. homeless 2013 stoping from pillar to post. poor old me, is that enough to go on ????????????????????????????? many thanks me xx

2020

19 FEBRUARY

Why do we want to feel more pain when we feel low? I couldn't stop crying on the way to work—it physically hurt in the pit of my stomach—but still I searched for his name in my inbox.

Five different messages popped up, all asking me to do stuff for him. Some banter, some serious. I could hear his voice saying each and every one of them. How I missed that voice.

But one from 2013 stood out. He mentioned his serious depression. Reading it made me take a sharp intake of breath. We had become so focused on the drugs, on his addiction, that we had lost sight of where it had all begun: his depression.

I thought back to 2013, before the world had been really ready to talk about mental health. I'd had a short period of postnatal depression, but it wasn't even on the same scale as Danny's suffering. I hadn't lost the zest for life that Danny had, and I'd had the comfort of a clearly identifiable cause. At the time, none of us were really equipped to understand what it meant for Danny. We probably told him to cheer up and move on. We didn't see then that being depressed wasn't the same as depression, or that being anxious wasn't the same as living with anxiety. We just saw a man we kept having to pull up; a loved one who began to spend a lot of time in bed. We saw the highs and the lows.

We were frustrated with him.

Uppers and downers. Uppers and downers.

26 FEBRUARY

'If someone mentions going to the grave one more time I am going to scream,' I tell Rachael. 'Sorry,' I add quickly, 'I'm just full of anger. It's pathetic—I don't understand why. I am just so angry at everything. With everyone.'

'Why are you angry?' she asks gently. She is calmer than I deserve. I'm being ridiculous and I know it.

'I don't know,' I continue, 'I just feel like we chose not to bury him and now we have ended up with a grave. *It's not a grave!*'

I go on to moan about how it makes me feel—how, every day, someone says they're going to go to the grave. Mum wanted me to agree to some kind of grave-tending rota so it stays looking nice after she and my dad die. It's all making me feel like I want to scream, and I don't understand why.

'Ignore me,' I tell her at last, before she can tell me I sound like a spoiled brat.

'Maybe you're angry because you don't want to accept he's gone,' she says, her voice soft like a therapist's. It has the desired effect. The tears begin to flow. *Bingo.*

'Maybe,' I sob.

'You're just finding it hard, Ali,' she tells me, 'this anger is normal. What you are feeling is normal. It's harder now. The longer it goes on, it's harder and harder. That's all this is.'

I know she's right and that what I'm feeling is probably normal, but it's affecting everything: work, home, commuting, kids, my bloody *grave-tending* duties, everything. We talk on the phone until we have exhausted my feelings. She moves us on to talk about kitchen tiles (hers) and colour schemes (mine). By the time we're finished, I feel better—the anger has subsided, and I ask how she is.

She tells me she's just keeping busy and, while I know it's true, I worry she's keeping her feelings locked away. I press her again but she insists she is doing okay before telling me she's now exhausted. So we say our goodbyes and each head off to bed.

27 FEBRUARY

I wake to find the angry feeling has returned. A quick scan of our WhatsApp group only serves to add fuel to the fire.

'Where's Nan?' Becky has asked.

'The grave,' is Hannah's reply.

Why? Why? Why does this get under my skin? I start Googling before I even get out of bed, and quickly find what I'm looking for.

A grave is a place with a body. What we have done for Danny is a memorial. It is not a grave.

I begin typing a reply explaining that they have the terminology wrong and could they kindly start saying 'memorial' rather than 'grave'. I quickly read it back and realise how bloody pathetic I sound. Why does it even matter? What should I care if they want to say 'I'm going to see Danny,' or 'We're going to the grave'? Why do I care?

I delete the message quickly, realising I sound like a madwoman. I know they'd be shocked and concerned to read something so bizarre. Besides, it's Mum I really want to say it to, and I wouldn't dare do that. It'd only upset her, and that's the last thing I want to do.

I go back to Google and type in 'sibling grief'. It's the first time I've looked for anything particular to me; everything else has been generic or about someone else—Mum, Dad, Shay. As I read, the tears flow hard and fast. I can barely read for crying. Every line hits home: suddenly being the oldest child in the family, the guilt, the sense of shared loss as your sibling knew your history better than the family you have created for yourself.

But the one that sticks, that hurts the most, is the line about how you lose your parents; how the relationship is irrevocably changed. And I realise then why 'grave' bugs me so much. It's because any time someone mentions it, usually Mum, I'm reminded of the incredible loss they're living with and of the fact I have lost my mum and dad. And I need them now, more than I ever did.

I'm angry because I feel incredibly alone.

29 FEBRUARY

One of the hardest things about mothering a child with anxiety is listening to him shout 'What will help me? What will help me?' amid rising panic. Neither Eddie or I have a good answer to this question. I tell him to breathe of course—*Keep taking those deep breaths, Peter!*— but the reality is that all we can do is ride it out. All I can do is stand beside him and hold his hand. When it's over—for it does always end—we move on with our day again.

As I sit on my train to work, I realise that, at the moment, I feel like Peter. I may not be vocalising it, but I'm screaming, 'What will help me? What will help me?' in my head, over and over and over again.

But, just like Peter, I know that no one can do anything to make how I feel go away. I just have to ride it out.

Last night, I told Eddie I'd had an awful day and that I'd cried on the way to school, hid my tear-stained face from the familiar mums at the school doors, and cried walking the kids home. I explained that I had spent the day researching options for Shay: counselling, education, living arrangements (I'd had this sudden desire to bring him in to live with us)— anything that might fix a broken child. And, while walking to school, I'd started to ask myself why. Why did it matter so much? What was I trying to do? It didn't take long to find the answer.

I had to fix Shay. I felt responsible. I had spent my entire life being responsible for Danny, and now I wanted to look out for his son. I immediately thought about the words I had written in Danny's eulogy only a few days after his death: *All the love we had for you will be poured into that boy.*

I should have spotted the signs back then. Someone should have told me. I was trying to replace one desperate need with another. I may have failed Danny, so I sure as hell couldn't fail Shay.

I explained all this to Eddie and he listened intently. He told me I wasn't responsible, that I'd never failed anyone, and that I'd done everything I could—more, in fact, than I should have. He listened to me protest for a while and then gently suggested I consider counselling. I was past the point of platitudes and hugs, and Eddie was beginning to get worried. I could see it on his face.

What will help me? What will help me?

I brushed the idea aside. I don't want counselling; an hour a week won't make it all okay. I don't want my friends and family either—in fact, I can already feel myself withdrawing from them. I no longer want to hear or read the same responses, to have them tell me they feel the same. I need something but I didn't know what.

I confessed to Eddie that I've been overeating again, stuffing my face whenever I'm alone. Chocolate on the way home, biscuits in the evening, cakes in the car—anything and everything to fill the gaping hole inside. It's not new. Food has been my drug ever since the postnatal depression. Of course, the kicker is that it only makes me feel worse. The more I eat, the more my trousers dig into my waist. The more I eat, the more I notice the double chin protruding from my face. The more I eat, the more uncomfortable I feel and the harder it is to move. And then comes the shame and guilt and disgust, which of course lead to yet more eating.

Eddie looked sad and helpless and reiterated my need to seek help. I felt overwhelmed with love for him, and grateful too—for his gentle support, for trying. For not knowing what to do.

What will help me? What will help me?

Danny. I need Danny. He always understood. We were the same—the same compulsions, the same shame. We did things that impacted our health, our families, and yet we did them anyway. I think of Shay living with the belief that he couldn't have been enough for his dad. I know he thinks that if he'd been enough, his dad wouldn't have been lured back in. And then I think of my own kids—the most important people in my life. And yet, when food calls, not even my love for them can stop me eating. Just like Danny's love for Shay couldn't stop him using drugs. It's not about a conscious choice; we don't feel in control.

But beneath all the murk, there's something crystal-clear. Danny and I both fought our own battles, but the ways in which we coped were strikingly similar. The difference was that while my bad habits can be compartmentalised, can fit into the spaces around my job, my kids, and my life, Danny's consumed everything they touched.

Now, alone, I desperately worry that I can't cope without Danny.

What will help me? What will help me?

I want Danny but I can't find him.

What will help me? What will help me?

'I'll look for a counsellor,' I told Eddie at last.

He kissed me on the head and squeezed my hand.

2 MARCH

When your mum, sister, husband, and best friend tell you they think you're struggling with depression, you have to take a moment to acknowledge that you may in fact be struggling with depression.

Over the course of one weekend, they'd all said the same. I seemed incredibly emotional, very low, and as if I was losing perspective. I needed to stop feeling responsible—for Danny, for Shay.

I should have saved you, Danny!

I told them I knew they were right. I could no more have saved Danny than anyone else. I knew, rationally, that it was his responsibility to save himself; that I should feel no more guilt, no more culpable. But, deep down in the pit of my stomach, I couldn't accept that. A part of me simply refused to let it go.

I thought back to the time I'd had postnatal depression and how my friend had pleaded with me to give myself a break. We'd known each other for under a year, but she'd quickly picked up on the fact that I set impossible standards for myself. It was okay for the other mums to do their best and get by—it really was—but not me. Why not me?

When I woke one morning and begged Eddie not to leave for work because I felt physically and emotionally broken, she had sighed because she'd seen it coming. She'd seen I was a woman pushing herself to the edge, stubbornly refusing to accept support or listen to the rational part of her brain. I was a new mum with twins and no family close by. My son had reflux, so cried constantly and couldn't be put down. I spent the majority of my time alone with the kids. Even I could see it was a recipe for disaster—and yet I refused to believe it was too much for me. Until, of course, it was.

While my brain lived on, entrenched firmly in denial and pushing all this nonsense about 'not coping' away, my body took over. One day, without warning, it decided it had just about had enough. When I begged Eddie not to go into work, it wasn't because I feared harming the children or myself; it was simply because I couldn't pick up a bottle to feed them. The simplest thing had become impossible. I was psychically and emotionally spent.

So I knew why my family and friends were worried now. I knew they'd spotted the signs earlier than I had. I knew I owed it to them to get some help.

On Sunday night, I made a list.

1. *Get on antidepressants* (Eddie's instruction).
2. *Start running again* (that was Kel).
3. *See a counsellor* (Rachael).

And then I added one from myself:

4. *Let him go.*

It wasn't your fault, Ali. You couldn't have saved him. You did your very best.

I so desperately want to believe that, but I worried I never would.

5 MARCH

It was the first time Shay had ever sent me a message that wasn't a response. He told me he'd been at school and had seen a couple of apprenticeships he was interested in. My heart burst with pride. I had to stop myself from driving to Leyland and throwing my arms around him.

Only a week before, his mum had been telling me he wouldn't leave his bedroom; school had definitely not been an option. He'd not been communicating at all—it was as if he was totally lost. Kelly was feeling the pressure from school, who were demanded he come back. The more they pressed, the more she put her head in the sand, unable to deal with the strain.

Stuck in the middle was a kid who had lost his dad and all sense of direction. He'd lost his sense of self.

So, with Kelly's permission, I spoke to the school. I talked them through everything from Shay's confidence to his mum's anxiety to his dad's death. I listened as the teacher described the version of Shay they saw at school. Apparently, he was just like his dad—quick to get defensive and give up; shy but full of bravado to hide it. I'd never seen that side of him before. The Shay I knew was sweet and kind and intelligent.

Together, we worked out a plan. Firstly me and the teacher, and then Kelly and my mum. Team Shay!

For weeks, my loved ones had been telling me I shouldn't feel solely responsible for Shay, and I knew they were right—but, at the same time, I could see he needed fighting for. His dad would have fought. Someone had to meddle to get us all working together and, when I got that text, I was so relieved that I had. There was a glimmer of light. He'll never be over it, but he can walk on. And we'd be with him, shoulder to shoulder, every step of the way.

9 MARCH

Dear Danny,

I saw Shay on Saturday. My god, you'd be proud.

He's moved your chair into his room at his mum's. It's made us all so happy to know that something so simple is giving him comfort.

He's so handsome, Dan, and so bloody smart. I have to stop myself throwing my arms around him and crying into his shoulder whenever I see him. I'm restraining myself on the hugging front—that is not cool—but I am yet to control the crying in front of him, although I'm working on it!

For the first time, I feel like he's going to be okay. He's back at school and we're all working together to make him feel supported. I do hope he feels that.

You did good, Dan. You did an incredible job with him. He is such a great kid. And I know he'll miss you forevermore, but he'll spend the rest of his life knowing how truly loved he was. You gave him something not everyone has: truly wonderful, unconditional, devoted, proud, firm, incredible love. And he'll carry that with him forever.

Love and miss you more than ever.

Your little big sister.

PS He showers twice a day! You'd be so proud. Ha, ha.

18 MARCH

The world has gone mad: an uncontrollable virus is sweeping the globe. Having begun in China, COVID-19 is crippling every country in the world. Right now, we're behind other European countries, like Italy, which is in complete lockdown. My cousin, Kat's told me they are building army hospitals in France, and it looks like we'll all be working from home for the foreseeable future. Like everyone else, I am overwhelmed by it all. I am worried for my loved ones, especially Dad, who's in the most at-risk group, and Becky, who is pregnant. More than that, though, I'm worried for humanity. People are stockpiling like the world is about to implode, not realising that it's exactly their stockpiling that'll *make* the world implode.

With so much going on, I have forgotten to grieve—or, rather, I've *parked* grieving. I've even been thinking he's better off dead—that's how crazy everything feels right now.

Except for yesterday, that is. Yesterday we got the news that Danny's insurance policy had paid out: a very healthy sum to put in a trust for Shay. A months after he died we discovered that the one bleedin' form Danny ever filled out by himself, turned out to be the one that most counted. I am overwhelmed with love. How proud Danny would be. How happy he'd be to know he did good by his boy. His final act: giving his boy some security and a head start.

Still, I feel bad for forgetting to grieve—so the floodgates open again.

Last night, as I walked in from work, I went straight into the kitchen, looking for Eddie. I wanted to tell him about Shay because it was a rare piece of good news amid all the madness. But, as I opened my mouth to speak, I found my voice wouldn't come. Eddie was by my side before I even knew I was crying. He was embracing me before the tears even started to fall.

I can't miss him with everything going on in the world—but I still do, more than ever. I still do.

I spend today trying to work. My new reality is a laptop on the kitchen table and a silent workspace. Waiting for the next conference call, I flick open Facebook and begin scrolling. Before I know it, there's a picture of him. He has his arms around his nieces—my Lily and Rachael's daughter Jessica—and he looks so goddamn happy. *So happy.* I cry and cry and cry. The world might have gone mad, I might be more scared and anxious than I have ever been, but I still want him back.

29 MARCH

Happy birthday to me. Happy birthday to me. Happy birthday, dear Alison. Happy birthday to me.

Except I'm not feeling very happy.

I spent the evening before crying. It was one of those nights where I didn't want to go to bed because I didn't want to face the next day. It was ridiculous—my kids were excited, and it was a good excuse to break the monotony of lockdown—but still, the prospect of my first birthday without a brother only made me sad.

Linda sent me a message Danny had sent her years before. I don't know why she chose that exact moment or why she chose to share it with me, but it really upset me. That same day we'd been sharing Danny stories on our family WhatsApp group, laughing about the silly things he did on his holiday with Rach and her family. Then, later on, Linda's message confirms he began using again shortly after coming home from that very same holiday. Who even was he? Did any of us really know?

I'm taken back to that time, to those calls where he insisted he was on medication for a chest infection. He was being sick a lot and kept trying to show me the toilet bowl to prove it. He told me he was wetting the bed— apparently, the chest medication wasn't agreeing with him. He desperately wanted me to react and be concerned, but I did neither. I was sure it was all lies. I knew he was using and he wouldn't admit it. Like so many times before, I couldn't be arsed.

I never understood why he kept calling. Why he continued trying to convince me when I quite clearly wasn't buying it. It must have just made him feel worse—I know it certainly did for me.

Eddie and the kids went to great lengths to make my day feel special, and it actually has been—I've had a lovely time—but I've not been able to shake the sadness.

I rarely saw Danny on my birthday. I've lived apart from my family for most of my adult life, but he always called. It was usually with a lame excuse about why my card was late or with a promise to buy me something on his next payday (he never did). But he always called. And today I missed it more than anything.

30 MARCH

My old school friend Michelle has asked me how my birthday was, so I tell her the truth. *Good in parts but mostly just sad.* I'm now forty-three—another year closer to his age. It doesn't feel right.

She replies telling me she understands and that she can't imagine how I must be feeling. We've spoken more since he died than we have in years, and I am reminded of the bond that we used to share. I'm grateful she's back in my life, because she understands what Danny meant to me. We spent our teenage years at each other's homes. Our dads became great friends and our respective families would always be a feature of the other's celebrations. Michelle still boasts about being the only one of my teenage friends to have never fancied nor had a dalliance with Danny.

'He was more like a brother to me,' she tells me, and I know it's true.

She spends the day sending me photographs from her endless albums to cheer me up. She has so many of Danny in his early twenties, far more than I do. He looks so handsome and happy and I feel pride and nostalgia rolled into one.

She sends me one of him with his then-girlfriend, Lisa.

'Is this the girl who put all those posters up around Leyland?' she asks.

I laugh as I'd totally forgotten. We'd awoke one morning to hear that someone had put up posters of Danny all over Leyland. Danny and his girlfriend had split up, and the posters told the world what a rat he was. I had no idea what had happened (I still don't to this day!), but I was determined that no one was going to humiliate my brother.

'No,' I reply, 'that was Julie. Or Julie's sisters, I think. Didn't we take them down?'

'Ali,' she replies, 'you did! By the time I got to Leyland you had single-handedly removed them all!'

I laugh. Yep, that sounds like me. I have only had two really major arguments in my life: one was defending Rachael and the other was arguing with Julie's sister about Danny.

I think back to those days. I must have only been about eighteen at the time.

'What was I like?' I say. It's a statement, not a question.

3 APRIL

All non-essential or public activities have been cancelled or postponed due to the coronavirus, so Danny's public inquest is off, at least for the foreseeable. We've been given the option of having the coroner proceed on paper, which would mean we can get a formal death certificate and, crucially, a cause of death. We've been weighing up the pros and cons as a family, but I'm in favour of going ahead. The future looks terrifying and I'm worried that, if we push things back, the inquest might never occur. In the UK alone the government is predicting 20,000 deaths, and that is the best-case scenario.

Fiona from the coroner's office called me. She agreed to send me all the reports so we can make our final decision and, since then, I've been refreshing my email constantly, waiting impatiently for them to come through. Finally, a window into what happened that night; part of me is excited, part petrified. There are so many things I want to know, but I know my deepest questions won't be answered. Danny is the only one who could fill in the gaps.

Still, I wait. *Refresh, refresh, refresh.*

2017

JUNE

'Helloooooo!' Lily yells, grabbing my phone off the counter and running away with it.

I roll my eyes and follow her up the stairs, calling, 'Who is it, Lily?'

'Uncle Danny!' she yells again before slamming her bedroom door. I can hear her animated voice but it's muffled; I can't make out what she's saying. I return to slicing the vegetables I was preparing before the phone rang.

It's some fifteen minutes before I hear her thundering down the stairs.

'Peter! Peter!' she's yelling.

Peter runs to his sister and takes the phone from her. He perches on the sofa in the living room as Lily runs out into the garden. I listen to his soft voice as he answers his uncle's questions. Unlike his sister, he is shy on the phone.

He giggles. 'I don't say that!' he protests, giggling hysterically.

Before I know it, Lily's back. She grabs Peter's hand and the phone drops to the floor as Peter's dragged out into the garden. 'Bye!' he manages.

I scoop up the abandoned phone with my free hand.

'I didn't do dat did I?' I hear Danny say.

'Erm, Danny,' I cut in, 'he's already gone. You've bored him!'

He laughs.

Oh, how I love that laugh.

'So, did you ring for the kids or to speak to me?' I ask.

'The kids of course,' he says.

'Yeah, likely story,' I tell him as I head back into the kitchen. I rest the phone on my shoulder and tilt my head to keep it in place. 'What do you need from me?'

'That is some cheek! How dare you?' he replies, mock-offended, before adding, 'but, seeing as you've asked, I know you're really busy but . . .'

And off he goes. Another day, another request to do something for him. I dutifully promise to do it once the kids are in bed.

'So, how are you?' I ask.

He sounds well. His voice is bright. I can tell when he is himself because he has all the time in the world for the kids. He adores his nieces and nephews, probably because he is such a big kid himself. He's fun and silly and talks to them on their level. No wonder they all love him so much.

'I'm good, Al,' he says. 'Me and Shay are going to come up and see you soon.'

'That would be amazing,' I tell him, because it would. I love hanging out with Danny and Shay. I love having my brother and his son in my world, especially when Danny's in a good headspace.

'How are you? I've been worried about you.'

His question is loaded because the last time we spoke I was in a bad place. Eddie and I had argued and I'd been feeling fed up. Danny thought the world of Eddie but sometimes felt he busied himself so much that he forgot to appreciate me. Of course, I'd certainly 'helped' Danny come to this view—I certainly moaned enough! Eddie and I were like night and day: I needed affirmations to feel loved and appreciated, but Eddie was practical. I'd lament the fact he hadn't bought me flowers or made a special effort for an anniversary, but then he'd surprise me by building a beautiful seating area in the garden so I had somewhere nice to read my books. It took many years for me to realise that we just communicated affection in different ways.

'We're fine,' I said. Things had blown over—it was another day. 'But I love you for asking.'

And I did. That was the other thing about him when he was in a good place: he bloody loved his family. He was fiercely protective of his sisters and, although I loved the fact he thought so highly of my husband, I dearly loved the fact he'd always, always have my back.

You really saw me, Danny. I love you for that.

We spoke for another ten minutes. He asked questions until he was sure I was genuinely okay.

'I've got to go, Al,' he told me at last, 'but text me when you've done it, will you?'

'Yeah, sure,' I told him before saying my goodbyes.

I dropped my phone back onto the counter and wiped my hands with a tea towel. Satisfied, I picked up a pen and wrote a reminder on the back of my hand.

Top-up Danny's phone. £15.

2020

6 APRIL

We decided to go ahead with the paper inquest. I felt like I had twisted Mum and Dad's arms but Mum insisted I hadn't. This wasn't something I wanted to force them into. I knew I could be persuasive, but this had to be their decision.

'We're sure, Alison,' Mum told me, 'we know we'll never get the answers we want either way.'

She was right. All those questions we had about the inconsistencies we'd read? They'd never be flushed out during an inquest. It wasn't a criminal trial; the accounts of what happened on the night he died would be taken as gospel. We weren't going to get the truth and we had to live with that.

I'd pored over all the documents already. The bundle came with a warning letter which, at first, I thought was a bit over the top. But after reading through everything, I began to understand why they'd included it. I had a dull sick feeling I couldn't shake.

I could picture him lying on the floor. I could imagine the paramedics darting around him, trying to save his life. I could picture the paraphernalia, hear the sounds—I could see his face. Unresponsive. Vacant. Danny but not Danny.

I kept reading and re-reading, hoping that, like some kind of master detective, I'd see through the cracks in the story. I'd be able to piece his final moments together and answer the questions we all had. *Why did he take it? Where did he take it? When did he take it?*

Why? Why? Why?

Instead, I faced a collection of statements that sounded so unbelievable they were laughable. His 'friend' just so happened to have a heroin antidote in his kitchen cupboard that the previous tenant had left behind. His other 'friend' had just happened to knock on the window when Danny was unresponsive.

The detectives hadn't found anything untoward. A dead man in his forties, anyone?

It didn't make sense, but I knew it didn't matter. The coroner wasn't looking to find flaws in the story; they were looking to establish how he'd died, and that was written clear as day in the toxicology report (joyful reading!). It was as we'd already been told: a cocktail of drugs and alcohol.

I guess that explains the sick feeling I can't shake.

I do the only thing I can, the only thing that makes me feel like I'm in some kind of control. I write a letter to the coroner.

I'm not sure if they'll even read it, but I want to make my (our) feelings known. It is disappointing that the facts weren't investigated fully because the details mattered to us. We understand that those involved with illegal drugs would lie to protect themselves, but those lies rob us of precious details into our loved one's last moments. How is that fair or right or decent? All rhetorical questions, but they made me feel better.

Once I'm done, I write to the guy he was with: the 'friend' who'd tried to save his life. I tell him I know he lied and that I hoped he would one day find a way to tell us the truth and help us fill in the gaps. But, I tell him, I'm grateful that he tried to save Danny's life. I finished by saying I hoped he was okay. I really meant that bit.

I keep coming back to the letter in the hours that follow. How can I draw a line under the events of Danny's death knowing the truth isn't clear? Why does it matter so much?

The more I think about it, the angrier I feel. It should matter to everyone, not just to those that loved him.

Why didn't the detectives investigate more thoroughly? Where did Danny get the heroin? Where did he take it? The 'friends' story didn't add up, but we had no experience of that world. Surely the detectives and paramedics could spot a cover-up a mile off. So why did they take it as the truth without investigating the facts?

But the more I think about it, the more I know why. Danny was just another drug-related death; just another man who'd died due to his own actions. They had a job to do, and they would tick all the boxes—but they would go no further. Another day, another druggy.

Except he wasn't. He was a man so full of warmth and love. He worked hard and held down a steady job. He was an incredible dad—even more incredible once we knew the extent of his struggles. He spoke openly and honestly about his addictions and his mental health. He worried about the medication doctors were going to put him on after his knee operation. He desperately didn't want to be in that place again. And yet he led himself to it. Drink weakened his resolve and he went for his 'one last time'.

The sick feeling, the one that doesn't go away—it's knowing that all anyone can see of my brother is the addict and not the man. He shouldn't be defined by his death, swept aside because he made a bad choice—he should be defined by his life. By all that he was.

I tell myself the only way I can shake the feeling, the injustice of all of it, is to keep writing. His inquest and his death certificate won't be his legacy. But my book will be.

7 APRIL

Linda and I had been exchanging texts about the inquest. I felt terrible asking her questions, but I knew she had more insight into Danny's recent drug-taking than any of us. He used to ask her to pick him up from his house so he could avoid having to walk past his dealer's house—such was the pull that drugs had on him, even when he was in a stronger place.

She'd told us that Danny had seen the guy who he'd died with the weekend before his death. He'd been in scruffy clothes and had looked gaunt. Danny had expressed sadness at this; he was worried about him. He'd known drugs had taken his friend to a dark place, and he knew this because he'd been to that dark place himself.

It takes one to know one, eh Danny?

Linda sharing that anecdote helped me see the world through Danny's eyes. He didn't see 'us' and 'them'; to him, these people that the rest of us might cross the street to avoid were just like him, only a little further down the road. I felt sad thinking about that guy, about Danny. About how horrible it must be to live in a world where you feel constant shame.

One of Linda's texts stuck in my head.

Danny wanted to be his friend. Not because they had drugs in common, but because he liked him. They had similar interests, they both had kids, and they both knew what it felt like to be chastised for your problems rather than supported.

Linda said Danny missed having friends, and it's those words that broke me. I couldn't comprehend how my brother, the most popular boy in high school, could have ever said those words. But it broke me because I knew it was true. His friends had gone—moved on. Maybe, like us, they'd felt annoyed with him. They'd seen changes they hadn't liked. Maybe they'd felt that he was beyond help. I'll never know. I daren't ask. But it all just made me feel desperately, desperately sad.

What happened to you, brother? Why do I feel like we all let you down?

5 MAY

Danny's inquest is due to take place at 11 a.m., and my family and I have arranged to raise a brew to him—we can't be with him in person, but I feel like we have to mark it somehow.

I spend the morning working, but find myself unable to concentrate as it gets closer and closer to 11. As the hour hand approaches, I allow myself a break and diligently make myself a coffee. Once I have the steaming brew in my hands, I snap a picture of myself.

'To Danny!' I say to no one, thrusting my mug in the air.

I send my picture to the family WhatsApp group and Mum replies immediately, confirming that she and Dad are having a brew too (with sugar for Danny's!).

I wish I could be there for you, Danny.

A stream of orange love heart emojis fills the group chat for a moment and then stops. I look aimlessly around my kitchen, feeling I need to do more to signal that I am right here with him. I look out at my stone step, the place I always look for Danny, and begin to talk to him. I'm just saying the first thing that comes into my head, and I don't even know if it makes sense, but I want him to know, in whatever way I can, that I am by his side.

It's late afternoon when the website is updated.

Suicide.

Suicide.

Drug-related death.

Suicide.

And then there it is. His name in full accompanied by a single word:

Misadventure.

Relief washes over me. This will mean a lot to Mum and Dad. Despite how far they have come in terms of understanding his addiction, they'll be comforted to know it won't say 'drugs' on his death certificate. Shay will be relieved too.

My sisters have seen it too and, before I know it, our WhatsApp group is buzzing again. We're all relieved and pleased. It's not long, though, that sadness comes following on the tail of our relief. He's still gone, and the inquest—the only closure we've been offered—is over.

Once the messages stop, I feel numb. *Misadventure. Misadventure. Misadventure.* I Google the meaning and roll the word around in my brain.

It means he did something that caused his death but that it was by accident. He didn't intend to die. And though I know this—deep down I've always known—it's comforting that some official independent party knows it too. He did not intend to die. And while I know that should give me some comfort, it does the opposite.

He did not intend to die.

He was in a good place.

He didn't know his time was up.

He just went back for a 'one last time'.

I wait until early evening to call Mum—she'll have needed some time to process things.

'How are you feeling?' I ask tentatively. I know she's been consumed by grief since the beginning of lockdown, which has been keeping us all apart, and I'm sure the inquest conclusion hit her hard.

'I'm relieved,' she tells me. 'I'm not ashamed, but I am glad it didn't say drugs.'

'I know, Mum. Are you okay though? You sound weary.'

'Yes, I'm okay. It's just your dad. He's ill . . .'

15 MAY

Before we'd really had time to digest the inquest, Dad was taken into hospital. It turned out he'd been especially unwell for weeks, but Mum hadn't wanted to worry us and Dad had hoped he'd pick up.

Dad had always been uncomfortable with hospitals, and now, with the threat of coronavirus looming large, he was especially worried. When he said he needed to go, we knew it was bad—but it got worse.

It was pneumonia which, on top of his COPD, made it impossible for him to breathe. He was taken away and put on oxygen. Within two days, the doctors said he had the virus too, and we were advised to prepare for the worst.

It was like losing Danny all over again except in slow motion. Rachael just shut down.

'I can't do this again,' she told us on a group call before hanging up.

I looked at Claire's tear-stained face. My mum wept.

No, no, no! You cannot do this to my family again. This isn't fair. You cannot take someone else we love.

We spent the first Sunday waiting for 'the call' but, by Monday, he'd picked up a little. Tuesday brought arguments with the hospital—how could he have caught the virus?! By Wednesday, we thought he was dying anyway so had to concentrate on that. By Thursday, a little hope rekindled—his blood tests were going in the right direction. On Friday, we just sat and waited.

He's having some chest physio. I am allowing myself to believe I'll see him again.

I can't lose someone else. I can't.

Don't take him with you, Danny. He's not ready to go yet.

I think of how sad Danny would be to see how much we are suffering. How he'd want to put his strong arms around Mum and tell Dad he was strong enough to pull through. And, if the worst happened (and I've thought about this a lot), how he'd greet my Dad with a cold pint.

1 JUNE

I inherited two things from my dad: his daft sense of humour and his scepticism. Dad had witnessed some unexplainable things in his lifetime but if you tried to put anything down to the afterlife he'd tell you that you were a bloody fool. I felt the same way; when Claire had been desperately seeking some kind of sign that Danny was still around, I refused to accept it. Dad and I took the piss and got a lot of enjoyment out of winding her up.

So when Dad said he'd nearly died in hospital and had seen Danny, I humoured him. When he said it the second time, I thought it must give him some comfort to believe that, and strength too; according to Dad, Danny had come to get him and he'd firmly told him, 'No son, not yet.'

But after weeks of fighting and days of wearing a mask that forced his airways open, he told us he was ready to let Danny take him. At that point, it didn't matter what I believed; it only mattered what he believed. If Dad said that Danny was coming for him, I wasn't about to argue.

It had happened: he was ready to die.

We're sitting in my mum's garden, socially distanced, together but apart. Mum and Rachael had been able to spend a bit of time with him before he announced he was tired and an incredible nurse called Louise had taken over. 'I'll be here until the end,' she told Mum.

And so we waited for the end; for the call that'd tell us our beloved, incredibly warm and witty husband and father had been reunited with his desperately missed son.

We watched as the sun sank over the horizon and the clouds receded from view. Beyond, twinkly stars flickered on in the dark, shining down on us. We were all looking for Danny. Without any one of us having said it out loud, we were searching the sky for him.

Rachael broke the silence. 'Give us a sign, Danny.'

No sooner had the words left her mouth than our eyes were diverted to the kitchen window. The lights flickered: one, two, three, and then off.

I felt shivers run down my spine. The hairs on the back of my arms stood on end. We all looked at each other, open-mouthed.

A few moments later, I lifted my gaze back to the sky and noticed what I can only describe as a tunnel like a white cloud hanging directly over our heads.

'Look.' I pointed upwards and watched as my family's gazes followed mine. We all went icy cold.

It's happening, I thought. *He is coming for you, Daddy.*

2 JUNE

And then, just like that, the worst happened. And he was gone.

When it came, when it was over, we let out now-familiar moans. Even though we knew a part of Dad had died when he lost his son, and even though we knew he'd been gravely ill and had suffered for long enough, it still tore through our hearts like a tornado.

Not Dad too. Not my dad.

Everything is so painfully familiar. We call Laura from the funeral home. We want Angela to deliver the service. I will write the eulogy. I'll read it with Rachael. Claire will sing.

It's like we all know what parts we need to play. We even know what coffin we want, where we'll get our flowers from ('Ooooh, they were lovely last time!'), and we know we'll drink endless cups of tea and coffee, because what else do you do?

Except, this time, we're mourning Dad, not Danny. Or maybe we're mourning both of them. None of us know.

As the days pass, a picture of Dad in a stark white frame is placed next to the picture of Danny and I joke that I'm going to have to get some decent pictures taken before it's my turn. It's not a time for jokes, but I'm acutely aware that they are what's missing. We no longer have Dad or Danny to lighten the mood.

I try to process all that has happened in the last month.

His breathing has dipped.

Not to worry, he's better again.

They're decreasing oxygen. He's coming home.

He came home.

Oh, he's going back in.

High dependency. Oxygen. More oxygen. CPAC. Ceiling of care.

And then, all at once, gone.

My wonderful dad. Gone.

Another beautiful light stubbed out.

You'd better look after him, Danny.

1998

SUMMER

Saturday nights were clubbing nights but Friday nights were reserved for the local pubs. Our friends would descend on our house (which was in the centre of town) and Danny would fire up his decks while my friends and I endlessly touched up our make-up in my room and the boys pranced around in front of the mirror in his. Doors were left open as my friends flirted with Danny and I flirted with Danny's friends. Getting ready was the best part of going out.

And in the midst of it all was Dad, freshly showered, clean shaven, and ready for a pint. He'd strut about making us all laugh, trying to be one of the boys.

'I'm gonna wear this,' he'd tell Danny. Then he'd appear in front of my big mirror in a black Dolce and Gabbana waistcoat over the top of a shirt Mum had bought him from the catalogue. The giant D and G letters covered the whole of his back and he grinned as he checked himself out.

Danny appeared and shook his head, laughing. He and his friends had developed a taste for designer clothes but, after a short stint of being label obsessed, had quickly moved on to items that were less obvious. Dad was reaping the benefits and happily migrating Danny's cast-offs into his wardrobe.

'Have you used my aftershave too?' Danny asked, leaning in and giving Dad a sniff.

'Danny," Dad replied, spreading his arms out, 'a look this cool needs a nice smell. I can't be wearing my Old Spice.'

Danny rolled his eyes and told him not to touch it again. Dad promised not to and shot me and my friends a cheeky wink.

He was a bloke in his fifties off to his local working men's club and he looked and smelt like he was a young man ready for a night on the town. He was our mate and his presence just made the whole ritual of getting ready more fun. Beneath us all, in the living room, sat Mum, getting ready to settle down to watch a movie with Claire as soon as all the chaos had left the house.

Dad always left first, swiftly followed by the boys, while me and my friends left only when we felt confident we'd drunk enough Bacardi and Coke. The first stop was always The Ship, the pub at the top of the road. Here we'd have a couple of drinks and work out who was 'out' before heading down to the busier places. But before that, we popped into the Con Club, Dad's club, for a quick drink. There Dad would be, centre-stage at the bar, making everyone laugh with a tale or two. He stood out like a sore thumb in his designer threads, as his friends looked like they'd gone for a pint straight from work. And in among it all were Danny and his friends, making the most of the cheap drinks and joining in the banter with Dad, the life and soul of the pub.

Dad's friends were winding him up about his new attire and Dad was lapping it up, not offended by the jokes that he was the butt of but rather enjoying every second. And as he laughed, Danny looked on, holding his pint glass across his chest and shaking his head. He was pretending to be embarrassed but he didn't fool me; I could see in his face that he felt exactly the same as me, and was thinking exactly the same thing:

That's my dad. You are bonkers but I bloody love you.

2020

12 AUGUST

I sometimes find myself crying without knowing who I'm crying for. I keep trying to stay positive and tell myself that we're so lucky to have had two people in our family who were so loved that they left huge gaping holes behind them—but it's hard to stay positive when everywhere I look there's a gap. The brown leather sofa where Dad used to sit in the living room. The vision of Danny in his bright orange work jacket walking past Mum's window. The 10 p.m. calls that don't come anymore. The jokes I want to share with Dad only to remember that he's no longer here to hear them.

Facebook keeps reminding of events from a year ago, and they almost always make me feel crushed. A year ago we still had a whole family: the complete set. And now two massive parts are missing. The men. The boys. The centrepiece of everything. Who even are we without those two winding us up and making us laugh? I fear none of us know anymore.

I have instantly switched from worrying about Dad to worrying about Mum. I can't comprehend how she'll move forward—first without her son, and now without her partner. She's lost Amber now too—Dad's beloved little dog and Mum's lifeline, managed less than two months without her dad before she gave up. I am willing my Mum to keep on keeping on with every fibre of my being.

But in my rare moments of calm and contemplation, I remember that I miss them too. I lost them too. And that's when the tears come.

Dad I hope I can come to terms with—it's the order of things, the circle of life. I will love him forever. I will miss him forever. But I always knew I'd have to spend some of my life without him.

But Danny? No. I just can't accept it.

You should be here, Danny. You should be here.

9 JULY

'I'm signing up for a sixty-day challenge,' I tell Eddie as we sit together in the kitchen.

He lifts his head from his tablet and nods in response.

'Do you think it's a good idea?' I press, desperate for some kind of response.

'Yeah, sure,' he replies absentmindedly.

I've put on more weight since losing Dad and we both know it, but Eddie's too kind to mention it. But now I want to talk about it and I need his support.

'Eddie,' I say, 'can we talk about this? It's important to me.'

He folds his tablet into his lap and turns to look at me.

'Yes, good idea,' he tells me, giving me his full attention, 'if you think you'll do it.'

I know he's heard it all before, he's supported me through so many diets and schemes; he's cooked the most marvellous meals to help me and he's never moaned when I dash off to the gym or for a run or whatever it is I've convinced myself will help me lose weight.

I tell him I think I will, that I'm ready—that I know I need to do something for myself.

He smiles and nods before picking up his tablet again.

'Do you think I can stick at it?' I ask. I'm aware I'm picking at a scab, almost willing him to tell me it won't work.

'Yes,' he tells me, 'but you need to figure out why you always give up.' He puts the tablet down again with a sigh and looks me in the eye. 'You always give up, Ali, and it's hard when you do because we can't talk about it—you won't let me, and I can't support you if you won't let me help you.'

I know he's right so, once again, I try to explain binge-eating and self-sabotage and the helplessness I feel when I fall off the wagon. I explain that I don't understand why I do what I do but that I am desperate to stop.

And he listens intently but I see in his face that he doesn't understand.

'You just need to stop yourself,' he tells me, confirming my suspicions. I realise he looks almost disturbed by what I've said, by my admission of guilt.

I've picked the scab.

I turn away so he can return to the tablet. The conversation is over. There's no point trying to make him understand. How could he unless he knew what it was like?

But then I think of Danny—of the conversations Danny and I had about addiction and compulsion. About the helplessness. The realisation you have done the thing you feared you would before you even had the chance to think about it, to have a word with yourself. And I think how Danny understood—better than anyone. Better even than me.

But, of course, Danny is gone. Now my shame is mine and mine alone.

I want to put food in my mouth to fill the gaping hole in the pit of my stomach.

20 AUGUST

C'mon, Shay. C'mon. I'm staring at my phone, waiting for a message to pop up. It's GSCE results day and I'm waiting for Shay to let me know how he did so I can confirm his place at college.

With Kelly's permission, I have taken on the role of next of kin for Shay and arranged a college place for him starting in September. He was offered numerous opportunities but failed to enrol, so I stepped in and convinced the tutors to allow him onto the engineering programme. It's something he's been interested in for a while, and I argued that it was better to offer a teenager something he was interested in than force him to do something he wasn't. I know Shay—he's like his dad. He'll look for an opportunity to say it's too hard or too boring. He'll look for a way out.

I've become that annoying auntie, that pain in the arse who nags him about the importance of education. I just want him to have something to focus on and enjoy.

I text Kelly and ask her to chase Shay for me.

'I just need to upload his results to confirm his place,' I tell her. I know I'll be stressing her out too, but college places are in high demand and I don't want him to miss out.

I check my phone again. Still nothing. I try to ring.

All the while, I think of Danny and how if, he were here, he'd be doing the same. He'd be frustrated with his teenage son's lax attitude to his education and would be nagging him too. The difference is that Shay would take it from his dad—expect it even. It's so different with me. I wonder how he feels about his auntie suddenly lodging herself in his life.

'You can't make him do it, Alison,' Mum tells me, and I know she's right. 'It's not your job to get him to college.'

But I also know Danny. *Look after Shay, Al.*

I genuinely believe in my heart he'd want—hell, he'd even expect—me to look out for his boy. And while I want to believe it's not my job, I simply can't accept that.

Lily is trying to get my attention and I put my hand up to hush her. We're packing to go on holiday and she's excited, but my mood is darkening by the hour.

I text again. I'm beginning to feel like I'm texting his father again, chasing him for the information I need so I can help him out. Something to do with Shay, perhaps, or a job application, or a website he wants me to set up—all favours he'd ask for and then not have time to contribute to. I remember the deep frustration I felt because I feel it now.

But I am forgiving of Shay; he's not his dad. He's a teenager and that's hard at the best of times, doubly so now he's going it alone. I can see he feels responsible for his mum, who's struggling with Danny's death. He feels like he has to be strong. He has to be okay.

And then there's the fact that Shay and I don't have the relationship that Danny and I had. I worry he'll cut me off, and that scares me—not just because it would mean losing the last part of Danny, but because I'd feel like I'd let him down all over again. I simply cannot allow that to happen.

'Try ringing the school,' I tell Kelly in a final attempt to get what I need. I can feel my blood boiling inside. I turn to Lily, who's patiently clutching the bag she has packed. 'Sorry Lil,' I say.

She opens it up to show me all the nail varnishes she's taking with her—every colour of the rainbow. She's also packed a teddy I haven't seen her pick up in years and a book she has already read.

I reach out and pinch her cheek. My beautiful, bonkers baby girl. And suddenly I feel all right again.

23 AUGUST

We're on holiday in St. Ives in Cornwall and it truly is stunning. The sky looks bluer, the sand whiter—it's like the world has been plunged into glorious technicolour.

I watch the kids attempt to build a sandcastle with their dad. Eddie is taking over, a grand vision for their masterpiece building in his mind, and the kids are happily falling in line, running back and forth to the sea to fill up their buckets. My mum relaxes in the sun, looking as glamorous as she ever has, a book lying unopened on her lap.

It's picture-perfect, yet I'm tetchy and irritable. My mood is hanging over us all like a dark cloud. Everyone is afraid to speak to me for fear I'll bite their head off and I'm afraid to speak for the same reason. I sit on the sand, running the fine grains through my fingers.

I can feel a headache coming on so I reach into my bag to grab some ibuprofen and guzzle them down with some water warmed by the hot sun. Mum asks if I'm okay and I just nod; I don't have the energy to talk.

I've stopped taking my antidepressants and, though I hate to admit it, it's almost certainly the reason I feel so bad. I've only ever taken them intermittently, blatantly ignoring my doctor's advice, because I'm still struggling to accept I have to take them at all. I thought that because I took them so sporadically in the first place I'd be fine to just stop, but that certainly doesn't seem to be the case.

I look up at the kids again and watch as they dutifully smooth down the walls of their growing sandcastle. My loves, playing together on this beautiful beach. I reluctantly reach into my bag again and find my foil packet. I take out a pill and pop it in my mouth. I can't ruin our holiday out of stubbornness. It wouldn't be fair.

I go back to sifting sand and try to imagine the chemicals seeping through my veins, hoping they'll work like magic, instantly lifting my mood and taking me back to my lovely family. I wonder why I have such a problem with taking them. I'd think nothing of it if it was someone else; I've even told plenty of friends in the past that they'd be silly not to take them if they'd help, but I refuse to follow my own advice. It's okay for everyone else but me—I should be able to handle it, shouldn't I?

I think back to the therapist I saw during my battle with postnatal depression. Through tears, I'd told her I wasn't good enough to be a mum, that my children deserved better and that I was failing them. She'd calmly and slowly walked me down a path I didn't know even know existed. When I'd finished gushing about my own lovely mum and my wonderful childhood, she sat back in her chair and asked me, 'Was your mum perfect, Alison?'

'Oh no,' I laughed, before reeling off a list of Mum's traits I hoped I'd not inherited.

Once I'd finished, she leaned forward and looked me in the eye. 'So your mum was lovely, Alison, and you love her very much. You credit her with giving you a wonderful childhood but you admit she wasn't perfect.'

'Yes,' I agreed, picturing my mum's lovely face as I did so.

'So, Alison, if you can say all that and admit your mum wasn't perfect, tell me, why do you need to be?'

29 AUGUST

Dirty clothes are piled high in my utility room. The washing machine is whirring in the background. All around are the remnants of a fun-filled holiday and a week away from home.

I clutch a cup of coffee in the kitchen and replay the events of the last week. Beach days, lazy days, laughter and fun with the kids days. And then I think of Mum. It was wonderful to take her with us, but it hurt too. She laughed, she smiled, she got involved, but there was an ever-present sadness she carried around. She's not the same woman she was. You can't help but notice it—she looks a little lost, like she doesn't know where she fits anymore. I want her to fit with me so badly. I want her to feel it's okay when she's with us, but I know, no matter how hard we try, she is only ever going to feel half of a whole. It was Mum and Dad. Dad and Mum. Pat and Pete. Ying and Yang. And now it's just her, left to silently and constantly mourn their lost son all alone.

She misses Dad. Of course she does—the companionship, the banter, the tea with two sugars, even the always moaning about money—but, most of all, the knowledge that she was part of a pair. Still, I know it is Danny she aches for. It's Danny's face she sees in the streets and Danny's shape she sees on every grown man with a bald head. When I look at her or think of her, I want to cry. She smiles, she always does, but her eyes don't twinkle like they used to. She's not the mum I knew and loved. Without Dad to prop her up, I worry she'll fall down.

I have another gulp of my coffee. It's lukewarm and I realise I must have been daydreaming for ages. The tears are flowing again and I begin to wonder if I'll end up with welts on my cheeks due to all this crying. How did we end up here, with this giant hole in our family? The tears flow faster now I've noticed them—I have unlocked the floodgates. I cry for my lovely, imperfectly perfect dad and my big brother. I cry for the family I once had. The mum who has been left behind, anchorless and grieving for a life she once knew. I cry for myself, for the feeling of being part of something safe and secure and for my life before I had to become the glue that tries to hold things together. I realise that's how I feel now: like the grown-up, the one in charge. I have to keep it together and find a way to fix us.

I look at the cup in my hands. Danny's cup. I allow myself to imagine his hands around it the way mine now are, two hands held tight as if the ceramic kept him warm. I can hear him slurping the hot liquid inside. Can picture him looking up and laughing at something someone said.

Suddenly, I am in my mum and dad's kitchen. We're all there: Dad, Mum, Danny, Rach, Claire, and all our kids. It's a madhouse. We're all talking over each other, every one of us trying to dodge being asked to make a brew, knowing it'll take forever to get through us all. Dad or Claire have put music on, I can't remember which, but it just adds to the noise and the sense of chaos. Mum is in the middle of it all, making sandwiches. No butter for Eddie and my kids. Eddie's outside, trying to keep away from the noise. My dad is desperate to join him, hoping to steal a crafty fag.

I am breathing it all in. Inhaling so deep it fills my lungs and makes my heart almost burst with love.

Why did I not know how special this was? This normality. This absolute chaos—I'd give anything to have it back. We are all so different now. We

309

smile and love and make time for each other; we gather in the same kitchen; we make the same brews. Mum fusses over us all, making food, wiping surfaces. But Danny and Dad are conspicuously absent. The scene is a painful shadow of what it once was.

I often think about their deaths and work out which hurts the most. It's like a really macabre game of Top Trumps, the kind I'd only ever dare to play in my head for fear of sounding like a madwoman.

Dad's had been painful because he'd known he was going to die. We all knew we were saying goodbye to each other and that, due to COVID-19, he would breathe his last breath without us by his side.

But we'd not been given the chance to say goodbye to Danny at all.

When I spoke to Rachael on that horrendous Monday morning, I remember feeling that it was impossible that you could get news like that and not be given the chance to put it right. He couldn't just be dead—there had to be some element of hope, even if it was tiny. To have it sat there, unmoving, as a cold, grim fact was simply too cruel. No one should just wake up to news like that; we should at least have had the opportunity to come to terms with it or, better still, to put things right.

I could have saved you, Danny. I should have saved you.

The holiday was wonderful. Blue skies, sun on our skin, and plenty of quality time with my truly marvellous kids. But Dad and Danny were never far away and the kids knew this. It saddens me to think my kids will only get a half-version of their mum now. They're already used to seeing me cry. They roll their eyes when I speak of Dad or Danny as they know my own will fill with tears. They've learnt how to cheer me up and to weave their grandad and uncle into everyday conversations. They know how to keep them alive, and I love them for that. But it makes me sad too; they are far too young to have to live around such loss. I wanted to protect them from pain for much longer.

The washing machine has finished so I stand up to gather the clean clothes. Another load will go in and the cycle will begin again. Just like that, life goes on. The cup goes in the sink, the memories away for a while.

Washing to do. Clothes to dry. A house to tidy. And on and on and on.

31 AUGUST

Shay sent me his results after all and I managed to get in touch with the college to confirm everything. I message him on Snapchat to update him and he replies immediately.

'Thanks, Auntie Al,'

My heart sings. Danny was the only person who ever called me Al. It's such a stupid thing, but it tells me I'm doing the right thing by continuing to help him. He's his father's boy.

12 SEPTEMBER

It's 9 a.m. on a Saturday morning and I am walking across a car park, outside the gym, holding a large kettlebell in each hand. A man who looked to be a similar age to me (and is as red-faced as I am) greets me, and I ask him how long he's been coming to the gym. He tells me it's his first week and repeats my question. I do a quick mental calculation and tell him I'm six weeks in. I feel a surge of pride—six weeks and I'm still here, keeping on keeping on.

As we get back to the wall to begin our next exercise, a young girl joins in our conversation. She is in her mid-twenties, with long brown hair swept up into a neat ponytail, perfect skin, and a body I would kill someone for. I immediately dismiss her as someone judgemental, but she quickly tells us it stays hard no matter how long you've been coming.

'I just love the feeling after though,' I tell them both, 'this bit kills me but I feel such a buzz when I'm finished.'

'And that's the thing that keeps you going,' she says, and it's clear she's serious. I immediately think of Danny and what the gym meant to him. Even though his work was much more physical than mine, he still wanted that routine, the buzz that I'm now feeling myself.

'My mum has just moved in with me,' I continue, 'and she's commented on how much energy I have now, so it must be doing me some good!'

The slim woman puts down the weight she's holding and places her hands on her hips, ready to move on to the next exercise.

'How come she's moved in?' she asks.

So I tell her. The colour and brightness drain from her flawless face as I explain how we lost Dad and Danny before him, and now little Amber. Saying it all out loud makes it sound ridiculous—you couldn't make it up!

She looks genuinely gobsmacked and sad and I realise I was stupid to assume she would look down on me, just because she had a polished appearance. She asks how Mum is coping and I tell her, truthfully, that she's doing as well as can be expected. She is lost, but we're all determined to help her find her purpose again. We're all in awe of her strength—she just powers through and keeps going. But despite this, I know she's vulnerable too; the prospect of her fall is never far from my mind.

'And how are you coping?' she asks, and I realise I've not really thought about it for a while.

'This helps,' I answer honestly. 'I think this is helping me keep my head afloat.' And as the words leave my mouth, I realise I mean them. I'm by no means a gym bunny but the routine, and the support of the owner, James, has injected some sense of control back into my life. I've been moving more, eating better, and, for the first time in a long time, feeling like I might just be okay. The tears still fall every day, my heart still aches for the family I used to have, but I'm getting better. For the first time in a long time, I don't feel like the wheels could come off at any moment.

As we walk back inside, another session under our belts, sweat pouring down my red face, I thank her for asking—not just for her concern, but for forcing me to think about it.

15 SEPTEMBER

I find it quite bizarre that I am feeling and looking better than I have in years and yet still living through the worst year of my life (so far!).

Thanks to the gym sessions and my improved diet, the weight is coming off and tone is coming back. If it wasn't for the loss of my brother and dad, I'd tell you I'm feeling better than I have in about five years.

I have more energy; I've weaned myself off the antidepressants and am trying to spend less time focusing on the loss of my loved ones and more time focusing on the joy they brought me. Peter and Lily are talking about characters from *Family Guy* and laughing about how Uncle Danny let them watch it with him in secret. I have no idea how often it happened, but it's clear from the way they talk that it was more than a few occasions! Part of me wants to scold him for letting them watch something so inappropriate, but another part—the biggest part—just feels so happy they have such fond memories of their beloved uncle.

'He always took us to McDonald's and Tesco to buy toys!' they tell me, 'and the duck pond!'

I'm instantly reminded of his desire to go for a walk every time we saw him. He always wanted to do something, to go somewhere—when he was in a good place, of course. And for the best part of a year, he was. We moved closer to home in February 2019 and saw much more of him, and he was so good—and when he was good, he made them feel the centre of his universe.

I'm so glad you remember that, kids.

They have no idea how much their uncle struggled; they just saw someone who was full of fun, who spoiled them rotten and genuinely loved their company. And I know my sisters' children feel the same.

It gives me so much comfort. So much to be thankful for!

You really saw him, kids, I am grateful for that.

26 SEPTEMBER

It's one of the last days of summer. Mum has sold her house and we're helping her strip the walls in her new bungalow. The kids are amusing themselves by having a water fight in the front garden—the sun is shining and the lack of traffic on the roads outside means that all I can hear is them giggling above the distant hum of a lawnmower. It's a day straight out of a Disney movie.

There is so much work to do but I can't get into it. Instead, I want to write! I slope off to the kitchen and take out my phone, jotting down thoughts and feelings in a now-familiar way. Writing takes me to Dad and Danny, and I need them today. As I look from Mum's kitchen window out on to her garden steps, I think of my own garden, my own stone step, the last place Danny ever sat in my home. I can't look out there without seeing him in his thick grey hoodie and shorts, smoking his last fag.

'I'm giving up tomorrow, Al.'

I want to see him there again. If I squint my eyes, I can picture him: he's smiling, his eyes crinkling as he does so. His pearly white teeth gleam in the sun.

You were so beautiful, my darling brother.

I look to the left and imagine the seat on my outdoor sofa at home, the one where my dad used to sit. His arm resting on the leg of his maroon trousers; his little dog by his side; a brew clutched in his hand.

I hope you're both together now. I hope you're looking after him, Danny.

I think through the pages and pages I've written. The lessons I have learnt, the understanding I've gained, and the promises I made to myself along the way. So many broken; so many on pause. But now, at long last, I feel I am starting to fix myself, to snap out of it and move on. Slowly, I'm learning to love myself again.

I'm just like you, Danny. But you always knew that, didn't you?

I realise I've been broken. Stuck in this limbo where I have refused to grieve properly as I don't want to accept that they are gone. Well, I can admit it now. That's why I have found visiting the cemetery so hard. I don't want to have to accept that it's real. Two headstones are there now, not just one—the harsh reality of a family torn apart.

I've desperately wanted to fix everything—Shay, Mum, the hole in our family. But as I sit in the kitchen, typing words into my phone, I know I can do none of those things. They are gone. We are broken. I am broken. We can't be fixed, not in the way I'd like. We just have to learn to walk on.

I immediately think of the Liverpool anthem, the song that has become famous around the world, and the words silently dance around in my head.

'Walk on, walk on, with hope in your heart.'

I cast my eyes around the kitchen in Mum's new bungalow and know now that this is what I must do.

I think about the relationship I had with them both. The men in my life: two people who shaped my view of the world. Losing Dad is something I will never get over. He was my first and greatest love; the person I wanted to impress more than anyone else in the world. And my brother? He was a part of me. It feels different somehow. As if I don't know who to be without him in my life. I can't remember not adoring him, not needing him to need me. I didn't see it at the time, but I do now.

Did you know that Danny? Did you know that even when I was cross, when I couldn't take anymore, that I didn't give up? Not in my heart. I never would.

The kid's giggling has turned to arguing. We've moved from Disney to horror in the space of ten minutes. One shouts my name while the other screams over the top: 'Stop! Stop!'

I glance out the window and know I have to go. They need their mum back. Besides, it's far too beautiful to be inside. It could be the last day of summer before the long northern winter sets in.

I have to stop this now, Danny. I have to let you go. They need me. I need me. You understand that don't you?

I think back to being a kid. While Danny's passion had been football, mine was writing. I found solace in stories and words. I always wanted to be a writer—I was forever trying to get my dad's attention by reading out my latest masterpiece. And, to his credit, he always encouraged it, always drove me to write more.

I laugh to myself as I think about all the books and stories that I've started and abandoned but, I tell myself with a satisfied grin, not this one. This one I have completed right to the end.

I didn't want to accept it before, but the fix I've been looking for was right in front of me all the time. I've spent all this time looking for lessons and meanings but the biggest lesson was staring me in the face: it was never my job to fix him; to fix anybody. It was simply my job to tell his story and to share mine.

That is the greatest tragedy of life. Of all of this. As the old cliché has it, you don't know what you've got until it's gone.

I put my phone in my pocket and head outside to the kids. I turn the stereo up as I leave the kitchen, and the music follows me out into the dazzling sun.

'Mum!' they yell in delight, as if I've just started a party. They stop arguing and begin squirting water at me, giggling in unison. Disney's back again.

I walk across to them, close enough to supervise but not close enough to get wet. The early afternoon sun feels wonderful on my face. I take a deep breath and look up at the sky, soaking it all up.

As the warm rays spread across my face, the music changes and our song, mine and Danny's, fills my ears: Danny Tenaglia, 'Music is the Answer'.

The familiar beat reaches my eardrums goosebumps bristle over my bare arms.

Music is the answer

To your problems

Keep on movin'

Then you can solve them

It feels like Danny is speaking to me. Music always was his answer to everything: happiness or pain.

At twelve midnight I'll be waitin' for you

So don't forget what you have to do

I hope you are, Danny. I hope this means I'll see you again. Someday, at the end of days, I hope I see your big outstretched arms and your beaming smile. I hope you are there to tell me it's all okay. That it was always okay.

Gotta keep on dancin'

And prancin'

Groovin'

Keep on movin'

Flyin'

Stop your cryin'

Choosin'

While you cruisin'

I know, Danny, I'm trying. Trust me, I'm really, really trying. But I just miss you so goddamn much and living without you is so, so hard.

If you feel that you can't take no more

And your feet are headed for the door

I do! That is exactly how I feel right now. I am *done*. I'm so tired of missing you and loving you and hating myself for not being able to save you. You see that, don't you, Danny? You've seen me teetering on the edge.

Music is the answer

To your problems

Keep on movin'

Then you can solve them

And right there, in Mum's new garden, surrounded by my wonderful family, I get it. I know that, as I've been writing, I've unravelled the complexities of his life and of the relationship he and I shared. I've discovered more about myself than I ever intended. Writing his story has allowed me to really truly understand who he was and the battles he faced. He's at peace—I see that now.

You fought a good fight, big brother.

I get why I had to lose him to understand; why I have felt an unexplainable compulsion to write every single word in this book.

His life won't be determined by how he died—we'll make sure of that. His legacy will be the impact he had; the ripples he left behind. The love and lessons he left will cascade through the coming generations.

And, as I listen to his voice in my head, I realise just how he would want our story to end.

He's telling me to forgive myself. That I did the very best I could, and more than I should have.

It wasn't your job to fix me, Al.

He's rolling his eyes again, winking at me, telling me to give myself a break, for god's sake. I can't fix anyone else, he's telling me—I have to fix myself.

My sister's beautiful, isn't she?

He's reminding me that he loved me, that he'll always love me. And he tells me he knows I love him back, grinning at his own pre-emptive strike. Then, his smile fades.

He asks me to let it go. To stop. To walk on.

Music is the answer

To your problems

Keep on movin'

Then you can solve them

He's setting me free.

Epilouge

counsellor

/ˈkaʊns(ə)lə/

noun

1. a person trained to give guidance on personal or psychological problems.
   'a marriage counsellor'.

During our last conversation, only a few days before he died, Danny told me he'd like to be a counsellor. I scoffed, but promised to look into it for him, as I always did. Still, I couldn't help but laugh. Danny? A counsellor? Really? Okay Dan, yep, I'll get right on that . . .

But I was wrong to laugh. Losing him taught me so much about strength and courage and how to fight, about what it is to be addicted. He taught me—and the rest of our family—how easy it is to misjudge and how it really doesn't matter what other people think.

Good counsellors (and I've seen enough to know the difference between good and bad!) guide you to find your own truth. They probe and steer you until, without ever seeing it coming, you stumble across your own conclusions. They help you understand what's important and how to shake the unhelpful inner narratives that sometimes occupy your thoughts.

Don't cry because it's over.

Smile because it happened.

- Dr Suess

In writing Danny's story I have learnt more about drugs and addiction than I ever thought I would. I've confronted aspects of my own life and behaviour that I'd hitherto ignored.

Danny has reminded me what is important in life. He has shown me that success isn't defined by money or fancy job titles; it's defined by the impact you have on other people's lives. He has taught me the value of love, of family–of being there for others as well as for yourself.

People will forget what you said.

They'll forget what you did.

But they'll never forget how you made them feel.

- Maya Angelou

We'll never forget Danny. I promise you that.

He taught me that being a good parent is about the lessons you teach your kids, not what you give them (and that includes time). It's about showing the kind of unconditional love that puts them first, even when it hurts you to do so.

He taught me, and I hope you, that real everyday people struggle with their mental health and that drugs are often used to self-medicate—not because someone is selfish or weak, but because they are hurting and need healing.

He taught me that it's not always about talking. It's about showing up. Being present. It might mean more than you'll ever know.

He taught me that music really *is* the answer. It offers a connection to the past, to the future, to those you love, and those you have lost. I will listen to music every single day for the rest of my life to connect with you, Danny.

He taught me (the hard way!) to never give up on someone you love. The pain of losing them will be greater than any pain they can put you through when they're alive. If you think watching someone you love self-destruct hurts, then you won't like the pain of accepting they're never coming back.

More than anything else in the world, though, he helped me understand his life and come to terms with his death. I feel like I have been guided to write every single word in this book; that every experience and moment paved the way to this point—this point right here, where I get to say, *I got you Danny*. I understand. Drug abuse is complex. You were complex. But then, aren't we all?

Do you know what made you so special? That you weren't so bloody special at all. You are each and every one of us. I see that now.

I think that makes you a pretty incredible counsellor, Danny. The very best, in fact.

Love you, big brother. Always and forever.

Your Al

x x x

Acknowledgements

I always knew (or should I say hoped) I had a book in me, but I can say with my hand on my heart that I never thought it would be this.

The process of writing this book has been equally cathartic and painful. I lost count of the number of times I had to stop editing to have a good cry because it hit me that the sad words I was reading were about my life.

But those who know me well will know I am incredibly driven and the prospect of leaving this book unfinished was never one I was going to contemplate. And it is those people who need to be credited here.

Firstly, to Cath, my number-one fan. Thank you for your unwavering belief in my ability to do Danny justice and for pushing me to keep going when I thought I had got to the end. Your wisdom knows no bounds and I am eternally grateful for your support and encouragement.

To Kelly. My best-friend and my absolute rock. You know me better than I know myself and I love you for that. The past year has been more bearable knowing you always, always have my back.

To Michelle and my cousin, Julie. You showed me the transformative power of this book early on and when I found I was struggling to continue I always thought of you.

To Helen, Kat, Alice, Jenni, and Emma, as well as countless other friends who read early sections and gave me incredibly helpful feedback. Thank you for making me a better writer.

My editor, Fred. How poncy does that sound? You literally took my book apart and put it back together. I valued every piece of feedback and learnt a lot through the process. I did. I did. I did.

And to my *frankly* incredible family . . .

My sisters, Rachael and Claire. If anything good has come from this last year, it's the reminder that we have an unbreakable bond. I love you both more than I can express and I am beyond proud of the wonderful women you are. I know Danny was too.

My nieces, Gemma, Hannah, and Becky—the other part of our WhatsApp group. Thank you for making me laugh and cry in equal measure and for reminding us all that we have to walk on.

To my darling Eddie. You have kept me standing up when I wanted to fall down. I am incredibly grateful for what we have and I'll treasure it always. Now, have a sit down and read this book!

My little teapots: Peter, thank you for the best cuddles and for wiping away my tears more often than any kid should have to. You and your Uncle Danny are the reason I'll continue to do my bit to educate people about mental health. And Lily, you are the kind of tonic every family needs. Thank you for being your bonkers self and helping me see the *sunny day* every time it felt dark.

To Shay (or should I say Heizenburg). Thank you for allowing me to share your dad's story with others. I will never stop telling you how proud your dad was of you. I hope you read his story one day and I hope you feel proud of him too.

Also to Shay's mum, Kelly. Thanks for ensuring that Shay remains an active part of in all of our lives and that his dad's memory is treasured.

My bloody lovely, exceptionally glamourous and unbelievably strong mum. Thanks for trusting me to tell *Dan-i-el's* story and fufil his legacy. I know this journey has been the hardest for you but he will help people, I can promise you that. They'll get to see how wonderful your boy really was.

To my late dad. I'm typing this with your fluffy dressing grown wrapped around me. I miss you so, so much Papa Luge. I wish you were here to read this, to see that I have finished something (for once!), because you are the reason I write. As a little girl, your encouragement meant more to me than anything in the world. I hope I continue to make you proud because I couldn't be prouder of you.

And finally, to Danny. I feel like our last conversation gave me permission to write this. You always did leave me the hard work to do on your behalf! Thank you for being the kind of brother that it has been so difficult to lose. I hope you are dancing in the sky.